Pearson
The Unlikely Gladiator

Lester B. Pearson was Canada's most successful diplomat, but as prime minister he was both controversial and paradoxical. He was the butter-fingered old smoothie, the cautious innovator, the anti-war warrior, the mild-mannered confrontationalist. The Pearson years were full of action and originality; Pearson had a strong team with bold, fresh ideas and their achievement was staggering. But there was also corruption in government, bitterness in Parliament, and turmoil on the home and diplomatic fronts. It was a period of both national accomplishment and national malaise, of a colourful new national flag and Charles de Gaulle's famous cry "Vive le Québec libre!"

In this collection of essays, leading academics, journalists, public servants, and politicians recreate and reassess Pearson's premiership from 1963 to 1968.

"Mike Pearson led us to a more tolerant, civilized, healthy, and prosperous country. This warm, generous, 'very ordinary' great man knew that great countries care for those who have little, nurture those who can do much, and bring in those who stand outside. Those were his values, his Liberal values, and they are the ones I continue to believe in and fight for today. His life was one of those rare and special ones that changed who we are." *Prime Minister Jean Chrétien, from the Foreword*

NORMAN HILLMER is professor of history, Carleton University, and co-editor of *International Journal*.

PEARSON

The Unlikely Gladiator

EDITED BY
NORMAN HILLMER

McGill-Queen's University Press
Montreal & Kingston · London · Ithaca

© McGill-Queen's University Press 1999
ISBN 0-7735-1768-5

Legal deposit second quarter 1999
Bibliothèque nationale du Québec

Printed in Canada on acid-free paper

McGill-Queen's University Press acknowledges the
financial support of the Government of Canada through
the Book Publishing Industry Development Program for
its activities. We also acknowledge the support of the
Canada Council for the Arts for our publishing
program.

Canadian Cataloguing in Publication Data

Main entry under title:
    Pearson, the unlikely gladiator
    Includes bibliographical references and index.
    ISBN 0-7735-1768-5
    1. Pearson, Lester B., 1897–1972. 2. Canada –
    Politics and government – 1963–1968.
    I. Hillmer, Norman, 1942–

    FC621.P4P44 1999   971.064'3   C99-900505-7
    F1034.3.P4P43 1999

This book was typeset by Typo Litho Composition Inc.
in 10/12 Palatino.

For Elizabeth Trowell, 1951–1998

Contents

Foreword

In 1963 I became a member of Parliament, and Lester Pearson became the new prime minister of Canada. Fresh from my rural Quebec riding of St. Maurice, I arrived in Ottawa eager to change the world and my country. Ottawa then was not the city we know now. It was a very English town, and I spoke almost no English. It seemed far from my home town Shawinigan and very far from being a capital where a francophone could feel comfortable.

I was 29, a small-town lawyer, and a French Roman Catholic. Mr. Pearson (as I always called him) was 66 years old, the son of a Methodist minister, and a Nobel Peace Prize winner. He had lived in grand embassies and dined with Churchill, Roosevelt and de Gaulle. His world seemed very remote from the factories and parishes of Shawinigan. He did not seem like the kind of prime minister with whom I could go fishing. When I met him, however, the miles between us quickly evaporated.

Mr. Pearson shaped my vision of what Canada could and should become. He once said to me that, "The biggest mistake we ever made in Canada was when Queen Victoria chose Ottawa over Montreal as the national capital. It was a bad move because the capital was an English city." Mr. Pearson was every bit as determined as I was to right that wrong. Very soon more people on the Hill, in Cabinet, and all over the city started to talk French. He began that great effort to make Ottawa the lively bilingual centre it is today, and to ensure that Canada reflected both cultures at the federal level.

Mr. Pearson loved Canada, loved it passionately. He knew from his rich international experience that a democratic and liberal country's true worth is measured by how it treats its minorities and how generously it shares its riches. He knew that Canada could be better, so did I, and so did the other young hopeful Liberal MPs elected from across Canada. We went to work to make it so.

Mr. Pearson established the Royal Commission on the Status of Women, whose ideals reflected strongly the views of his wife, Maryon, and his daughter, Patricia Pearson Hannah. His government fought long and hard – into the parliamentary nights – for a new Canadian flag. I was proud when he put on his war medals, summoned up his courage, and announced before a hostile Royal Canadian Legion audience that Canada would never again fight a war or keep the peace without its own national symbols.

We said that the Canadian immigration process would be colour blind. We introduced the Canada Student Loan Plan, which made university education possible for so many more Canadians. When I was a boy, parents like mine worked long hours, mortgaged houses, and saved every penny to put, perhaps, one or two of their children through university. Only one out of 50 Canadians graduated from a post-secondary institution in the 1950s. Today it is more than one in five, the highest rate in the world. We brought in the Canada Pension Plan and gave working Canadians a new security of which my father's generation had only dreamed. We legislated Medicare – over the objection of entrenched interests, over the heckling of the Conservative government of Ontario, and over the opposition of richer provinces and many richer people. This social program has saved thousands of lives, and has also saved Canadians billions of dollars as compared to their American counterparts.

Mr. Pearson led us to a more tolerant, civilized, healthy and prosperous country. A better country. This warm, generous, "very ordinary" great man knew that great countries care for those who have little, nurture those who can do much, and bring in those who stand outside. Those were his values, his Liberal values, and they are the ones I continue to believe in and fight for today. His life was one of those rare and special ones that changed who we are. I know it changed my life. And, even more important, it changed Canada's.

Jean Chrétien

Pearson

INTRODUCTION
Pearson and the
Sense of Paradox

NORMAN HILLMER

His contemporaries recognized in him some of the chief qualities of diplomacy – patience, tolerance, flexibility, a sense of proportion, and moral imagination. But they also noted a distaste for confrontation, an emotional distance which my sister and I came to know as children and to exploit at times. Able to see both sides of any dispute, he would turn it aside with a joke or a story. He reached always for the middle ground … He witnessed at an early age the brutality and squalor of the First World War and, like others, may have suffered some darkness of the soul, to be repressed or overcome by a quick wit and a sense of paradox.

Geoffrey Pearson[1]

Lester B. Pearson's years as prime minister of Canada from 1963 to 1968 were a contradiction. They vibrated with action and creativity, strong ministers and brilliant advisors, and state activism on a breathless scale; yet scandal, bitter partisanship and a chaotic air of crisis management undermined accomplishments and threatened to sweep them from memory. National achievement competed with national malaise. Glittering celebrations of the country's centennial year coincided with a social and political upheaval in Quebec which caused doubt that Canada could be held together. A powerful red maple leaf flag symbolized Canadian unity, but it came at the expense of six months of divisive debate which "dominated the House of Commons, disrupted it, and led many to despair about the future of the country."[2]

Presiding over all the success and confusion was a man bristling with incongruities of his own. Pearson was a realist with idealist sensibilities;[3] a cold warrior hating conflict; an old smoothie who seemed to drop the ball as often as he held on to it; an innovator most cautious about change; a francophile with almost no French at his disposal; a quiet diplomat by training and disposition who risked the souring of relations with Lyndon Johnson's United States over the war in Vietnam.

Commentators were quick to note the inconsistencies. Parliamentary correspondent Richard Gwyn observed that the Pearson government was one of the most legislatively productive administrations in the country's history, but it lacked the essential magic spark, the link between the governed and the governing.[4] Somehow Pearson, by all appearances the most accessible of men and certainly the most celebrated of Canadians, could never quite touch the electorate. Peter Newman's highly critical journalistic assessment of the Pearson era, *The Distemper of Our Times*, commented on the prime minister's personal blend of the detached and companionable, pragmatic and idealistic, profound and lighthearted. Newman saw the prime minister as a good man in a wicked time. "Lester Pearson was easy to caricature, impossible to paint. Those who knew him best believed the outward paradox mirrored accurately a paradox within."[5]

Outward flexibility was no precise predictor of inner toughness. Robert Fulford, writing in *Maclean's* two days before the election of 1963, understood that the Pearsonian style and personality could be deceiving. In a profession of obsessive talkers who loved the sound of their own voices, he listened more than he spoke. He appeared cooperative, not to say malleable, bearing the imprint of the last person who visited him and giving the impression of being what others wanted him to be, "a kind of mirror for their ... ideas and anxieties." Intellectuals thought him one of their own, despite his lack of interest in abstract thought. Diplomats believed he had never left that craft, though he had been a practising politician for 15 years. His colleagues in the Liberal party were even, after many false starts, beginning to consider him an expert politician. The left wing of the Liberal party claimed him and so, by and large, did the right wing.[6]

There was danger in indirection. The long-serving Liberal prime minister, Mackenzie King, had employed ambiguity as a devastating tactic, but his pale political persona seldom raised hopes or enthusiasms. Pearson was so believable, his character was so evident, that he risked disillusionment when he eventually took a stand. Advocates both of a strong defence and disarmament believed he was their ally until his closely hedged decision, in the prologue to the 1963 election, to support the acquisition of nuclear warheads from the United States for Canada's armed forces. He shattered those (the Quebec academic Pierre Trudeau among them) who associated him with the Nobel

Peace Prize he had won for fashioning a diplomatic solution to the Suez Crisis. Yet at the same time Pearson said that he hoped to give the weapons back to the Americans as soon as possible, failing to satisfy the defence mavens because of his refusal to take an unequivocal stand in their favour. Fulford noted the disappointment on both sides of the debate, and rightly predicted more of the same when Pearson became the country's chief executive.[7]

Sometimes the paradoxes were simply personal growth in disguise. Pearson had lived a life of relative comfort and was at ease with the rich and sophisticated, but his government greatly expanded the range of social programs available to all Canadians. During a long public career he had never been known as sympathetic to Canada's francophone population, but he demonstrated a sensitivity to the need for major reform to make Quebeckers feel at home in their own country. He had a poor relationship with Cabinet colleague Judy LaMarsh, and he refused to name any more women to his government on the grounds that one was enough; nevertheless, he appointed, with far-reaching consequences, the Royal Commission on the Status of Women. For his fine biographer John English, Pearson "refused to cling to what he knew, and the ambiguity and uncertainty that marked his career and his personality were the counterpart of a remarkable generosity, an openness to the new and to the 'other' that is rare in our times, and especially in our politicians."[8]

Near the beginning of this book, Denis Stairs explains that Pearson was a classical liberal centrist – anxious to contain power, resolve conflict, accommodate difference, combat dogma, promote tolerance, balance interests and build consensus. His greatest strength, frequently identified as his greatest weakness, was the ability to view an argument beyond his own point of view. He had "a kind of instant receptiveness" and "all the tricks of a negotiator," a newspaperman of long acquaintance remembered. "Finding out how one side felt, then playing it back to the other side, and vice versa."[9]

The characteristic went far deeper than subterfuge. The Liberal leader told a party meeting in 1966 that "I have not the divine certitude that I am always right or that I am one who has been called upon by God to save the country. I even admit that I can see both sides of a question when, as is usually the case, there are two sides, unless there are four or five."[10] The arrogance that there could be absolute truth was apt to make a leader "believe that he is only doing what God would do if He had all the facts." From there it was only a short step towards extremism and dictatorship.[11]

From the liberal pluralist perspective, the essential ingredient in the political art and practice was an appreciation of the complexity of human affairs. Those who governed had to understand that different people saw the world through different lenses, from the standpoint of different circumstances, and with different imperatives. Even first principles competed and conflicted, creating paradox everywhere, requiring in turn nuance and qualification.[12] Pearson understood the complexities, and valued them because they made it more difficult for the simple-minded or messianic to have their way. Paradox, as Stairs puts it, yields "fluidity, and fluidity gives room for manoeuvre. Deals can be struck, trade-offs can be made, coalitions can be engineered. At another time, and for another cause, they can be rearranged ... Everyone can get a piece of the action."

Pearson's intellectual stance was the unavoidable consequence of a collision between environment and experience. Born late in the nineteenth century, he was a child of Methodism: his minister father was a decent, moderate and intelligent man, although apparently not an imaginative or ambitious one. Pearson was a child, too, of Ontario and of the British Empire, at a time when the association with the mother country was the defining staple of Canadian life. He enlisted in the First World War, but collapsed under the strain. John English makes a strong case that the twin pillars of his youth, Christianity and imperialism, disintegrated as "he realized how the world he expected to live in had been made still-born by the events of 1914–18. He stumbled for a while in the new terrain, and his breakdown of 1918–19 deeply affected him, forcing him to limit his range and to resist close emotional ties with others and with faiths or ideologies that demanded intense commitments."[13] Ever after he was described as hard to know and devoid of obsession.[14]

Pearson left imperialism, but not necessarily the Empire. Robert Bothwell's opening essay depicts the war as a nationalizing but also an internationalizing experience. "There was, obviously, a world beyond Canada, and even a world beyond the Empire." Pearson and Canadians hesitantly stepped out of colonialism towards nationhood, but the British Empire was still the context in which they operated, and not simply in the realm of external affairs. That institution was more real to them, if also more vulnerable, after four years of sapping Anglo-Canadian collaboration against the enemy. In the 1920s there was a movement towards self-government in the international arena to match what had been achieved in domestic affairs in 1867, with the result that a decentralized British Commonwealth replaced the Empire. Britain, however, was still the centre of attraction, or in some instances repulsion, still the country that mattered most to Canadians. Pearson attended Oxford University from 1921 to 1923, forging lifelong friendships and reinforcing the loyalties he had taken from his fervently pro-British family. He was often critical of Britain, but he was always more comfortable there than in the United States, where he had lived for the first time during a brief business career immediately after the war.[15]

In 1928 Pearson entered the Department of External Affairs, then the preserve of Dr. O.D. Skelton, the under-secretary and Prime Minister Mackenzie King's closest advisor. "Mike," the airy nickname acquired from his squadron commander during the war, was a little too offhand for the aristocratic Vincent Massey, the Canadian diplomatic representative in Washington, who complained that there was "something curiously loose-jointed and sloppy about his mental make-up which, as a matter of fact, is reflected in some measure in his physical bearing." Skelton agreed with the appraisal, but he was "not wholly convinced that all entrants to External Affairs should combine the mind of a mathematician with the posture of a Grenadier Guard."[16] Pearson had written the best entrance examination, and Skelton, bent on building a foreign service based on ability rather than wealth or family connections, judged the 31-year-old had "very distinct capacity" and "attractive personal qualifications."[17]

There was little to do at first. Mike (even the very formal Skelton soon called him that) was rushed to Ottawa from his teaching position at the University of Toronto to take up his grand new duties, but found himself housed in cramped quarters in a dank attic on Parliament Hill and given as a first job the preparation of routine background material for an international conference on the causes of death. That was followed by requests for materials relating to lighthouses in the Red Sea and the protection of women artists living abroad. Even after many months of such work, Skelton was not sure Pearson was up to rigorous analysis: he seemed better at compiling information than distilling it into something useful.[18]

The under-secretary was more at fault than Pearson. Skelton had inspirational integrity and intelligence, but he was a poor developer of talent because he was unwilling to delegate responsibility. Pearson chafed under Skelton's administrative strictures and King's lack-lustre foreign policy. On New Year's Day, 1936, Pearson revealed his ambition and the extent of his unhappiness with External Affairs in one of his intermittent diary entries. In neat, child-like handwriting, he coveted Skelton's job and vowed he would do it better: "Lord, how I would like to be given the job of pulling External Affairs & the Foreign Service apart & putting it together again, with a few pieces left out." Despite his fine qualities, Skelton had no interest in or aptitude for personnel and organizational questions. He was " 'not ruthless enough; won't hurt people'; and 'won't fight for his subordinates.'"[19] Later on, Pearson's colleagues and staff would say precisely the same of him.

It was as a diplomat, far away from Skelton, that Pearson flourished. His first foray abroad was to the London Naval Conference, where he caught a glimpse of the glittering world of international negotiation and loved it. He was part of the Canadian delegation at the League of Nations during the Manchurian and Ethiopian crises in the early to mid-1930s. Superiors got themselves into trouble, but he stick-handled skilfully around their muddles and made sure Ottawa knew he had no part in them. Under High Commissioner Vincent Massey, by now a warm supporter, Pearson served at Canada House in London from 1935 into the Second World War. Again, the observer of his life has to live with contradictions. He supported collective security through the League, but he feared that it might draw Canada into a European war which had little to do with the national interest. He cherished the British connection, but he realized the dangers of getting too close; seeing England's imperfections at close range intensified his Canadian nationalism. In May 1940, as the Nazis subjugated France and drove the British Expeditionary Force off the continent, he exclaimed, "Never have I been so glad to be a Canadian as in these last days – at least we are not responsible for this mess."[20]

When Skelton died in early 1941, Pearson expected to get his job. He had to settle for the number two position at External Affairs headquarters under the less experienced Norman Robertson, a setback he described as the greatest professional disappointment of his life.[21] Within a year he was posted to Washington, where he remained for the rest of the war, becoming ambassador in January 1945. There was nothing left of the sloppiness which Skelton and Massey had observed almost two decades earlier. He had become the consummate professional, imaginative, articulate and diligent, the undisputed star of a young diplomatic corps which was rapidly winning good notices in foreign offices around the world. He had a wonderful humour, resilience and detachment which gave him perspective and a capacity for finding middle ways.

The foreign affairs commentator James Eayrs, gathering his evidence from Pearson's memoirs, eloquently matched the job to the man:

He bobbed about in the swirl and eddy of diplomatic life, enjoying rather than enduring the interminable round of parties and receptions, buoyed by his gregariousness and the sense of fun that would sustain him even through the rigours of a political campaign ... That the diplomat more than most professionals can be a tragic figure – an artist compelled to be an artisan, a painter forbidden to paint, a poet forced to ghost-write the gibberish of nations – seems never to have occurred to him, much less caused him sleepless nights. He became adept at drafting evasions ("we found suitable compromises on these points by resorting to ambiguous or meaningless phrases"), suppressing qualms ("I compromised with my conscience by speaking unemphatically") and meeting the press ("I learned to make new bricks with a minimum of straw"). The boredom did not bother him a bit – if need be, he could add to it: "Of course no one here has any idea as to what the Canadian attitude towards this conference is, or even if there is a Canadian attitude. But I was reluctant to say that, so I chatted amiably for fifteen minutes."[22]

Son Geoffrey adds that Pearson was "rarely depressed by failure or daunted by obstacles." Nor was he over-impressed by tradition or formality. "At a later stage, as Party leader, he was perhaps too prone to listen and to sympathize rather than to instruct and to command, but as a diplomat the qualities associated with the smile and the handshake served to gather support for the policies he advocated and pursued."[23]

Pearson was marked indelibly by the two wars and a brutal economic depression which demolished so many of the years in between. He observed the corrosive excesses of nationalism, totalitarianism and violence. He saw Canadian unity and democracy strain under the pressure of deprivation and danger. He watched the League of Nations disintegrate because it could not adapt to the circumstances of the 1930s and lacked the collective instinct to survive.

Balanced and credible institutions were inoculations against the ever-present danger of chaos, devices for recognizing diversity and accommodating difference. Pearson's generation, in Bothwell's words, "thought it only natural to apply the lessons of depression and war, which suggested the largest possible government instruments, and national leadership and action." Further afield, but closely linked to indigenous forces (foreign policy was simply "domestic policy with its hat on"), Pearson and his friends learned that Canada lived in and would be shaped by the wider world. Multilateral arenas like the League and its successor, the United Nations, had the opportunity to contribute to international amity and collaboration, while at home federalism could build bridges between Canada's English and French populations. It is not surprising that, as prime minister, so many of Pearson's responses to the Quebec problem were structural – the introduction of bilingualism into the public service, for example, or the "opting-out" mechanism of cooperative federalism. These, according to Denis Stairs, are telling examples "of the liberal pluralist's dedication to practical flexibility in the construction of 'sound institutions.'"

For all his success at representational diplomacy, Pearson had some disdain for it. He wanted to be at the centre, to be a *working* diplomat, "to face the challenge of being a 'great man.' "[24] In 1946 he was a strong candidate for secretary-general of the United Nations, but the Soviet Union would not accept him. Instead he got his old wish to be made Canada's under-secretary of state for external affairs. By this time, however, the rumours were rife that this was simply a way station on the route to political office, and indeed the prime minister raised the question of becoming foreign minister even before Pearson took the under-secretary job. On 19 September 1947, Mackenzie King, after 21 years of power, told him he expected Louis St. Laurent soon to be the next party leader and that Pearson, if he would enter the Cabinet, was likely to be prime minister after St. Laurent.[25]

Almost precisely a year later, not yet a member of Parliament, Pearson became secretary of state for external affairs. The great international events of the next decade – the early cold war; the founding of the North Atlantic Treaty Organization (NATO); the building of a multiracial Commonwealth; war in Korea; the Suez Crisis and peacekeeping – were his events, and he was Canada's connection to them. Christina McCall remembers how powerfully he personified the idea that the country had an existence beyond its parochial self, inspiring young Canadians to make a difference in the world, "just like Mike."

Pearson succeeded St. Laurent, with whom he had had the closest possible working relationship, as leader of the Liberal party of Canada. But not as prime minister. John Diefenbaker, a mercurial western Conservative, had unexpectedly won the election of 1957, bringing St. Laurent's political career to an end. Then Diefenbaker almost finished Pearson off in the election of 1958, when the Liberal party sustained its greatest political defeat. He was left with only 49 seats (14 of them in Ontario and none in the west), compared to Dief's 208.

Pearson hung on, and the authors of this collection give him high marks as an opposition leader. Although not a natural House of Commons man, he and what was left of the St. Laurent front bench fought back hard in Parliament. Often against the grain, he opened the Liberals to fresh ideas and new people. He set out progressive views on French-English relations and social policy. He listened, and had the self confidence to delegate – to Walter Gordon, for example, went the responsibility for rebuilding the party organization, while Tom Kent took on the work of designing a liberal social policy. J.L. Granatstein writes that "no one should forget the way Pearson and a few Liberals steadily chipped away at the Tory edifice. Mike Pearson was sometimes too tentative, too rational, but his persistence and his ability to learn the details of Canadian domestic affairs ensured that he evolved into a fine opposition leader."

The Pearson-Diefenbaker rivalry dominated the turbulent tenth decade of Canadian political history. Opposing one another in four increasingly bitter election campaigns over seven years, they were usually portrayed as complete opposites of experience and temperament. Granatstein and McCall, however, explore the notion that they were (in the latter's phrase) "unlikely gladiators," and thus more similar than Canadians ever imagined. After all, the two men were of and from the same age,[26] born not far from one another and shaped by similar influences of Empire, war and depression. Each served rather unhappily in the First World War, was among the small number of their contemporaries who graduated from university, and chose public service as an outlet for their considerable ambition. They were products of the "old" Canada but they came to represent modernity, Pearson as the forward-thinking citizen of the world, Diefenbaker as "the harbinger of a more egalitarian Canada," the prairie populist out to bust the central Canadian grip on federal power. As prime minister, both disappointed, ultimately seeming out of step with their times, anything but new.

Mild of disposition, cautious by instinct, Pearson was a less likely gladiator for change than the restless and dynamic Diefenbaker. Yet the Conservative boss held tight to the past, while Pearson transcended his limitations. Despite the Liberal leader's years (he became prime minister just before his 67th birthday), he recognized the social, economic and political forces that were overtaking the country and met them, even if not always head on. Granatstein acknowledges the Pearson government's hesitations and inefficiencies, but credits an impressive record of performance under patient and realistic guidance. McCall highlights the Pearson role in the coming of the modern social service state, his attempts to understand Quebec's aspirations and, particularly, his sensitivity to the struggle for women's equality. It was not, she argues, that he pulled Canada to the left, as conservative analysts insist. "It's that he helped consolidate a political culture north of the American border that centred on the value of government, rather than on its venality."

Pearson carried high expectations with him into office, along with the liberal glow of his ally, President John F. Kennedy. Mike had the media enthusiastically on his side in the election campaign of 1963, and the "new politics" of slick image-making were much in evidence. "In fact," Patrick Brennan argues, "the Camelot of the North seemed to have everything – ideas, style, and a blizzard of 'forward looking' policies – everything, as it turned out, but a Kennedy." Pearson promised "60 days of decision," but the only success he had to show for his first two months in office was a trip to meet Kennedy at his summer home in Hyannisport, Massachusetts, where the new government agreed to bring nuclear weapons into Canada forthwith.[27] Finance minister Walter Gordon's first budget was so inept that it made many, including many Liberals, hope it would be his last.

Thus Gordon, advertised as the government's superman, was severely weakened within days of taking office, his program to limit American influence on the Canadian economy stillborn. He offered to resign. Pearson simply asked him if *he* had sufficient confidence in himself to continue. Gordon never lacked that, and so he carried on, but he felt betrayed, not for the last time. Stephen Azzi's examination of Pearson's ideas on foreign investment looks closely at his relationship with Gordon, showing the prime minister's capacity to live with contradictory views without excessive discomfort, while giving encouragement to all sides. In dealings with Gordon, this tendency was reinforced by Pearson's reluctance to become involved in economic policy. The venerable journalist Bruce Hutchison, Pearson's friend extending back to his days as a diplomat, recalled that "Even when coached by the great economist John Deutsch he could never put his heart into the dismal science ... to him economics was territory more foreign than foreign affairs."[28]

Beginnings can be fatal, or nearly so. The 1963 budget fiasco made the Liberals backtrack furiously and punctured their promise to return efficiency to national government. The media sniffed weakness. Brennan characterizes them as an increasingly adversarial breed, embracing "the 'libertarian' cat-among-the-pigeons philosophy that the media were the guardians of the citizens' rights and it was their duty to uncover and expose ineptitude and hypocrisy wherever and whenever they found it." Pearson had his loyalists like Hutchison, but even he became skeptical, and the old cozy relationships between Ottawa's elite and the press were no longer thought proper. Television, which accentuated "the leader," was no kinder to Pearson: his avuncular, soft-edged, bow-tied persona was not well suited to McLuhan's "cool" medium, while the program *This Hour Has Seven Days* cruelly documented his half-steps and missteps. These continued on a regular basis throughout the five years, making rich sport for journalists and obscuring what by any standard was a spectacular list of achievements:

a new Canadian flag, important reforms in parliamentary rules and the committee system, a reorganization of government departments, the foundations of a bilingual federal civil service, the redistribution of constituency boundaries by an independent commission, important changes in federal-provincial relations, the beginnings of constitutional reform, a new bank act, new regulatory agencies for transportation and broadcasting, a new labour code, the Canada Pension Plan, the Canada Assistance Plan, a guaranteed minimum income plan for old age pensioners, medicare legislation, the setting up of a health resources fund, youth allowances, the liberalization of divorce laws, industrial research incentives, provision for technical and vocational training schemes, a doubling in the External Aid program, the abolition of capital punishment for a trial period of five years, new bankruptcy, company and consumer legislation, the unification of the armed forces, collective bargaining for the civil service, establishment of the Order of Canada, new feed grain and crop insurance legislation, a fund for rural economic development, a new immigration act, and the setting up of several important new agencies, including the Economic Council of Canada, the Science Council, a corporation to encourage the Canadian film industry, the Company of Young Canadians, and a corporation to manage and phase out the Cape Breton coal industry.[29]

Pearson got little credit for this welter of legislation. A poll taken just before he stepped down as prime minister showed that 70 percent of Canadians could not conjure up a single beneficial accomplishment during his administration of government. In *The Distemper of Our Times*, Peter Newman grudgingly admitted that, "even if his government was worse than it should have been, it was better than it appeared to be," an "impressive stream of useful reforms" having been squeezed from two minority governments. Pearson himself, however, was accorded the role of a bemused bystander, not so much "governing Canada as presiding over its survival." He unleashed novel forces and pressures, but he could not control them. He initiated radical social change, but could not explain, rationalize, or exploit it. Worst of all, it seemed to critics like Newman, he made the wrong "impression," the mortal sin of the modern media age.[30]

The judgement of scholars has on the whole been kinder than the opinion of contemporaries. When *Maclean's* recently asked a panel of academics to rank the prime ministers of Canada, Pearson was complimented for his legislative record in social policy and innovations in federal-provincial relationships, achieved despite being the first prime minister never to have a majority in Parliament. In the view of political historian Blair Neatby, he "fundamentally altered Canadian identity by introducing the flag, Medicare, a national pension plan and comprehensive welfare measures, and by focusing attention on Quebec's challenge to national unity." He also won praise as a happy warrior – modest, reasonable, self-deprecating and internationally respected, embodying Canada, in the words of University of Saskatchewan political scientist David Smith, "as Canadians wished others to see it." Nevertheless, as Smith asserted, "leadership in policy was not matched by a similar command of Liberal party organization or of Cabinet." Pearson failed to achieve a clear victory in four national election campaigns and, while in power, did not convince either as a politician or administrator.[31]

The articles in this volume give conflicting assessments of his leadership skills. The focus of Greg Donaghy, a historian at the Department of Foreign Affairs, is on Canada's Asian diplomacy in the context of Canadian-American relations and, in particular, on Pearson's relations with Paul Martin, the secretary of state for external affairs. The prime minister's experience and expertise in the field were unrivalled, but he felt constrained by his friendship and rivalry with Martin, whom he had known since the 1930s. "The reserve which characterized their uncertain partnership, and a reluctance to undermine his minister's authority, obliged Pearson to tread carefully when he entered Martin's domain." Their paths veered, however, with Martin wishing to carve out a more independent path in Asia. Thinking the foreign minister's approach rash and seeking to minimize differences with the United States at a time of rising anti-Americanism, Pearson eased Martin to one side.

But he could not obliterate the differences, and did not wish to. He encouraged cautious initiatives to seat Red China at the United Nations and to moderate the war in Vietnam. Donaghy reveals a leader confident and sure of step, and fully understanding the puzzle of Canada's American tie, the habitual desire to be distinct from the United States but very close at the same time. Pearson's Temple University appeal for the suspension of the bombing campaign against North Vietnam is the most enduring image of 1960s Canadian-American dealings, but it was a misleading indicator of the prime minister's overall purpose and approach.[32]

Longtime diplomat Ross Campbell wants to resurrect Pearson's commitment to power as well as to peace. Pearson was a visionary but also a pragmatist, aware that Canada was vast of size and small of population, and determined to defend it with collective security undertakings and credible armed forces. He supported the best while preparing for the worst: his government was the last one "to observe and preserve this prudent sense of balance in international security affairs." The *Globe and Mail*'s Andrew Cohen is less impressed by Pearson's global achievements as prime minister than by what he stood for in international affairs – conciliation, moderation, patience and, when all that failed, imaginative ambiguity. "He thought Canada could be the successful mediator, the builder of institutions, the exemplar of humanitarian assistance." The realist in him knew his and Canada's limits, but the idealist recognized the "obligation of compassion."

Cohen traces Pearson's liberal internationalist legacy in Canadian prime ministers since 1968. Pierre Trudeau began with an explicit rejection of helpful fixing and honest brokering, but he transformed himself into an alliance-builder and peacekeeper and ended his time in office with an utopian peace crusade to save the world from nuclear terror. Whether in South Africa or in *la francophonie*, Brian Mulroney had Pearson's fingerprints all over his policies, though he was incapable of putting moral distance between Canada and the United States, as Pearson did over Vietnam. The Chrétien administration has, lamentably in Cohen's view, put an accent on the promotion of national economic interests, but even here there is strong and observable continuity of collective engagement with the world. "Pearsonianism" is inescapable.

Like Donaghy, P.E. Bryden has studied Pearson on the basis of close and extensive documentary research. The author of a major study of social policy in the 1957–68 period,[33] Bryden concludes that Pearson established himself as "a leader of considerable foresight and courage" during his time in opposition, when he oversaw and stimulated innovative planning in spite of little background or interest in the area. But in government, his natural tendency to delay took hold, conflicting with the party's promise that the "sixty days of decision" would bring contributory old-age pensions and national Medicare. In the case of pensions, hesitancy yielded reward, because the original scheme was flawed. The eventual Canada Pension Plan, coming two years later, was a prudent federal-provincial compromise, although it had the odour of weakness and retreat. Universal health care moved much more slowly, with Pearson procrastinating mightily over its implementation, which he did not wish to carry forward without unanimous support, well into his second minority term. In this way he jeopardized a program which came to be regarded as synonymous with his premiership. Bryden regards him as a prime minister who cannot be said to have achieved greatness, but he governed during a period when great things were accomplished.[34]

Tom Kent and A.W. Johnson, Pearson's key 1960s social planners, tell the story rather differently. They emphasize how much was done and how quickly, pointing to the huge improvements that programs such as the Canada Student Loan Plan or the equalization of provincial revenues brought in the "human well-being and the dignity of individual Canadians," especially at middle- and lower-income levels.

Kent attributes the "Pearson burst" to society's reforming mood and the Liberals' political opportunism, but also to the leader himself. He had promised real change in the 1962 and 1963 campaigns, and he delivered, despite self-doubts and the doubts of others which impressed him perhaps too much. For Johnson, the source of Pearson's commitment to equality-directed reformism lay in his values, stemming from the religious and liberal influences of his youth. They made him "consistently humane, consistently concerned with fairness, consistently related to governance that would unite Canada through serving all its inhabitants."

Monique Bégin associated these principles with Pearson, even though she entered the Liberal party too late to know or even to meet him. He was a point of reference, an authentic Canadian who "nurtured the best in us" and "made us dream." When she became minister of national health and welfare in 1977, Bégin had his social inheritance very much at the front of her mind, hoping to extend it through the establishment of a guaranteed annual income for Canadians. Instead she had to confront the neo-conservative shibboleths that were much in fashion at the time; she clung tight to the Pearson tradition in order to "save for my fellow citizens the best acquisitions of the past." Bégin and Kent regret the recent blows against the social service state, and with each slash the attenuation of the Pearson legacy.[35]

Pearson's appeal to a young francophone woman like Bégin had something to do with his empathy toward Quebec. The Liberal party which they shared, as Blair Neatby reminds us, was founded on accommodations between English and French Canada. Pearson, the year before he became prime minister, selected Maurice Lamontagne's advice from among conflicting voices and decisively promised in the House of Commons to work towards a true "partnership" with French Canada. It was in that speech that he put forward the ideas of a royal commission on bilingualism and biculturalism and equal and full access to government services for both language groups. John A. Macdonald, the country's first leader, had said that the French would act generously "as a free people do" if they were treated "as a nation." Call them a faction, however, "and they become factious." Pearson agreed, quoting Macdonald with approval. Right at root, he believed that tolerance and a respect for diversity were essential bonds of a civil society, as they were of a peaceful international order.[36]

Claude Ryan, the 1960s editor of the influential Montreal newspaper *Le Devoir*, and University of Ottawa historian Michael Behiels have quite different interpretations of Pearson's complex responses to Quebec's new nationalism and the threat to Canadian unity. Ryan applauds the prime minister's initial flexibility and generosity of spirit: Quebec, he announced in the House of Commons during his first term, "in a very real sense is not a province like the others"; it was a nation "in the historical and linguistic and cultural sense." Thus the "B and B" Commission, cooperative federalism, shared cost programs and enriched francophone participation in the Ottawa government.

But circumstances changed in mid-decade, and with them Pearson. Fellow Liberal Jean Lesage, difficult though he was, was replaced by the even more assertive Daniel Johnson as premier of Quebec. Within Pearson's team of ministers and advisors, there was a shift towards ardent federalism, with the brilliant Pierre Trudeau in an increasingly prominent position. English Canadians, moreover, began to react to the accumulation of "concessions." The fear of an independent Quebec mounted, reinforced by the province's incursions into diplomacy and the impact of French President Charles de Gaulle's emotive cry, "Vive le Québec libre," from the balcony of Montreal's city hall. Pearson, Ryan speculates, had been divided between his desire to acknowledge Quebec's distinctiveness and "his profound commitment to Canada and its federal system of government." The second impulse, already the stronger, increasingly took control. Quebec was returned to life as a province like the others.

Behiels makes many of the same points, but to a contrasting end. His contention is that Pearson got better rather than worse in his handling of the Quebec file, and was at his peak in 1967 and 1968, when he publicly rebuked de Gaulle and covertly worked to install Trudeau in the prime minister's office. He agrees with Ryan that there was too much vacillation and indecisiveness, but his overall assessment of Pearson is more favourable, in part because he promoted "such pan-Canadian achievements" as Medicare, the flag, and regional economic expansion. Behiels makes a good deal of the enormous transformation that Canada was undergoing during the decade – in population, culture, gender, class – and urges that Pearson's extensive reforms "contributed in small and large ways to the maintenance and promotion of social and political cohesion in a society undergoing serious strains at all levels."

The Ryan-Behiels discourse is part of a larger national debate about the history and future of Canada and Quebec – the direction they have taken since Pearson was elected, and the course they ought to follow if the country is to be preserved. Gordon Robertson, Ottawa's most influential bureaucrat when secretary to the Cabinet in the 1960s and 1970s, prescribes finesse rather than confrontation for the constitutional malady. He is certain that Pearson would never have brought the constitution home from Britain without the participation of the Quebec government, and almost as sure that he could have saved the Meech Lake Accord. "We might not now be at the edge of the abyss if we had had his healing talents for a few years longer."

Thirty years after he left power, Pearson's memory remains powerful and controversial. In 1997–98, the *Globe and Mail* heaped praise on foreign minister Lloyd Axworthy for reviving "a Pearsonian sensibility in foreign affairs, most notably with his strong – and effective – championship of the landmines treaty."[37] Columnist Allan Fotheringham excoriated the Chrétien government for lacking Pearson's modesty and forthrightness: "Lester would be ashamed."[38] Commentator David Frum recalled that the maple leaf flag "splendidly symbolized the new bilingual, bicultural country Lester Pearson hoped to build." But, he added, the "Pearson project" was impossible, "nonsensical from the start."[39] The Lester B. Pearson Centennial Symposium in Ottawa-Hull, on the one-hundredth anniversary of his birth in April 1997, attracted 225 people on short notice, including academics, businesspeople, public servants, politicians of all stripes, journalists and students. Criticisms and critics were in evidence, but few disputed the recollection of former Prime Minister John Turner and ex-Conservative leader Robert Stanfield that Pearson brought unique personal qualities of "freedom and fun" to the country's leadership, combined with a high level of courage and creativity.[40]

I ought to declare my biases. As his Carleton University assistant in 1972, I spent a great deal of time with Mr. Pearson, finding him as accessible and elusive as others did. After watching him teach several graduate seminars, I decided to tell him that he was spending too much time reminiscing and ought to stimulate more interchange with and between the students. He had a way of encouraging such frankness, but I was enough of a coward not to put the matter to him directly. I wrote a memorandum, thinking he would see it at his office downtown. The next time we met, however, he extracted my note from his briefcase and said that he would read it on the spot so that we could discuss it. He did, and then we did. I squirmed, but I need not have. He told me that I was right, that he agreed completely, and that he would instantly alter his ways in light of my perceptive criticisms. In the classroom, alas, nothing changed, and I found myself added to the list of thousands who had been told what they wanted to hear. He gave no hint of the illness that caused his death late that year. His warmth, wit and intelligence remained intact right to the end.

Canada's Moment:
Lester Pearson,
Canada, and the World

ROBERT BOTHWELL

Canada has the reputation, outside its borders, of a steady, dull, reliable country, economically advanced but spiritually bucolic. Its quarrels and stresses, to non-Canadians, have a whiff of self-indulgence. How could such a fortunate place, rich and remote, have anything but "small problems," as Henry Kissinger once called them? Canada, Kissinger believed, was a country of the ordinary. This is, admittedly, not the view from inside the country. "Canada is the most difficult place in the world to govern," as prime minister after prime minister has discovered. Managing Canada can be an extraordinary achievement, drawing on qualities of imagination and reserves of principle.

For five years in the middle of the twentieth century, Canada was led by an unusual Canadian, ordinary and extraordinary at the same time: Lester B. Pearson. Pearson's ordinary qualities, an easy charm foremost, topped off with a disarming smile, appealed to his fellow-citizens – appealed just enough to permit them to award him two grudging mandates to govern them. Pearson had the opportunity to learn the hard way that Canada was a very difficult country to govern. By the end of his prime ministership, in 1968, he knew that most Canadians thought it was time for him to go. Affectionately but grumpily, they waved him good-bye, and with him a generation of politicians and, many thought, the problems the politicians brought with them.

Pearson's identity, and Canada's, was not just a product of domestic life or concerns. He was, in the words of the British author and humanitarian Barbara Ward, "that shrewd yet visionary voice," who had in his time helped change the world, and for the better. Ward praised Pearson as a citizen of the world and as an idealist with realist sensibilities.[1] In Pearson's case, international praise is reinforced by international symbols – the Nobel Peace Prize of 1957, a recognition of his work, as Canada's external affairs minister, in establishing a United Nations (UN) peacekeeping force and ending the Suez crisis of 1956. Although sometimes forgotten at home during Pearson's lifetime, the peace prize has been an enduring and important factor in Canadians' self-regard and self-definition.

How did this apparently ordinary Canadian, albeit with extraordinary gifts, become a citizen of the world? The prospects at the time of his birth, in a hamlet outside Toronto in 1897, must have seemed dim. Lester Pearson was born into a Methodist parsonage in what was then a far corner of the British Empire, in a place, Canada, whose inhabitants were not even sure it could or should be called a country. English-speaking Canadians took militant pride in being called British subjects, a notion that helped shut out the shrieks of the American eagle across the border, even though that bird spoke with almost the same accent as Canadians north of the lakes. As for the French Canadians, they accepted English pretensions with resignation, and in the hope that the English would not interfere too much or too often in their daily affairs. And so Canada lumbered on through the first 14 years of the twentieth century.

There was little that was remarkable or atypical about Pearson's early life. A Victorian Canadian, a British subject, a Protestant in a world where sectarianism supplied those parts of identity that citizenship left out, Pearson and his generation had no particular need to question the assumption that God was an Englishman and lived, part of the time at least, in distant London. When Great Britain went to war in 1914, there was no doubt that the Empire's cause was also God's and Canada's. Pearson, by then a student at the Methodist Victoria College in the University of Toronto, followed the young urban males of his generation into the army and, eventually, to the war in Europe.

Pearson did not enjoy the war but, as with so many other young Canadians, the war had a large impact on him. For his generation, it was both an internationalizing (perhaps the term should be "deprovincializing") and a nationalizing experience. There was, obviously, a world beyond Canada, and even a world beyond the Empire. The Empire, mighty as it was, had its limits; its militaristic symbols, so important to the generation before 1914, proved even more drastically limited in a world of trenches, machine guns, and bombs. With the Empire enfeebled in the Canadian imagination, English Canadians stepped, uncertainly, out of colonialism toward nationalism.

The University of Toronto processed its honoured veterans in a perfunctory way at the end of the war and turned them loose to find their ways in civilian society, equipped with degrees if not an education. Pearson, a veteran with university certification, was again not atypical. Granted, veterans were a minority of the population, but they were a very large minority; while the university-educated were also a minority, they were plentiful enough to bring their skills to bear – in Pearson's case, skills that were innate or acquired through experience rather than classroom learning.

They would do so, of course, if they stayed in Canada, but that was not a good bet for the postwar generation. In the early 1920s, more than 600,000 Canadians or residents of Canada emigrated to the United States in search of opportunity. Canada, in the view of many contemporaries, resembled a headless pyramid. What should have been the top had moved to the United States. Lester Pearson and his brother Marmaduke (called Duke for obvious reasons) headed south. Duke stayed, but Lester left, via Canada, for Oxford University in 1921.

Oxford in the 1920s had a much greater impact on the young Pearson than had the University of Toronto in the 1910s. As his biographer, John English, has elegantly demonstrated, Oxford gave him a polish, an experience and a self-confidence previously lacking; it also provided a context, making for lifelong friendships with young Englishmen that left Pearson appreciative and affectionate toward the mother country, but not awestruck.[2] The experience did not automatically confirm his attachment to Canada, but it made him less a colonial. The Oxford interlude lasted two years, until 1923, when fate intervened in the form of the University of Toronto, which offered employment in its history department. Pearson returned to Toronto and Canada.

Pearson was remembered as a popular if not especially profound teacher, resourceful, adaptable, and likeable. He married a student and fathered a child and then, like many optimistic members of the professoriate, discovered that his university income did not match his aspirations. In the inflation-ridden 1920s, university salaries had not caught up. There was no point and little prospect of changing universities, but there was a new opportunity on the horizon. The Mackenzie King government in Ottawa had authorized the creation of a new professional foreign service for Canada, and Dr. O.D. Skelton, the under-secretary of state for external affairs, was looking for recruits. Better still, he was prepared to pay. Pearson sought out Skelton, who encouraged him to sit the competitive civil service examination (set by Skelton himself) in 1928. Pearson came in first and was offered a post. Pearson had found a living wage, a job, and his métier.

A living wage was an important commodity, as the prosperity of the 1920s turned into the bleak Depression of the 1930s. Politically, the Depression reached into every Canadian household as unemployment rose and gross domestic product plunged, creating a profound crisis of confidence in the existing political and economic system. Pearson witnessed this side of the Depression at first hand, acting as secretary to the Royal Commission on Price Spreads, investigating the employment and competitive practices of Canadian business. Then and later, Pearson was impressed by the case for reform, and for government action, but not so impressed that he joined the ranks of central planners, the political and social engineers of the 1930s and 1940s, as so many others of his generation did.[3] Like other young and concerned Canadians of the period, however, Pearson became convinced that any possibility of coherent government action must be centred in Ottawa. It was a natural conclusion for Canadians with experience abroad: Canada's tiny population – slight by comparison with the United States, or Great Britain, or even Spain or Romania – suggested that Canadians could compete or compare only by concentrating their resources.

Pearson spent time abroad – in Washington, at disarmament conferences, at the League of Nations and, finally, from 1935 to 1941, in Canada's principal mission abroad, the High Commission in London. Pearson thus had a ringside seat as Hitler's Germany embarked on its career of expansion and domination, and finally brought the world to war in 1939. Equally remarkable was the feckless and futile diplomacy of the great western European democracies, Great Britain and France, as they failed to block Hitler either through concerted action or by force. Reluctant to go to war and mindful of the horrendous cost in lives and morale of the First World War, the governments of Great Britain and France preferred a course of "appeasement" – attempting to satisfy Hitler by conceding, piece by piece, to his demands.

The Canadian government, for its own reasons, strongly supported appeasement, even though Mackenzie King, the prime minister of the period, privately feared that war was inevitable. King lived nevertheless in hope that appeasement would succeed, because an absence of war would mean an absence of the bitter divisions between English and French Canadians that the First World War had brought. King prepared for war by avoiding any policy that might antagonize any important interest in his fragile country. He knew, too, that if appeasement failed it would show that Hitler was truly insatiable and dangerous, and that the democracies' cause in resisting him was just.

The failure of appeasement imprinted an indelibly bad name on what was, up until then, merely a technique of diplomacy. Pearson, in his memoirs written in the 1970s, left the impression that in the 1930s he was an opponent of appeasement.[4] That was not quite right. Pearson was certainly sensitive to the nature of the Nazi regime in Germany, and at times he was a supporter of what was called "collective security" – multilateral action against international disorder. On the other hand, his opinion of the British government and its capacities and intentions was low, mirroring that of Dr. Skelton, his overseer in Ottawa. Pearson had no influence on Canada's policy on this matter: it was ultimately determined by Mackenzie King as he judged best, and very much against Skelton's wishes.

Pearson's waffling on the subject of whether he had indulged in appeasement reflects his eventual conclusion that appeasement in the face of aggression was a great folly. Like many others of his generation, he was governed by the "lessons of the 1930s," lessons that gained force from the very near escape from catastrophe that had followed the outbreak of war in 1939. Canada was involved, of course, as Mackenzie King had always intended and, as it turned out, King's political bulwarks at home held. French Canada did not turn on English Canada, or vice versa, and Canada emerged united from the war, with no lasting damage to its political system. That certainly did not mean there were no incidental unhappinesses, even inside Canada's diplomatic service, between English and French, but on the whole a recognition of the benefits of unity prevailed. A secondary lesson, not uncommon among those who witnessed and reflected on the rise of totalitarianism in the 1930s, was of the superior (if deplorable and immoral) political concentration of the totalitarian states. Diplomacy alone, certainly not diplomacy of the classical kind, based on shifting coalitions and temporary interests, would not carry the day. The creation of Anglo-American harmony and a unified approach to grand strategy between 1941 and 1945 showed that the democracies could do what was necessary. But what would happen after?

Pearson's career advanced during the war, though not as fast as he would have liked.[5] He ended it as ambassador in Washington, where his easy ways and affability assisted a shrewd and hard-working intelligence. Experience in Washington sharpened Pearson's diplomatic instincts at a time when bland harmony was the official tone of Canadian-American relations. From the American point of view, Canadian interests were not so much opposed as forgotten: simply getting recognition for Canada meant struggling hard for a seat at the table. Pearson's later diplomacy was criticized for thrusting Canada into improbable places for the sake of dubious objectives, and sometimes the critics had a point. It is impossible not to see the insistence on a Canadian presence as a reflection that nobody else could be trusted to guard Canadian interests – even Americans, whom Pearson considered to be great and good friends.

The Second World War drastically altered the international balance of power. It temporarily reduced Germany and Japan to impoverished client status. It sapped British resources, economic and political, and marked a further stage in British decline. It boosted the power and position of the United States. It left the Soviet Union militarily preponderant in eastern and central Europe, as well as ideologically attractive to millions of Europeans craving order and accepting the inevitability of a totalitarian future, Soviet-style. Wartime advances in weaponry, especially aircraft and missile technology, and the creation of the atomic bomb, reduced and even abolished the oceanic defences that had sheltered Canada from the unwelcome attentions of overseas powers.

It was a new world, packed with danger, and an unfamiliar world that very few Canadians could even begin to imagine. Pearson, by temperament and experience, was one of the few who could.

The years after 1945 are often described as a Golden Age of Canadian diplomacy. Certainly they were a Golden Age for Lester Pearson and his generation of diplomats. Drawing on the negative experiences of the Depression and appeasement, statesmen celebrated the virtues of action and unity. Pearson, becoming under-secretary of state for external affairs in 1946, was among them – not unique, but increasingly prominent because he expressed so well, and managed so skilfully, the agenda of the postwar generation.

The agenda was not entirely willed or intentional. At first, presiding over victory and preserving unity among the victors took pride of place: international organizations, some enduring like the UN, some abortive like the World Trade Organization, were the signature of the time. They were quickly overshadowed by dissension between the Soviet Union and its western allies, expressed in the 45 years of the cold war between communism and western liberal democracy.

There was never any question that Canada would take its place among the nations resisting communism, or that Pearson would guide Canadian policy in that direction. History, geography and ideology made that inevitable. Canadian political parties were united on the issue, barring, of course, the Canadian communists and their fellow-travellers who sank steadily in reputation, if not self-esteem, as their subservience to Moscow became apparent.

Canada was a fortunate land, especially in the late 1940s. Prosperous, with a rising standard of living and full employment, Canadians approached the world with confidence. Canada had played a respectable part in the Second World War and would naturally play a large part in securing the peace, if not at the UN then in combination with Canada's allies, Great Britain and the United States. The Liberal party, which under Mackenzie King guided the country through the war, remained in power during the peace under a new leader and prime minister, Louis St. Laurent.

Just at the end of the King regime, in September 1948, Pearson moved effortlessly from the civil service into the Cabinet, as minister for external affairs, a post he held until the St. Laurent government was defeated in the election of 1957. The period is remembered as politically tranquil, which is not completely accurate, and as a period of consensus on foreign policy – a proposition which is true in parts. Enough parts, as the Liberals discovered, for the conduct of foreign policy to be a political asset to the government.

Pearson, with his trademark grin, a shock of diminishing hair dangling over the forehead, and his bow tie, became a political icon to Canada's burgeoning television audience. Rumpled, respected, reliable: identifiably Canadian, at least as Canadians liked to see themselves, and on display at the UN, at international conferences, and in the gatherings of the great, such as the Americans Dean Acheson and John Foster Dulles, the British Anthony Eden, the Russian Khrushchev. Khrushchev was the most difficult, since friendly contact frequently involved endurance drinking; Pearson remained proudly upright, unprepared by Methodism but favoured by 30 years of diplomacy.

There is an interesting parallel between Pearson and his contemporary, Dean Acheson, the American secretary of state. Acheson, like Pearson, came from a Canadian clerical family, but Anglican rather than Methodist. Acheson's father moved to the United States and became a bishop, but the family's British-Canadian background lingered in Acheson. He played on a larger national field than Pearson, but the two men, colleagues in wartime Washington, nevertheless found their basic objectives compatible. The United States, in Acheson's time, was paymaster to the western world, and an occasionally impatient alliance leader, in part because of the difficult and convoluted nature of its domestic politics. Representing a powerful country, the most powerful country, Acheson used power as the currency of influence – in a good cause to be sure, but one in which means shaped ends. The needs of the moment were so overwhelming that Acheson's horizons contracted, causing him to take an exasperated view of those who, like his friend Mike Pearson, insisted on gazing at more distant goals and measured achievement by slightly different standards. When Pearson insisted on including a clause (eventually Article 2) in the North Atlantic Treaty Organization (NATO) Treaty, looking to cultural and economic cooperation, Acheson sighed and acquiesced: no good would come of it, he murmured, then and later, in his memoirs and in essays. "Stern daughter of the Voice of God," Acheson called Pearson's Canada, an international scold, upholding impossible ideals and preaching unachievable ends. Article 2, Acheson noted, remained inert. That was true, but it was also true that NATO limped badly when economic and sometimes philosophical differences developed among the allies, as they inevitably did in its lengthy lifespan.[6]

Inside the Canadian government, Pearson's masterful summaries of international affairs, and the steady support he received from St. Laurent, kept the Cabinet on course through the approval of NATO (1948–49), the Korean War (1950–53), and the Suez Crisis (1956). At ease at home and abroad, Pearson seemed to live a charmed life.

The Suez Crisis of 1956 exemplified Pearson's diplomatic objectives, his values, his skills, and his limitations. Pearson's *objectives* were plain: the Suez Crisis disrupted the western alliance and cast doubt on the link between Great Britain and the United States. Pearson's first priority was to bridge the gap and restore the alliance. Pearson's *values* also came into play: he was, after all, a British Canadian with strong sentimental and personal ties to Great Britain. He was more content in the British system than in the American, and he believed that the British government had blindly ignored British interests and values in plunging ahead in a bloody neocolonialist adventure. Many of Pearson's British friends agreed.

It is Pearson's diplomatic *skills* that are remembered from the Suez Crisis, his grasp of the instruments offered by the UN and his imagination in putting them to work in the western interest, which he carefully identified with the larger interests of world peace and the equality of peoples and nations. Pearson had earlier identified the importance of links to the Third World, especially to India, a democracy with a political culture close enough to Canada's to allow a useful interchange of ideas. Pearson's far-sighted cultivation of India sometimes went awry in practice, but in 1956 it proved a diplomatic pearl without price. Yet in his solution to the crisis – the creation of a peacekeeping force – there were *limitations* which reflected Canada's limitations and those of the international system. Pearson would have preferred a much tougher mandate, with the capacity to override local Egyptian sovereignty in the larger interests of world peace and UN authority. He did not prevail, nor could he have, but it was a road he very much regretted not taking, even though insistence on this point could well have scuttled the entire peacekeeping operation.[7]

In the crisis Pearson discounted the problem of Canadian public opinion. Not surprisingly, Canadians had not kept up with the sweep of international history. What Pearson saw as a rescue operation for a declining British power was seen by many Canadians as a betrayal of Canada's great friend and ally. The embittered reaction in parts of Canada helped speed the Liberals' electoral demise in the 1957 election, although it was only one element among many.

Pearson nonetheless won the Nobel Prize for Peace as a result of his diplomacy in the Suez Crisis. The award was due recognition, to be sure. He got not only the Nobel Prize but, shortly afterward, the Liberal leadership. There was a connection, but it was not as direct or automatic as has often been assumed.

In his acceptance of the Nobel, Pearson gave an elegant and memorable speech and his fellow citizens again basked in the rays of his reflected glory. Unfortunately, some acquired a taste for the Nobel sun (or possibly sunlamp): not a few of Pearson's successors as foreign minister encumbered their, and their country's, diplomacy with the futile quest for another Nobel – the politics of spurious imitation.

Pearson's achievements were real, but they mirrored the circumstances of his generation and its "moment" in Canadian history – the immediate legacy of war, the temporary diminution of Europe, and the nature of the alliance politics of the 1940s and 1950s. In Pearson's hands, Canadian policies kept the United States at a tolerable and friendly distance and maintained a functioning and very close relationship with Great Britain. Then circumstances, as well as personalities, changed.

Pearson became Liberal chief in January 1958 and lost his first election as a party leader two months later. He spent five years and another election warming the opposition benches in Parliament. It is proverbial that governments lose elections and that oppositions do not win them. (Certainly the election of 1957 that terminated the St. Laurent government was an event lost by the government.) Yet like most political nostrums, even those elevated via scholarly equations to theories or, worse still, "laws," this one has its many exceptions. Governments certainly must lay the groundwork for their demise, and in this the Conservative Diefenbaker government of 1957–63 became a high achiever. Uncertain and incoherent, the prisoner of its lack of strategy, the Diefenbaker government floundered in perennial indecision, defended only by its leader's flashes of tactical brilliance. It was a vulnerable government, and Pearson in opposition made the most of the fact.[8]

Pearson proved to be a most successful opposition leader. He and his associates – Paul Martin, Jack Pickersgill, Lionel Chevrier and Paul Hellyer, the remnants of the St. Laurent government – consistently outperformed the Conservatives in a Parliament where the

Liberals were heavily outnumbered and enjoyed few of the resources available to parliamentarians today. Outside Parliament, Pearson's long-time friend, Walter Gordon, oversaw the rebuilding of the Liberal party as a national force, while Tom Kent, recruited from the *Winnipeg Free Press*, devised policies that made the Liberals attractive to progressive voters. Outmanoeuvring the Conservatives in Parliament, the Liberals under Pearson outflanked the New Democratic Party on the left and established a political position that endured for the next generation.

Pearson therefore returned to government in 1963, as prime minister. Outside and inside Canada, there was a sigh of relief. Pearson was not John Diefenbaker. Government had returned to competent hands and expectations were high. But Pearson did not have, and never had, a majority in the House of Commons, and in his five years as prime minister could never be entirely certain whether his government would survive from week to week.

Curiously, the domestic record of Pearson's prime ministership proved more substantial than the achievement in foreign policy. The recovery of Germany and Japan, the development of the European Common Market, the decline of the Commonwealth and British power, American distraction in the Vietnam war – all lessened or marginalized Canadian influence in international diplomacy. The expulsion of the UN peacekeeping force from Egypt in 1967, much to Pearson's irritation, symbolized the disappointment Canadians felt at the trend of events and suggested that an inward-looking policy, concentrating more narrowly on Canada, was the proper response to a world where Canada's role was no longer appreciated. The most lasting change in foreign relations, the Autopact with the United States, was signed in the shadow of the Vietnam war in 1965. Yet Pearson gave it only a perfunctory justification in his memoirs, reflecting his preoccupation with other issues he considered to be of greater importance.[9]

The most intractable of these was the question of Quebec and, more generally, Canadian federalism. The generation of 1945, including Pearson, thought it only natural to apply the lessons of depression and war, which suggested the largest possible government instruments, and national leadership and action. Quebec, though under a Liberal government directed by a friendly Jean Lesage, thought differently. Pearson was unsuccessful in solving the resulting impasse, but he swiftly promoted the problem to the top of his priorities and was tireless and frequently imaginative in his responses to the needs of a modernizing Quebec. Pearson's advisors were less certain: Quebec's quest for autonomy could not be satisfied at the price of excessive devolution or through a special status for the province that would diminish its responsibility for, and connection with, national affairs. Pearson's relations with his Quebec caucus were never entirely smooth and, at times, as during the parliamentary scandal sessions of 1965–66, his authority over his own members was seriously in question.

Politically, Pearson was less successful as prime minister than as opposition leader. However, he never made the ultimate mistake that would have lost him, and his party, power. Moreover, he left the Liberals in sufficiently good shape on his retirement to help them to win the 1968 general election, and with a majority. A mixed record, to be sure, but not a disastrous one. Pearson had learned, as most of his predecessors had, that Canada is a very difficult country to govern.

Pearson responded to his country and was shaped by it. He saw his country changing and tried to awaken Canadians to the fact. He reminded them, in and out of season, that Canada must live in and be shaped by a larger world. Some foreign observers thought Pearson a man larger than his country; but not too large for it, as it turned out.

Lester B. Pearson
and the Meaning of Politics

DENIS STAIRS

Lester B. Pearson was a liberal.[1] How do we know? Not because he joined the Liberal party. For philosophical liberals in Canada, there were in his time, as there are now, other possibilities.[2]

We know, instead, because he wrote like one and because he behaved like one. The purpose of the discussion that follows is to explain what this observation means and to explore its implications for Pearson's practice of the political art, both at home and abroad.[3]

In describing Pearson as a "liberal," I am not using the term in the currently popular American sense (now also becoming fashionable in Canada) of someone who takes an expansive view of the proper role of the state in addressing the ills of society and starts with an optimistic conception of the remedial value of social engineering. Such a view, reflecting the conviction that the social and economic miseries of the human condition are caused more by environmental circumstance than by failure of will or weakness of character, was perfectly consistent with Pearson's practical performance in the construction of Canadian public policy. The record of the government that he led from 1963 to 1968, replete with the introduction of Medicare and the Canada Pension Plan, clearly sustains this point. But the acquiescence, and sometimes the active support, that he gave to the projects of those who were stationed on the moderate left of his party's centrist ranks were not in themselves the most direct of the consequences of his political philosophy (though they may have been so at several steps removed). The core of that philosophy was represented more by a particular view of politics itself than by a specific array of public policies or a predisposition to favour this or that sector of society.

Pearson's views had their roots, no doubt, in a murky combination of upbringing, education, personality and professional experience of the world. Only the most incautious of observers would attempt to weigh the influence in relative terms of these variously formative forces. Nonetheless, the last – professional experience of the world – may have been especially important in determining where, within the liberal corpus as a whole, he thought the emphasis should lie, for his practical experience began with the world abroad, not the world at home. His political education, in other words, may well have come more from the international than the domestic environment; more from watching at first hand the interactions of states in the state system than from observing the endless competition for public protection – and public largesse – that defines the politics of almost any polity at home, and democratic polities most of all. Academically, of course, he was steeped in modern British history.[4] He therefore understood the evolution of the British liberal tradition, and he valued the qualified individualism that went with it. But the lessons that weighed upon him most vividly came more, I think, from a proximity to the politics of the real world, and from their consequences as he perceived them in the raw. These were located in the international domain, and they made him above all a pluralist.[5]

In Pearson's conception, as in the conception of others in his tradition, politics is ultimately a manifestation of differences of interest, actual or perceived. It is at once an *expression* of conflict and the means to its resolution. Given that resources are limited, whereas "appetites" (needs and wants) are endless, the interests in play can never be fully satisfied. Hence, politics is permanent. It follows that it is not a disease that can be cured. If it is a disease at all, everyone has it. It is intrinsic to life. About the best we can hope for is to manage our experience of it in a reasonably civilized fashion, and seek in the process to inhibit the appearance of its most unpleasant symptoms. To the extent that we are successful in doing so, we have made "progress."

It follows from this that a "good" politics is a politics that does a good job of resolving conflicts. Resolving conflicts well is taken to mean resolving them peacefully by means of bargaining, negotiation, and a measure of give-and-take. A good resolution is thus one that provides reasonable satisfaction to the conflicting parties, while ensuring that the conflict itself neither deepens, nor escalates, nor spreads needlessly to other players. In the normal course of events, these results are achieved on a continuing basis in a given society whenever successive government responses to competing demands are widely accepted as having been fairly distributed overall – that is, when they are regarded as having been delivered with a tolerable measure of balance. By the same token, a "bad" politics is a politics that responds to conflict through the exercise of force or oppression, leads some interests to be the consistent winners and others to be the consistent losers in the contest over time, and produces in consequence a de-stabilizing intensification of unresolved differences.

On this account, at least two elements are necessary for "good" politics to occur. These are *sound institutions*, and *sound attitudes*. Sound institutions are institutions that secure the effective representation, as well as the articulate expression, of the interests in play. For this, the precondition is the assurance of liberty – particularly, but not solely, the liberty of the individual. Sound institutions also provide efficient, rule-governed procedures for resolving the differences that the representation of competing interests serves to express. Sound attitudes, it hardly needs to be said, are the attitudes that are necessary to ensure that such institutions actually work.

In politics, more often than not, *institutions* are established by *constitutions*. In the liberal view, constitutions must be devised, and their conventions followed, with precisely these sorts of considerations in mind. They must be based also on the understanding that their purpose is aimed more at ensuring that the competition will be fairly conducted than that any particular construction of the content of the "good society" (apart from the procedures that should govern it) should be guaranteed. The constitution of a free society thus makes it possible for pluralistic interests to express themselves, and for their differences to be settled by means that are neither oppressive nor authoritarian.

As a practical matter, a society that is organized on liberal pluralist premises in this way can only function effectively if its inhabitants have tolerant dispositions. In August 1949, while still fresh from the public service in his new role as public politician, Pearson chose to exposit for the benefit of the Couchiching Conference what he later called his "philosophy of politics and government."[6] His opening line was a flat statement: "The essential lubricant for a free society is tolerance."[7] The tolerance he had in mind was the tolerance of diversity and the requirement for compromise. In any society ruled by the consent of the governed, there must be both understanding and acceptance of the need to give, as well as to take. In the absence of this disposition, conflicts cannot be amicably resolved, disagreements are intensified, and the system as a whole comes under stress. If the deterioration is allowed to advance to extremes, the system itself may actually break down.

A corollary of all this is that the interests of no single group can be allowed to prevail at the expense of another – not consistently, at least, and not in ways that the losing interest, or the interest that has to pay the price, regards as fundamental. This proposition is more easily expressed than implemented, and buried in the principle itself are difficulties sufficient to torture many a philosophical mind, John Stuart Mill's prominently among them. For Pearson, this was one of the prerequisites for the effective functioning of all "free" societies – for all societies, that is, that are established on liberal foundations. And it was a requirement that had particular force in Canada. Canadians were committed "to the principle that by compromise and adjustment we can work out some sort of balance of interests which will make it possible for the members of all groups [listed elsewhere in the same passage as "racial, geographic, economic, religious or political"] to live side by side without any one of them arbitrarily imposing its will on any other."[8]

The very multiplicity of the interests that Pearson identified in expressing this view was at least as significant as the interests themselves. For it is essential to the liberal pluralist conception that interests be perceived as multiple, so that the politics they generate can be interpreted as kaleidoscopic. The polarization of a political community along any single dimension, or through the coalescing of differences in tandem with any single cleavage (over religion, for example, or language, or race, or – as the Marxists would have it – class) is a recipe, not for resolving conflict, but for ensuring that it will persist and become more intense. It makes the balancing of interests that is so essential to stability and to the conduct of an amicable politics an immensely more difficult, if not impossible, aspiration. The liberal pluralist is grateful for complexity, for overlap, for paradox. They all yield fluidity, and fluidity gives room for manoeuvre. Deals can be struck, trade-offs can be made, coalitions can be engineered. At another time, and for another cause, they can be re-arranged. Multiple portraits of reality, moreover, each of them true but incomplete, can be constructed in response to almost any interest's need for self-legitimation, and for the assurance that its demands have been reasonably taken into account. Everyone can get a piece of the action. None, no doubt, will be satisfied in full. But most will be "satisficed." And that is enough to maintain the stability of the state, along with the acquiescence (and, for most of the time, the amity) of its citizens.

All this leads the classical pluralist to think well of some things, but not of others. Among the latter are concentrations of power. It goes without saying that these can threaten the security and welfare of the individual.[9] But at the level of public policy, they can also distort the equilibrium, the "balance," that must characterize the responses of government to the issues of the day if the requisite satisficing of multiple interests is to occur. In the end, they leave too many interests standing outside the pale, where they are neglected and deprived of community succour and reward. Also to be avoided is an attachment to dogma, an addictive and infectious condition which inhibits both the pursuit and the acceptance of the compromises upon which the survival of the liberal order as a whole depends. A further hazard is ignorance of the world, along with related sources of tunnel vision, for the latter, too, enfeebles the capacity to understand the needs and perspectives of others. In so doing, it undermines the empathy that makes compromise acceptable. Emotional habits of mind are sometimes a cognate affliction. They nurture the politics of passion at the expense of the politics of reason, so that the detachment necessary to the weighing of interests (in the long term as well as the short) is lost to the process of give-and-take. Overly grand designs can similarly get in the way by depriving the responsible political practitioners of the flexibility they need for the effective performance of governmental tasks – the making of trade-offs not least among them.

What the liberal pluralist *likes* is largely the opposite of these. Particularly favoured is the diffusion of power. But where power cannot be diffused, its containment – by institutions most obviously, but sometimes by countervailing forces – will do. A pragmatic disposition – informed by principle, certainly, but guided also by a deep understanding of practical limits – is similarly preferred, along with the capacity for detached analysis that its exercise routinely demands. Tolerance is essential, and with it the empathy that is sometimes associated in its most sophisticated form with a liberal education and, perhaps more generally, with an upbringing (often religious) that assigns a particularly high moral value to compassion.

Taking all this into account, the liberal pluralist gravitates naturally, as Pearson himself conceded, to the "middle of the road"[10] – there being in the pluralist vision, of course, not one road, but many, upon which to find the middle way. The roads themselves keep shifting their place as history unfolds, kicking up new issues and ideas, and with them new interests and new sources of conflict. In most cases, the middle of the road is philosophically the easiest place to be, since its justification often demands little more than a reference to the principle of compromise itself, along with an invocation of the rules of fair play. Beyond that, the pertinent philosophical arguments are supplied directly by the disputing players. The pluralist in power has only to respond. In responding, he or she soon discovers that the middle of the road is not only the easiest place to drive from the philosophical point of view, but also the most rewarding place to drive from the political point of view (even if it leads to pot-shots from the ditches on either side). On some accounts of the history of Canada's politics, the Liberal party has been consistently more astute than any of its rivals in finding the middle of the roads that are bearing the greatest traffic and, in consequence, it has had the most enduring enjoyment of the privileges of office.

The party's rivals, on the other hand, would answer that this is not a function of its political acumen, but of its lamentably pragmatic want of principle. Pearson understood the meaning of this charge. He may even have felt its weight. Pluralists often do. But they cannot escape their overwhelming sense that political reality is what it is. This awareness of reality – of limits, of what they think is constructively possible – is what drives their position in the end. But their pluralism, and with it their distrust of concentrations of power, does lead them to become at least the "champions-in-moderation" of interests that might otherwise always lose. Pearson himself once asked the central question: Is the middle way "merely the political line of least resistance along which drift those without the courage of their convictions, or simply without convictions?"[11] His answer showed that he knew the danger was real. "It is," he said, "*or should be*, far more than that." [author's emphasis] This implied that it sometimes might not be. But what he *wanted* it to be was clear enough. Part of it was a reflection of the liberal's preoccupation with the individual – with (as Pearson put it) "human values," and "the integrity and worth of the individual in society," together with "the emancipation of the mind," and "personal freedom and well-being." The approach of the principled liberal, he went on, "is irrevocably opposed to the shackling limitations of rigid political dogma, to political oppression of, and to economic exploitation by, any part of the community. It detests the abuse of power either by the state or by private individuals and groups. It respects first of all a person for what he is, not who he is. It stands for his right to manage his own affairs, when they *are* his own; to hold his own conviction and speak his own mind. It aims at equality of opportunity. It maintains that effort and reward should not be separated and it values highly initiative and originality. It does not believe in lopping off the tallest ears of corn in the interests of comfortable conformity."[12]

Given the emphasis on the realities of power, on the persistence of difference, on the importance of having the freedom to express it, and on the permanence of politics as the ultimate consequence, the liberal pluralist is a reformer, and not a utopian. Certainly Pearson was not. There was evidence in his writings of a modest belief in progress, just as there were signs in his behaviour of an impressive determination to make things better. But the perfect society was in another world or, at the very least, a long way off. His practical interest was therefore in practicable projects, not in wish-lists, no matter how noble the intentions that gave them birth.

The liberal pluralist, as I have implied, has enormous respect for power – so much so, that its containment is at the centre of the liberal project. This is worthy of further elaboration. For with the respect for power as a force of history goes a certain recognition of the inevitability of its effects. By appropriate mechanisms of state, its impact can be diffused. But it cannot be diffused entirely. Nor can its exercise be completely contained. On the other hand, with luck, with effort, with rightly designed institutions and the help of appropriate understandings of how politics works, it can be more constructively directed. To this extent, the pluralist is a realist, although not a fatalistic one. There is room for manoeuvre. In the pursuit even by the powerful of the most coveted of their interests, there is always the possibility of a usefully constraining enlightenment. The Lords Beveridge and Keynes, who together did as much as anyone to create the postwar Western consensus on the functions of government, argued in favour of state intervention not from compassionate motives alone, but because they knew it would be the best protector of capitalism in the end. (It is possible to argue that the lesson needs to be re-learned once again, the hard-faced advocates of unfettered market forces having apparently forgotten, in the exuberance of their globalized endeavours, that they can still be mightily inconvenienced by states that have been aroused to action by the politics of their disaffected.) As Pearson himself put it, "To the extent that the influence and power of any individuals or groups within a nation is greater than their recognition and acceptance of responsibility and of the rights of others – to that extent democracy is merely a word and not yet an achievement."[13]

In the specific case of the domestic politics of Canada, as Pearson viewed it, the capacity of the powerful to exact mischief at the expense of the weak had been confined to reasonable levels by a system of representative and responsible government that had been conveniently coupled to the federal principle. By the same token, the attractions of dogma – another of the enemies of a free society – had been undermined by the wilful diversities of the country itself, which gave short shrift to the inflexible and the doctrinaire. The appearance of emotionally excessive forms of Canadian nationalism had likewise been inhibited (at the federal level at least) by these realities of difference, and by the differences between English-Canada and French-Canada most of all.[14] Their effect was to force-feed a politics of compromise that made immoderately nationalist projects hard to sell.[15] Such political dogmas as could be rooted in religion, moreover, had been largely driven from Canadian politics by the separation of church and state. There was no need in the Canada of the postwar period (not in most of it, anyway) to inveigh, as Laurier had had to do in the late 1870s, against the destructive polarization that would come from creating parties of Catholics and parties of Protestants. In making his case to his opponents in 1877, he had displayed in the most explicit terms the pluralist's perennial fear of the destructive effects of irreconcilable difference. "You wish," he said, "to organize all the Catholics into one party, without other bond, without other basis, than a common religion; but have you not reflected that, by the very fact, you will organize the Protestant population as a single party and that then, instead of the peace and harmony now prevailing between the different elements of the Canadian population, you will throw open the door to war, a religious war, the most terrible of all wars?"[16]

In combination with the individualism of the liberal tradition, the diversities of geography, language, and ethnicity had also served to prevent the emergence in Canadian politics of a significant contest between irreconcilable classes. The contest was certainly there, and those on the left were given to taking great notice of it. But it was a muted engagement, diffused by cross-cutting conflicts of other kinds.

In all, it seemed hard to think of a country more closely matched than Canada to the pluralist view, or more suited to its practical application.

These awarenesses may actually have come to Pearson rather late. As I have already observed, his formative political tutoring came more from international than from domestic affairs. Here, the pluralist premise had a special pertinence and, as it turned out, a special calling.

For Pearson, there was a sense in which the most distinguishing feature of the politics of the international environment was that it was pre-constitutional. Compensating for that void, and perhaps in some measure attempting to fill it, was at the heart of his mission, and it profoundly influenced the way he responded in his mature professional life to such opportunities for initiative as the course of world affairs presented. The stakes in the international context were in some respects more obvious than they were at home. Certainly they were more violent. It was the spectacle of violence, experienced initially in the First World War, that probably moved him most.[17] For Pearson, as for others of his generation, the problem of international politics centred on war and peace, which he defined in stark and simple terms. It had to do with the killing and maiming of people, and with the destruction of property on a horrendous scale, by wilfully violent acts of state. In our present era, we can think of the problem of security as having many dimensions, some of them related to disease, poverty, the degradation of the natural environment, and the depletion of resources. We can think this way because we know such phenomena do a lot of killing in their own rights, because we believe they are also among the more fundamental of the causes of war itself, and because (for the moment, at least) we are not so deeply distracted by the sorts of immediate and dramatic threats to security that in Pearson's day dominated the international agenda. There was certainly evidence in his career after 1945 of an interest in promoting the more ancillary of the conditions of peace – the economic prosperity of the disadvantaged abroad not least among them. But in the end he was under no illusion that the wars of Europe, with which he was most familiar, or latterly those of Asia, had much to do with poverty or disease or environmental decay. Like most of his contemporaries, he certainly believed that they were facilitated by the absence of democracy, and by the ability of dictators in his own time to both cultivate and feed upon the resentments emanating from economic hardships, of which some were widely attributed to the Treaty of Versailles.[18] Ultimately, however, he knew them to be rooted not just in the *concentration* of power, but in its *abuse*.[19] This was particularly the case in the workings of dogmatic ideologies and nationalisms, in the principle of state sovereignty and the anarchical circumstances to which it led, and in the imperialism of the most powerful states. There was not, perhaps, a great deal that could be done about the way in which other states governed their internal affairs. But perhaps something *could* be done about the institutional structure of the international environment itself, and about the way in which inter-state conflicts were managed, contained, and resolved. In a sense, Pearson viewed the international community in the way a Madisonian liberal might survey the state of nature.[20] It was diversely composed, as Canada was. It was also under-institutionalized, as Canada was not. It was therefore in need of a social contract. If a full contract could not be obtained, a series of partial contracts would at least be an advance.

There is a serious danger in this sort of exposition that the subject will be given a greater coherence than is really there. Distorting chaotic realities so that they can be made to fit with an economical construct is one of the persistent temptations of academic life. Politicians do it, too. Such activities are useful, even essential, to the comprehension of our world, but the process can be abused. It needs therefore to be closely watched. And it is true that Pearson did not himself say everything that I have said about what I think he believed. But he said much of it – enough, in fact, to allow his behaviour in response to the political dilemmas of the real world, and his commentaries upon them, to fill in the gaps. Perhaps a few small demonstrations will suffice, starting first with some of his reactions to the world abroad.[21]

Here, it may be useful to begin with the question of institutions. Sound institutions, as we have already noted, are crucial to the taming of concentrations of power and to the construction of rule-governed procedures for resolving conflicts among competing interests. Without them, a "good" politics is hard to get. Their absence is especially dangerous for the weak, but it creates hazards for the strong as well. It follows that the institutionalization of the international environment is a potential first order of business. For Pearson, it became so. As Peter Gellman has tried to demonstrate,[22] he was not an unqualified supporter of the principle of "collective security." Such a principle demanded far too much from sovereign states that were far too powerful in an environment that they regarded as far too primitive, and hence far too unworthy of trust, to warrant their taking the risk. In the absence of a *perfect* world order – an order in which all states could count on the reliable enforcement of the public peace – an *im*perfect order would still be an advance over no order at all.

This preoccupation came early, perhaps triggered initially by the First World War and the Wilsonian aspiration. It was evident – we might now think strangely – in an early, if conflicted, affection for that particularly accommodative "order-in-diversity" that was represented by the evolving British Empire and Commonwealth.[23] It surfaced most explicitly in the interwar period in Pearson's response to the awkward dance of the League of Nations (and the Canadian government) over the Italian invasion of Abyssinia.[24] The essence of his position was clear. The League should have been made to do as much as it could, but should not have been asked to do more than it could, it being understood that the limits of the possible were determined in the end by the pervasiveness of the sovereignty principle,[25] in combination with the will (or want of it) of the greater powers. The best should thus not be pressed home in preference to the good, for it would certainly be defeated and bring the good down with it.

In this sober calculus can be found the kernel of Pearson's approach to the construction of the postwar international order – an approach that was shared in general, if not in every detail, by most of his senior colleagues in the foreign service. International institutions were to be created, encouraged, nurtured. Since the process could advance only by the consent of the players, and since the consent of some of the players (the most powerful ones) mattered more than the consent of the others, it ought not to be pushed beyond the limits of what the greatest of them would regard as acceptable. Otherwise the legitimacy of the enterprise would be lost. This would certainly be the result if the distribution of decision-making entitlements were not designed so as to be reasonably in accord with the distribution of capacities, and hence of obligations. The smaller powers might rejoice in the principle of state equality, but if they were to *insist* upon it, the great powers would pick up their marbles and go home. The cause of a peaceful world order, along with the interests of the weaker states, would then be no farther ahead.

John English has reminded us that Pearson's "direct influence on Canadian policy and on Canada's work at the San Francisco conference," which finalized the essentials of the United Nation's (UN's) constitution, "was not great."[26] Despite his pragmatism, he was frustrated by the general instruction from Ottawa that Canadian delegates "do nothing to endanger American, Russian or British acceptance of the charter." In the bargaining over the extent to which the great-power privileges enshrined in the Dumbarton Oaks draft might be modified to make room for the more active participation of states of lesser rank, he thought it led too often to retreat.[27] This was a reaction not to the policy itself, but to how it was applied. Politics was still the art of the possible. The only issue in dispute concerned the judgement of what was possible and what was not.

In the middle of the conference, Pearson took time out to give an account of the Canadian position to the Town Hall Club of Los Angeles. He was a public servant. His address reflected the government line. But its themes were obviously amenable to his own way of thinking and they warrant attention here. The interest in institutionalization, the recognition of the realities of power, the desire to leaven the future politics of the UN by ensuring that its own diversities would be taken adequately into account, the concern to ensure that the best not be pursued at the expense of the good, the gradualism of the liberal's preference for evolutionary reform, the distrust of idealism taken to excess – all these were clearly evident.

First came the accommodation of the principle of state sovereignty with the pervasiveness of power – an accommodation that the great powers had built for themselves into the Dumbarton Oaks draft, and that the Canadians now wished to see extended to powers of the middle rank. "We agree," Pearson told his apparently appreciative American listeners, "that power and responsibility should be related, that absolute equality in any world organization would mean absolute futility. No country will be able to play its proper part in international affairs if its influence bears no adequate relation to its obligations and its power. This, however, means not only abandoning the fiction that Salvador and Russia are equal in the World Security Council, but also abandoning the fiction that outside the group of four or five great powers, all other states must have an exactly equal position."

The new organization, he went on, had to be universal. There was "no permanent basis for a world organization on any alliance of a few powers, however great. There must be an international framework within which great powers can work with each other, but also with all other powers. The world organization must be a symphony, not a string quartet," although it would still have to have a leader. The leader would be the "Big Three" (the United States, Britain, and the Soviet Union), who would have to work amicably together if the system were to be effective.

In offering these observations, Pearson freely conceded their realist premise: "Canada's preoccupation with San Francisco is based," he said, "on the hard realities of the existing international situation." There were "dangers in seeking perfection." Whatever emerged from the conference would be "a compromise." It would not, and could not, be "ideal." "If we insist on perfection, we might not get anything. We would merely make the *best* the enemy of the *good*." [Pearson's emphasis] Canada's "main purpose" was "to get an organization going which everyone will accept and which will help to ease international difficulties by adding to the machinery for international co-operation." It accepted the fact that not all of its own preferences would be met. The charter would have to "represent the highest common denominator of agreement among the four great powers. The veto, for instance, [was] "unavoidable ... simply because unanimity among the great powers was essential."

Canada was particularly interested in the proposed Economic and Social Council: "What we are trying to create here is a league for peace, not a league for war. There must always be in reserve overwhelming force on the side of peace, but the use of that force, or even the threat of its use, must become the deplorable exception, not the general rule. The new international organization must therefore come to think and act less and less in terms of force and more and more in terms of forces – the forces that create or destroy international amity and goodwill, the forces that create poverty or promote well-being."

The UN was only the beginning of the process of establishing a system in which *all* states, "great and small," would "co-operate in the work of ensuring peace and promoting welfare," and would be committed to the ultimate objective of bringing "national force" under "international control." This objective would not be easily attained. There would be "counterattacks." The process would be "slow" and "tough." There would have to be "superb organization" and "brilliant improvisation." There would also have to be "[a]t times caution;

at other times, a willingness to run great risks for great objectives. At all times a refusal to permit temporary reverses to shake our belief in ultimate victory. Above all, there must be no false optimism about the possibility of an early victory. There is no easy and upholstered way from the foxhole to the millenium. We shall not secure victory over war at San Francisco ... But we must be very sure that we get ... as large and effective a beachhead as possible ... If we fail, then we might as well agree with the cynic who referred to this war as 'the little one before the last.' "[28]

The premises of these arguments crop up again and again in Pearson's observations on world affairs in the immediate postwar period, the period of the "creation." They were at the foundation of his own role in the development of some of the UN's "specialized agencies."[29] They were at the root of his approach to the construction of the North Atlantic Alliance. The distrust of grand designs, the will to cooperate, the insistence on realistic assessments of the distribution of power, the emphasis on the eclecticism of causes and effects, the belief in multilateral arenas as vehicles for the encouragement of accommodation, the conviction that pragmatism is inescapable and the most constructive way to go – all these ingredients of the pluralist view were routinely evident in his disquisitions, public and private alike. In early 1948, for example, he instructed the Vancouver Branch of the Canadian Institute of International Affairs in "Some Principles of Canadian Foreign Policy." "Foreign policy," he said, was merely " 'domestic policy with its hat on.' " It reflected an array of "domestic factors," among them "[g]eography ... climate, natural resources, the racial composition of our population, historical and political development, our dependence on foreign trade, our physical and economic relationship to the United States, our historic association with Britain in a commonwealth of nations ..." These were "the factors that influence, and often determine, the decisions which the Canadian government has to make on individual problems which require action." It was "the collectivity of these decisions, made in a variety of ways, with great thought or little thought, for good reason or for no reason, which make up what we call 'foreign policy.' " In addition, of course, Ottawa's options were "limited also by the policies and attitudes of other governments."

Given all these constraints, foreign policy could not take the form of "clear-cut, long-range plans and policies under national direction and control." Canada had power, but it should not be exaggerated "by talk of sovereign rights and unrestricted independence." Few of its objectives, in any case, were "concrete or positive, except in the realm of international economic policy, where again the major decisions are outside our sole control." Its "modesty" or "timidity" in foreign affairs reflected, in part, the recognition that it could "most effectively influence international affairs not by aggressive nationalism but by earning the respect of the nations with whom we co-operate, and who will therefore be glad to discuss their international policies with us." Canada knew "instinctively" that it could not "easily secure and maintain prosperity except on the broadest basis of multilateralism," which was "another name for internationalism."[30]

Canada's interest, in short, lay in the cultivation of institutionalized international regimes within which there was a willingness to "deal." That willingness to deal, however, depended for its success on attitudes and norms, as well as on institutional frameworks. It required, once again, tolerance, moderation, an affinity for compromise, a preference for the "middle way," a rejection of extremes. In the real world, these were in scarce supply, being cut off at the source by forces inimical to empathy, to reason, to an understanding of the inevitability of difference and of what that inevitability means. Among them were not only the blinkered perceptions of political leaders caught up by their adversarial circumstances, but sometimes also the constraints upon flexibility that flowed from the unreasoning demands of an emotional, untutored and aroused constituency. The more severe the conflict, the more inflamed the response. In such circumstances, the preference of the pluralist is the instinct of the diplomat: cool the temperature, contain the damage and, if necessary, work to persuade the parties that their dispute is a matter of interest, not of principle. Principles cannot be traded off; interests can.

Evidence of these tactical precepts or "instrumental beliefs," as political scientists at one time were given to calling them,[31] can be found as commonly in Pearson's writings as in his professional practice. In the second volume of his memoirs, for example, he comes to the defence of "quiet diplomacy," the purpose of which is to promote the constructive resolution of conflict. The public, he says, is entitled to "full information on the principles determining our foreign policies and on the practices followed in applying those principles," and it has a right to expect "publication of agreements made or of commitments undertaken." But this does "not mean the issue of a statement every day on the progress of negotiations, or on the Canadian position ... on every detail ... This would make give-and-take bargaining and compromise impossible." Publicity is sometimes necessary as a political weapon, but it is then "an admission of the failure of diplomacy," not an extension of it.[32]

In *Democracy in World Politics*, he observes that "if diplomatic representatives are to have the freedom of manoeuvre which is required to bring about agreement, and if 'face' is to be kept in its proper place, negotiations *in camera* are often better than those before the camera." More fully, "The purpose of negotiation is the reconciliation of interests, the exploring of a situation in an effort to find some common ground, some possibility of compromise, the seeking of agreement through mutual adjustments. Such adjustments are not made easier, and may well be made impossible, when the negotiators fear that any concession or compromise will within the hour be printed, pictured, or broadcast back home as a capitulation."[33]

This is standard stuff for students of diplomacy, and Pearson has no trouble finding quotations from Sir Harold Nicolson, de Callières, George Kennan, and even Louis XIV, in support of his argument. But there is more to his position than mere advice on technique, for the technique is the mirror of the substance. Pearson was writing when the cold war was still frigid and nuclear holocaust was still a prospect. His fear of the consequences of dogmatic judgement is palpable:

If … it is true that the function of negotiation is the reconciliation of opposing interests, it is also a stubborn fact of international life that different nations have interests which do strongly oppose each other. Those who ignore that fact or, at the other extreme, try to explain differences of policy solely in terms of all white on one side and all black on the other, live in a world of unreality. To the extent that such men's myths and bogeys determine policy, disaster is likely to result. That is undoubtedly one of our greatest dangers today. It also obstructs and frustrates that reconciliation which is the main function of negotiation …

In my view, nothing could be more dangerous in this divided world than a final and complete failure of man's ability to communicate with man across whatever differences of regime or race or economic conditions, across whatever curtains of fear, or iron, or prejudice may exist. As I see it, one of the most vital of our diplomatic purposes should be to keep open and to develop these channels of communication, so that some day, and may it be soon, when *both* sides are willing, they may be used for the process of negotiation and eventual agreement.[34]

These observations were delivered at Princeton University. Americans were supposed to take note.

In the light of these convictions and his preference for the "middle way," it is not surprising that Pearson internationally was so often (as John Holmes would have put it) in the middle of the argument. His enjoyment of the position was undisguised. Of the 1949 discussions in London on the question of how the Commonwealth might accommodate India's new status as a republic, he reported later with obvious satisfaction that "I was in a rather easy position as this was a battle that could be left to other delegations who took extreme views on one side or the other and my efforts could be devoted to finding compromises between the extremes."[35] If the foundations of a disagreement were such as to make a resolution manifestly impossible, of course, it was safer not to be driving on the road at all. Following a visit to India and Pakistan in 1950, for example, he concluded that the dispute over Kashmir was for the time being insoluble, and therefore suggested to Ottawa "that we should extricate ourselves from any special responsibility ..."[36] He had similar hesitations in the Middle East. As he recalled in his memoirs, "I heard some pretty wild speeches at the United Nations during the Cold War by Mr. Vishinsky and others, but nothing to equal the venom and the fury of the Arabs ... This was genuine; this was sincere; this was from the very depths of their being. And one of the things that made this rather different from other disputes at the UN was that Jewish feeling was equally deep and sincere. This was no diplomatic conflict; it was a life and death confrontation between two peoples. It still is."[37]

There were occasions when even Pearson was tempted to step out of character and offer a vigorous pronouncement by way of sending a signal to a foreign power. The usual result of the exception was to reinforce the rule. In the spring of 1951, for example, responding to American cold-war warriors whom he thought to be out of line over Korea, he offered in public a lengthy commentary during the course of which he observed that "the days of relatively easy and automatic political relations with our neighbour are ... over." The outcry on the American side of the border was such as to lead him to try to explain himself to Hume Wong, the beleaguered Canadian ambassador in Washington. In so doing, he observed that he was "more worried about extravagant praise from Canada than abusive criticism from Americans, because it shows how easy it would be to work up a strong anti-American feeling in this country at this time. The danger is obvious, and that is one reason why, having now said my piece, I will lapse back into the traditional Canadian-American speech pattern unless specific events and developments make that impossible, when I shall do my best to say nothing – in public!"[38]

Some 15 years later, as the American involvement in the Vietnam War was rising to its greatest height, Pearson, now prime minister, risked suggesting in a speech at Temple University that thought be given to a pause in the bombing of North Vietnam as an experimental encouragement to Hanoi to agree to diplomatic negotiations. President Lyndon B. Johnson invited him to lunch at Camp David the next day. Treated at first to a rude display of indifference, as if he were not there at all, he was then assaulted by an unprecedented and explosive presidential harangue. The gambit had failed. He could only have come away with his deeper instincts reinforced.[39]

It should not be concluded from the evidence of Pearson's preference for a pragmatic approach to the politics of give-and-take that he had no strong views about the respective moralities of alternative forms of government. Totalitarian politics and autocratic regimes do not sit well with liberals. Pearson's attacks upon "the armed might, the aggressive ideology, and the totalitarian despotism of the Communist empire of the USSR and its satellite states under the iron hand of one of the most ruthless tyrants of all time [Stalin]" could rival the rhetoric of the most dedicated of the anti-communist ideologues of his day. The Soviets had to be opposed in every way – militarily, economically, politically, philosophically. What he called the "Atlantic Vision" was dedicated to the defence, not just of a territorial arena, but of an entire civilization. But as a matter of practical politics, this did not mean that westerners should allow their antipathy to the communist experiment and its leadership to prevent them from engaging in bargaining and negotiation. When the Chinese entered the Korean War, the Americans insisted on branding them in the UN as aggressors. Pearson had no quarrel with the charge, but thought the making of it would prolong the war. With the help of others, therefore, he sought successfully to delay it for a time, pending the pursuit of a negotiated settlement. When the Americans finally lost patience with the attempt, the first display of pragmatism gave way to a second: Pearson called the resolution "premature and unwise," but voted for it anyway as a means of maintaining allied unity. Here, as elsewhere, empty gestures were to be avoided. Politics was a pragmatic art. It was also a practical one. There was no virtue in siding with the angels unless doing so could help the angels' cause. A serious acceptance of moral responsibility meant dealing in the hard choices kicked up by the real world, not in ostentatious but ineffectual displays of affection for ideal principles.

For smaller powers, it should be observed, this commitment to practicability often meant working at the margins of the great issues, not at their core – which was the special domain of the big battalions. Canada might try to amend, to modify, occasionally even to moderate, the behaviour of governments with resources substantially greater than its own. In this enterprise, it was necessary to work with others, and multilateral institutions helped to expand the opportunities. But in the practice, as in the theory, the aspiration should not exceed the grasp. In Korea, for example, the fundamental decisions to intervene in the hostilities in the first place, to launch a counteroffensive through Inchon, to cross the 38th parallel into North Korea and to condemn the Chinese as aggressors, were made by the United States. The Canadians, in league with others, could try to amend the terms of reference, to influence the diplomatic tactics, to fiddle with the timing. Beyond that, given their interests in the long term as well as the short, they were wise to go with the flow.

All this required, of course, a certain capacity for detachment. At the personal level, Pearson had this in bountiful measure. It was, after all, the other side of humour. But as he knew very well, his capacity to exercise it was the product also of Canada's fortunate geopolitical position. In many of the disputes in which he played a conflict-moderating role, the Canadian interest was more in the *fact* of settlement than in the *terms* of settlement. The 1956 Suez episode was the classic case, but not the only one. Canada, he had once pointed out, had "no territorial desires, having already quite as much geography as [it needed]," "no expansionist political ambitions," and "no inherited legacies of hatred or distrust with which to inflame and excite" its people. It worried, of course, about the ability of the US "to use its great new power in a way which will ensure peace and security for the world and will not infringe [Canada's] own legitimate national rights." Even that was "not a worry" to be expressed "in any positive way." It led only to "an 'on guard' posture."[40]

There is not here the space to establish at length the extent to which Pearson's pluralist view of the politics of the world was also reflected in the way he conducted himself first as leader of the opposition and then as prime minister at home. In the latter context, especially, there is a distracting clutter in the tale. Colleagues in his Cabinet were too prone to getting into ostentatious trouble. Their shenanigans exercised the press, gave fodder to the opposition, and overpopulated the agenda. In any case, the forensic partisanship of the domestic political process made the exercise of Pearson's preferred approach to the resolution of conflict a trifle difficult. Early on, he even tried to tone it down – a futile endeavour, particularly in an environment shared with John George Diefenbaker. As his memoirs later recorded, "I began to emphasize the need for a new kind of politics based more on national consensus and less on party conflict. What I had in mind was the kind of politics a nation will accept if facing defeat in war, but rarely, if ever, when confronted with disaster in time of peace."[41] In making the pitch to an audience composed largely of Toronto Liberals in early 1964, he paid homage to the importance of party politics as "the very foundation of Parliamentary democracy." But he wanted "a new politics" that would drop the "narrow and nasty, short-sighted and selfish partisanship." Some would think this idealistic, but it was "realistic too," because it was necessary if Canada was "to meet new and unprecedented challenges." "The new politics," he went on, "is, in a sense, merely good citizenship, a citizenship based on a deep pride in our country and its strength and its unity as one nation ... It is a citizenship more concerned with discharging duties than in proclaiming rights. It is a citizenship desperately anxious to find solutions to our social and political and economic problems and in the search is willing to rise above special and narrow interests." It would require everyone's involvement, without which we would be "spectators betraying our democratic responsibility and our democratic rights." It was that betrayal which paved "the way for the extremists, for their noise and for their violence, all the more dangerous because [the] uproar [was] given so much publicity." The rational pluralist was here hard at work. Soften the polarization; offload the intolerance and the extremism, along with the emotive vocabulary and the accusatory rhetoric; bring a reformist spirit to the challenge of change; focus on finding practical solutions to real problems. As he later ruefully observed, the "appeal had little or no effect," and the "country was unmoved."[42]

With regard to the more substantive matters of state, problems of economic policy, as John English has indicated, seemed not greatly to interest him. On the other hand, his belief in the importance of balancing interests, and in the liberal principle of equality of opportunity, led readily enough to support for significantly redistributive initiatives in social policy. Initially, he gave his blessing to Walter Gordon's ill-fated attempts to contain the power of foreign capital, although, in typical accommodation of forces that he came to think were beyond the government's political capacity to overcome, he retreated in the end.[43]

It was probably in the area of French-English relations that the premises of his political *praxis* were most clearly evident. As he later put it, "My passionate interest when I was in government, apart from the ultimate question of peace and war, was in the national unity of our country. In some respects this was the most important issue of my career." Characteristically, he described it as "a problem of many facets embracing, among other factors, the constitution, federal-provincial relations, and the bread-and-butter issues of tax-sharing and equalization grants." But he thought "the problems of culture and language [were] pre-eminent."[44]

He encouraged bilingualism and biculturalism, the purpose of which was clearly intended not only to help francophones feel fully comfortable and at home in Canada, but also to create the fabric of mutual understanding and empathy upon which support for essential policies of practical accommodation would have to depend. "I wanted French-speaking Canadians to feel deeply that they were and were recognized as an integral part of Canada," he wrote later. He also wanted "a nation-wide recognition of the cultural and linguistic fact which they embodied so that they would be content to remain within confederation, and thus make Canada strong." For he could "see no way of holding our country together unless English Canada adopts a new attitude towards the intention of our French-speaking compatriots to maintain their identity, their culture, and their language as a special fact of life within Canada. Those who persist in telling us that we must do away with this idea, that we must insist on talking about our country, race, and nation as one and indivisible – these are the real separatists."[45]

Imbedded in this position was Pearson's perennial distrust of abstractions that get in the way of pragmatically balanced responses to the demands of competing interests. His support of biculturalism and bilingualism led to his being "attacked as a believer in two nations." Exasperation ensued: "Our critics were trying to crucify Canada on a cross of words. It is a dreadful experience to see disputes develop over semantic differences (this time over the word 'nation'), especially when there are those who for reasons of their own are eager to distort those semantic differences into differences of substance. This misrepresentation is so easy, and has been tried so often, that one is almost afraid to use the word 'nation' at all. The French in Canada are a nation in the sense that they are a separate people. As Sir John A. Macdonald said of them: 'Treat them as a nation and they will act as a free people do – generously; call them a faction and they become factious.'" There was a point beyond which the federal government could not go, and Pearson had never argued that "two *political* nations [his emphasis]" could "exist within one country." But this did not mean that the francophone identity could not be recognized and accommodated.[46]

The practical manifestations of Pearson's understanding of the national unity problem, grounded as always in the recognition of difference, were probably represented best by the Royal Commission on Bilingualism and Biculturalism,[47] and by the "opting-out" features of his doctrine of "cooperative federalism." It would be hard to find a more telling example of the liberal pluralist's dedication to practical flexibility in the construction of "sound institutions" than the latter, or a more persuasive demonstration of the attempt to cultivate "sound attitudes" than the former. On the other hand, the limits beyond which he was not prepared to go were reflected most visibly in the firmness of his response to Quebec's attempt – supported by the France of Charles de Gaulle – to establish itself as an actor with an internationally recognized entitlement to operate in world affairs in a manner that was independent of the government of Canada.[48]

Lester Pearson was certainly a liberal. He was also a realist. He understood difference and what it means to politics. He also understood power and what it, too, means to politics. From the combination of the two came an array of attitudes and operational rules that were fundamental to his practice of the political art both at home and abroad. The latter came first, and the experience reinforced the native disposition.

Pearson's conception of politics is not the only conception. It may not even be the best conception – not *always*, at any rate. There are places, times and circumstances in which other views may yield better service.

In our current time of crisis in Canada, it is easy to sustain the argument that we risk our own destruction for want of precisely Pearson's understanding of what our survival as a country requires most of all – tolerance, empathy, understanding, and a willingness to give as well as to take. We speak much of our liberal rights, collective and individual, and of our entitlements. We speak little of our obligations. None should think these characteristics are manifested among *Québécois* secessionists alone. They appear elsewhere, too, and much less defensibly. For elsewhere, they are expressed most vigorously by the richest and the best served within the Canadian majority.

Canada could disintegrate because too many of us have abandoned the "sound attitudes" that are essential to ensuring that our "sound institutions" work.

Pearson and Diefenbaker: Similar Men?

J.L. GRANATSTEIN

To suggest that Lester Pearson and John Diefenbaker were "similar men" can produce a reaction of near outrage. Most everyone believes that Pearson and Diefenbaker were as different as chalk and cheese. Pearson was a great diplomat, a fine human being, an honourable man who grew into a fine parliamentarian. John Diefenbaker, on the other hand, is widely perceived as a politician with a mean streak, a man of low cunning whose greatest achievement, usually offered grudgingly, was that he was a superbly effective, if destructive, leader of the opposition. Few, except for the dwindling band of Diefenbaker loyalists, would disagree with either description. And yet, there are more similarities than are apparent on first glance.

The obvious one is that they were both born at roughly the same time in late nineteenth-century rural Ontario, though the Diefenbakers soon moved to the then-Northwest Territories. Their circumstances were different, the familial comforts of the Pearsons rather more middle class than those of the Diefenbakers, but they nonetheless shared certain British values in common, certain Protestant traditions, a certain base of knowledge. Both also went to university – Pearson to Victoria College at the University of Toronto, Diefenbaker to the much newer University of Saskatchewan in Saskatoon. At a time when only a tiny percentage of Canadians went on to higher education, this was a uniting trait. Both proved very intelligent, practical young men able to marshal words, but neither Pearson nor Diefenbaker was easily capable of abstract thinking, although that has never been an impediment in Canada. Probably neither could be judged to have possessed "first class minds" in the academic sense.

Their births in the mid-1890s also meant that they were of age to serve during the Great War, and both did. Pearson went with a Canadian hospital unit to England and then to the Salonika front; then, pulling "strings in a good cause" and using family connections to Minister of Militia and Defence Sir Sam Hughes, he wangled a transfer to officer training in England and then to a pilot's course with the Royal Flying Corps. Diefenbaker trained as infantry officer in Canada and proceeded overseas to England. Neither man made it to service on or over the Western Front and both thus survived, unlike so many of their fellow infantry lieutenants and green pilots. That Pearson and Diefenbaker had nervous crises ("neurasthenia," the term then in use) that spared them from combat is no sin, nothing of which either should have been ashamed. Even so, both camouflaged the inglorious end to their service more than slightly. Pearson's story was that he was hit by a bus in the blackout and invalided out of service, nothing more. John English tells it differently in his definitive biography. Diefenbaker said, among other things, that he had been injured by a shovel in a training accident in Sussex. His biographer, Denis Smith, has a much fuller account based on military and medical records.[1]

Their careers and lives soon diverged dramatically. Diefenbaker returned to Canada to attend law school at the University of Saskatchewan and to set up practice in Wakaw, a tiny town in that province. Pearson returned to Victoria College when he was demobilized, completed his degree and, after a brief period of employment in the United States, won a Vincent Massey fellowship that took him to Oxford, where he "read" ice hockey. Then it was a position teaching history at the University of Toronto.

Both men married before the end of the 1920s, though only Pearson had children. It soon was apparent that each, in his different way, had entered into a difficult marriage with a sharp-tongued woman who had substantial influence on him. Diefenbaker in fact would have two such marriages.

Egotistical and ambitious to a fault, John Diefenbaker was the first to seek entry into partisan politics, but the voters repeatedly rebuffed him, defeating his efforts in federal, provincial and municipal politics until, in 1940, swimming against a massive Liberal tide, he finally captured a seat in Parliament.

Pearson had more success early on, though there seemed few flashes of enterprise in him at the University of Toronto. In 1928 he secured a post in the Department of External Affairs through competitive examination (perhaps helped by Professor W.P.M. Kennedy's letter of reference that commented on his "distinct success with his students ... as an organizer"[2]) and rose steadily in that still-new service. Pearson was by now displaying every bit as much career-oriented drive as Diefenbaker, but he always felt a certain Methodist guilt about his ambition and hid it better than the Prairie lawyer. Still, he worked hard, charmed everyone he met and by 1935 had been appointed an Officer of the Order of the British Empire for his work with the Royal Commission on Price Spreads. He soon had increasing responsibilities on the staff of the High Commission in London, the perfect place to serve abroad in the critical prewar era. Pearson was more isolationist in his sentiments than Diefenbaker – a man who had struggled because of his Germanic surname during the Great War and who was a perfervid supporter of the British Empire as a result – but both supported Canada's entry into the war in September 1939.

The two were in Ottawa at the same time for many of the years after 1941; the chances are good that they met early and often. For much of that period, however, Diefenbaker remained an obscure backbencher, an underachieving disappointed political striver. His overweening ambition led him to consider seeking the Tory party's House of Commons leadership in 1940 at the very first caucus he attended as a newly elected member of Parliament, but, not surprisingly, he drew back: "I couldn't hope to get anywhere as everything was too cut and dried."[3] He did put his name forward for party leader in December 1942 and again in 1948, but he lost first to John Bracken and then to George Drew. Bitter disappointment ever after clouded his judgement, though he developed a mesmerizing oratorical style that captivated many small-town and rural Canadians in an era when stemwinding speeches were still a form of entertainment.

Pearson, on the other hand, had a slightly stumbling style of speechmaking, not least in French – he once commented that he spoke it "fluently only when under the influence of alcohol."[4] That interfered not at all with a steady upward climb that saw him named Canada's first professional diplomat to be an ambassador and, moreover, the Canadian representative to innumerable wartime agencies and conferences at which, with brilliant effectiveness, he played an increasingly important role for a nation that was feeling its oats – and its new power.

Nonetheless, the very competitive Pearson had not won the post he most wanted, under-secretary of state for external affairs, in early 1941, after Dr. O.D. Skelton's death. From England, Pearson had unhappily watched the choice fall on his friend and colleague, Norman Robertson, a more intellectual and less personable man who was his junior in the foreign service and in age. Robertson, however, was trusted by Prime Minister Mackenzie King and, most important, he was on hand. Even so, it is arguable, at a minimum, that King might have made the same choice even if Pearson had been in Ottawa; Hume Wrong, also Robertson's senior, was in Canada, and King passed him over too. Robertson felt guilty that the hand of fate had fallen on his shoulder. Pearson was furious, though he loyally pitched in with enormous effect to help run the Department of External Affairs when, in mid-May 1941, he was brought back to Ottawa.[5] Still, just as Diefenbaker never forgot those who denied him the party leadership in 1942 and 1948, so Pearson always remembered his disappointment at Robertson's better fortune.

After 1948 and his entry into politics at the top, a development which seemed in retrospect all but inevitable for one who had enjoyed the limelight in a most un-civil service-like way, Liberal external affairs minister Pearson sat across the floor of the House from Tory frontbencher John Diefenbaker. They clashed on occasion, but there was no special bad blood between them. Their views on the failing Empire/Commonwealth were different in emphasis, as the Suez Crisis of 1956 demonstrated. Pearson won the Nobel Peace Prize for his work in finding a peaceful end to the affair; Diefenbaker and many British-oriented Canadians thought he had let the British down and supported the Americans too readily. Pearson, however, had had sufficient trouble dealing with Washington that he probably was almost as suspicious of the Americans as was Diefenbaker. Certainly there are memoranda by Pearson worrying about Canada's growing dependence on trade with the United States,[6] and he likely had a hand in seeing Walter Gordon, whose growing doubts about American economic penetration of Canada Pearson had heard frequently, get the chairmanship of the Royal Commission on Canada's Economic Prospects.

John Diefenbaker took the brass ring first. He had no Nobel Prize (though he claimed that he had proposed United Nations peacekeeping before Pearson put it into effect at Suez[7]), but his minority victory in the federal election of June 1957 put him in command, and his enormous victory in the general election the next year, won over Pearson's Liberals with devastating effect, seemed to bid fair to make the rest of the century a Conservative one. It was a sweet victory for the Prairie lawyer – to triumph over Pearson was apparently a justification of the old ways and old virtues over the new ones that Pearson, the modern man, appeared to embody. But no one should forget the way Pearson and a few Liberals steadily chipped away at the Tory edifice. Mike Pearson was sometimes too tentative, too rational,[8] but his persistence and his ability to learn the details of Canadian domestic affairs ensured that he evolved into a fine opposition leader; he was arguably better in that role than as prime minister, just as Diefenbaker was.

Diefenbaker's government was an administrative shambles, his Cabinets wallowing at sea much of their time. Was Pearson's, in power from 1963 to 1968, much different? He had not been a notable administrative success in the Department of External Affairs,[9] and his ability to control his government was little better. The legislative record Pearson's administrations established was far better than Diefenbaker's and, given the conflicting viewpoints around the Liberal Cabinet table, it is difficult not to give much of the credit for that record to the prime minister whose combination of diplomatic skill, pragmatic management of affairs and hard-headed realism were sorely needed. Yet the vaunted efficiency that Pearson's government was supposed to offer in 1963 turned to ashes even before his promised "60 days of decision" were concluded. Pearson's ministers broke ranks and squabbled in public, leaked Cabinet secrets to the media, and became involved in serious scandal. The ineffective management of the Diefenbaker and Pearson governments was such as to suggest that competence had suddenly disappeared from Ottawa. Pearson did not share the corrosive suspicion of the public service that preyed on Diefenbaker's mind, but his government – and its leader, too – had almost as much difficulty in making up its collective mind and in protecting Cabinet secrets. Both leaders suffered very critical responses from the media, and neither ever developed a thick skin.

There was perhaps another similarity. Diefenbaker had a cruel, sometimes sadistic, streak that let him prolong and enjoy the discomfort he could inflict on others. He disliked those who had let him down or worked against him years earlier, and he could use his sharp tongue against Cabinet miscreants. Pierre Sévigny, for example, was regularly upbraided by the prime minister for his sins, while Ellen Fairclough recalled Diefenbaker's constant threats to replace her.[10] Pearson had some of this, as well. In 1966, when he was creating the Royal Commission on Security, he called in his old friend, Norman Robertson, who had been serving the government in trade negotiations. As Robertson noted, Pearson had talked about the commission, dangling the chairmanship before him but not offering it. "I knew that he wanted me to ask for it," Robertson told his wife, "but I wouldn't do that."[11] For Robertson, who had been under-secretary of state for external affairs for a second time from 1958 to 1963, and who had struggled to put his capacious intelligence at Diefenbaker's service, the difficulties of working under the two men were not all that different. Nor was the way they could use their power. Still, Pearson lies buried in the same tiny cemetery that Robertson (and Hume

Wrong, another friendly rival) occupies, suggesting ultimate unity of purpose.

Pearson had not used muckraking and scandalmongering as a weapon in opposition, and his government suffered grievously from Diefenbaker's mastery of it after 1963. Pearson could never have countenanced the implicit and sometimes explicit anti-*Québécois* racism that Diefenbaker and his members revelled in, and he despised the Tory for that. Nonetheless, he allowed himself to be dragged down to Diefenbaker's level during the scandal-ridden parliaments of 1963–66. When the two men met in the prime minister's office on 10 December 1964, to discuss the Munsinger case Pearson had learned of from the commissioner of the Royal Canadian Mounted Police, the prime minister noted that Diefenbaker "seemed tired and more than usually nervous." Pearson laid out what he had learned. Diefenbaker responded that, after interviewing Pierre Sévigny, the associate minister of national defence who had had an affair with Gerda Munsinger, a German-born Montreal prostitute who was suspected of having links with East German security agencies, he had satisfied himself that no security had been violated. It seems certain that Pearson hoped to persuade the opposition leader to cease the allegations of scandal that his party was levelling against the Liberal government by implicitly threatening disclosure of the Munsinger case.

Pearson thus delicately held a pail of slops over the opposition leader's head, in George Bain's telling phrase.[12] Not surprisingly, Diefenbaker responded in character, as Pearson noted in his memorandum of their meeting: "[he] indulged in his own form of blackmail by telling me that when he took office, there was a very important security file – from Washington – in which I was involved. He was surprised, I think, when I identified it, said I knew all about it, would have no worry if it were ever made public and had, years ago, told the U.S. State Department just that!"[13] This may have been the single most unedifying moment in Canadian political history, the time when a prime minister's attempt to silence the opposition was met with a counter-blackmail effort, both men relying on confidential security files for their ammunition. The two leaders rolled in the muck together, neither emerging with much credit.

This appalling incident notwithstanding, Pearson was nonetheless a much more decent and honourable man than John Diefenbaker. He had more ability, more charm, more justifiable international renown. He listened, even if sometimes too closely, to people and their representations.[14] Diefenbaker, on the other hand, talked and postured.[15]

Their memoirs ultimately differentiate their characters, even though the same researcher-ghost who helped Mike Pearson with his three volumes of reminiscences shortly thereafter went to work for John Diefenbaker in the production of *his* three-volume autobiography. John Munro did good work for both men, yet the resulting memoirs were very different and, ultimately, profoundly truthful. Diefenbaker's were venomous, self-serving and notoriously unreliable; Pearson's were self-deprecating, funny and much more accountable to the facts.

While men can be similar in many ways, they can still differ in the most important ways. There is no doubt whatsoever that, if the battle in the House of Commons between John Diefenbaker and Lester Pearson might fairly be called a draw, the battle in history thus far has been won hands-down by Pearson. John Holmes, the long-time diplomat, historian of foreign policy, and friend of Pearson, captured this most presciently in 1965. Holmes wrote a friend that he had spent several evenings discussing Pearson and his government with "several shrewd and neutral observers who expressed the opinion that the critics of the government and of the Prime Minister in particular were keeping their eyes on short term affairs and neglecting to notice that the Prime Minister was in fact riding hurricanes very successfully, leading the country the only way in which it could be led and that historians would undoubtedly look back upon him as a very forceful and effective Prime Minister."[16]

Holmes was precisely correct. The rating of prime ministers sponsored by a *Maclean's* panel of historians in 1997 placed Pearson "sixth" (just behind Trudeau and ahead of Borden in the "High Average" category), while Diefenbaker was "thirteenth" (at the very bottom of the "Average" category) out of our 20 prime ministers. This seems entirely appropriate. The high rating of Pearson is notable, when four of the first five places went to leaders (King, Macdonald, Laurier, and Trudeau) who had very long terms in power and won election after election. Pearson lost his first two elections as party leader and twice won only minority governments, but the record of his government nonetheless was most impressive. *Maclean's* scholars rewarded that record and, moreover, they recognized that Pearson's qualities of mind and heart were vastly more impressive than those of John Diefenbaker.[17]

Mike Pearson was the *beau idéal* for many Canadians who came to maturity in the 1950s and 1960s, and rightly so. He was also a very successful prime minister, the leader whose governments delivered the Canada Pension Plan and Medicare and laid the foundations of a bilingual and bicultural federal state.

The Unlikely Gladiators: Pearson and Diefenbaker Remembered

CHRISTINA MCCALL

When I first heard the title of Jack Granatstein's paper, "Pearson and Diefenbaker: Similar Men?" it seemed to me a mind-boggler. How was it possible that those warring titans whose palpable differences defined the public discourse in my green years as a political writer could be seen by such a renowned historian as being even vaguely alike? But after I had turned the notion around in my head for a few minutes, looking at it upside down and sideways, I realized that there was a time in the 1950s when I would have accepted Professor Granatstein's hypothesis with ease.[1]

After all, both men belonged to the generation of Anglo-Canadians who were born before the turn of the century, were called to the defence of the British Empire in the "war to end all wars," and energetically engaged in public life thereafter as members of the young dominion's small educated class. Men whose responses to the exigencies of the Depression and the Second World War led them to prominence in the old Canada – that long-lost homogeneous society whose citizens were connected to each other not by six degrees of separation, as the American playwright John Guare would have it, but by only one or two.[2]

For many people in the Anglo-Canadian middle class of the early postwar period, Diefenbaker and Pearson were as familiar as distant relatives and talked of in much the same terms. Certainly, they were in my parents' house in Toronto and in the houses of my friends.

My father was an Ulsterman who had immigrated to Canada as a boy and had involved himself in the Presbyterian Church and the Conservative party. John Diefenbaker's maternal uncle, Duncan Bannerman, was a member of the same Tory riding association, an adopted Celtic cousin who shared my father's prejudices and his hopes. They both loathed the condescensions of the English, the boosterism of the Americans, and the perfidies of the arch-Liberal William Lyon Mackenzie King.

To the barely pubescent me, Bannerman seemed a scary old character, with fierce pale eyes and the noxious habit of smoking cigars while expressing his immutable opinions after a roast-beef Sunday lunch. He convalesced at our house once from a mysterious operation. ("What was wrong with him exactly?" I asked my mother. "It's nothing for you to worry about," she replied. "It can only happen to men.")

When Diefenbaker, then an opposition MP from Saskatchewan renowned as an advocate for the underdog, came to Toronto to make a political speech – probably part of his doomed attempt to beat out the Ontario premier George Drew for the leadership of the federal Conservatives in 1948 – he fitted into his schedule a duty call on his uncle Dunc. In a fit of shyness, I hid in my room while Diefenbaker was in the house, but I could hear his voice reverberating up the stairwell as he addressed his tiny Tory audience of three while consuming tea and cakes. (Diefenbaker was a Baptist teetotaller and, out of respect for his convictions, my father and Mr. Bannerman must have decided to forego the occasional dram of whisky they enjoyed.)

After Diefenbaker left, waving grandly from a taxi, I listened while the adults talked about John's anti-Bay Street ideas and eloquent concern for the unjustly accused and unfairly disadvantaged – the very first time I ever heard an expression of western rage against the central Canadian hegemony.

Five or six years later, when I was studying at Victoria College in the University of Toronto, Lester Pearson, then leading a charmed life as the peripatetic secretary of state for external affairs in Louis St. Laurent's Liberal government, was much talked of in the college as its illustrious graduate, the honorific college chancellor and a power in cold-war diplomacy.

One Halloween, students from Burwash Hall – the men's residence where Pearson himself had lived as an undergraduate – burned in effigy the red-baiting American senator Joe McCarthy. After their prank was reported in *The Varsity* and picked up by the Toronto dailies, the college buzzed with the news that Pearson had written censoriously to the college principal about this profoundly illiberal act, even though – or perhaps because – he himself was suffering from the scrutiny of McCarthy's senatorial committee on American security. That episode – and the fact that Pearson's radiant face could be seen occasionally in American news magazines as he went his conciliatory way in the world – seemed to connect us directly to great events beyond parochial Canada. Undergraduate women seeking political sophistication as members of the university's international relations club could bask in Pearson's reputation when we toured the United Nations (UN) headquarters in New York; and undergraduate men – gangly boys from the same Ontario towns where Pearson had grown up as the son of a Methodist preacher – talked of the possibilities of "going into External" after they graduated and "making a difference in the world, just like Mike."

My parents looked on Pearson as a man who transcended party politics; he might have been a protégé of the hated King and a favourite of the suspect St. Laurent, but they knew a good man when they saw one. A close friend's parents, Cambridge classicists turned Canadian academics who were founding members of the social democratic Co-operative Commonwealth Federation (CCF), sympathized as Pearson tangled with the forces of American reaction. At the same time, they approved of Diefenbaker's advocacy of a citizens' bill of rights.

The cosy postwar Canadian consensus that this "approval across party lines" represented began to crumble as the 1950s wore away. With the bitterly fought pipeline debate of 1956 which proved to the electorate that the Grits were as arrogant as the Tories claimed. And with the Suez Crisis later that year, which brought both Lester Pearson's Nobel Peace Prize and the disaffection from him of die-hard British Imperial Canadians who saw his role in that tangled affair as a heinous betrayal of "Mother England."

These events, thought to be cataclysmic at the time, led to the Liberal party's fall from grace and to Diefenbaker's electoral triumphs of 1957, when he defeated the sadly aged St. Laurent, and 1958, when he overwhelmed the still boyish-looking Pearson, by then the Liberal leader.

When Pearson displayed embarrassing ineptitudes in his first two years as opposition leader, a job he approached with well-founded misgivings, and Diefenbaker enjoyed surprising successes in his early years as prime minister, a job he had been longing for most of his adult life, it looked as though the heyday of the old consociational Canada, elitist in its democracy and centred on the alliance of Ontario and Quebec, had passed forever, and that it would be Pearson's unenviable lot to oversee the steady decline of the Liberal party that had been so instrumental in its creation.

By the time I began to work in Ottawa in early 1960, as a young magazine writer recently married to a political journalist reporting from the Parliamentary Press Gallery, anybody expressing the bizarre notion that Diefenbaker and Pearson were "similar men" would have been laughed off Parliament Hill. Pearson was viewed as an overly genteel has-been, Diefenbaker as the harbinger of a more egalitarian Canada, fuelled by the rambunctious energy of the emerging West.

Animosity between the two men burgeoned as Pearson tried to adjust to being out of power and confined to dealing with mostly local (i.e., Canadian) affairs, and Diefenbaker struggled to wield power while turning away from traditional Tory ideas and traditional Tory supporters in the business community and seeking to appeal to both the emerging multicultural middle class and his natural agrarian constituency.

Among old Ottawa hands left over from the King-St. Laurent era, it was thought to be only a matter of time before some suitably important job abroad would be found for Mike by his international friends, since his foray into domestic politics was so clearly a disaster.

But before 1960 was over, *Fortuna* began to turn again in Pearson's favour. That was the year when Diefenbaker's errors of judgement in foreign and economic affairs, his ineptitude in managing his Cabinet and caucus, and increasing alienation from the intertwined business and bureaucratic elites began to tell. The year when monetary policy conflicts between the prime minister and James Coyne, the bloody-minded governor of the Bank of Canada, began to surface. The year when the opposition Liberals were heartened by their provincial counterparts' victories in Quebec (under Jean Lesage), and New Brunswick (under Louis Robichaud); by the election of the liberal Democratic candidate, John Kennedy, as president of the United States; and by the demoralizing effect their determined attacks in Parliament were having on Diefenbaker and his inexperienced front bench.

Senior mandarins in the bureaucracy and senior commentators in the press gallery began to express in private their grave concerns about what would happen to Canada if the renegade Diefenbaker wasn't stopped before he did Canada irreversible harm. As they toyed with their oysters at the communal table in the Rideau Club at noon and sipped their dry martinis in the bar of the Roxborough at nightfall, the Ottawa men began to tell each other, and their attentive junior colleagues, that only Mike could save the country.

For reasons particular to my circumstances, I watched this drama unfolding from one of the best seats in the house. The man I was married to then and I both wrote for magazines – still a powerful national medium – he for the old bi-weekly *Maclean's* and I for *Maclean's* and *Chatelaine*, with some side excursions into CBC radio and television. I also functioned as his researcher and editor, an extra pair of eyes and ears. In that guise, I went in his company to Question Periods, private bureaucratic briefings, and off-the-record interviews with politicians of a kind that women rarely attended and at which I listened mutely to constant talk about the urgent need for change.

Because of the restrictions on the subjects that women were thought capable of writing about then – commenting on Cabinet decisions of consequence, particularly when they had to do with the economy or international affairs, was thought to be beyond our scope – I also saw the Diefenbaker/Pearson era from the perspective of voters who were not privy to confidential briefings but were experiencing this need for change in their everyday lives as the postwar consensus faltered along with the postwar boom.

Some of the suitably "soft" issues that had not yet become central to the public policy agenda and could safely be assigned to a woman writer like me included proposed reforms of the archaic divorce laws; the failure of the social welfare system to meet the needs of the growing numbers of the unemployed; the problems experienced by the Inuit trying to leap for their lives into the twentieth century as white men brought their technology, their addictions and their diseases to the North; the ideas of the sociologist John Porter on how the class system worked against the interests of Canadians of non-British backgrounds; the causes and consequences of the brain drain to the United States; or – and this one came closer to home, or at least to Ottawa insider briefings – the hard lot of politicians' wives.[3]

Researching major articles on Olive Diefenbaker and Maryon Pearson was at least as revelatory of the marked differences in their husbands' experiences and attitudes as listening to the two men rail at each other across the Commons floor, or observing them closely at press conferences, political meetings, and social gatherings. Blair Fraser, the great liberal gentleman journalist of the postwar Liberal era, told me once that official Ottawa was a village where everybody knew everybody else, and it was important for political writers to be aware of its dangers as well as its charms, a perception that took on a heightened acuity when I interviewed the leaders' wives.

Encountering Mrs. Diefenbaker at 24 Sussex was like visiting a prairie parsonage presided over by a sweet-natured minister's wife who had an unexpectedly shrewd eye for the vagaries of his parishioners and the ways in which they might do him harm. After discussing with disarming frankness the details of her everyday life, she showed me the separate bedrooms where she and her husband slept; took me into the prime-ministerial kitchens and introduced me to the domestic staff; displayed for my admiration the best set of dishes used for queens and presidents, and the second-best set, used for practising politicians and assorted lesser lights; retrieved from the safe the modest jewellery that had been given to her as the Conservative leader's wife; told me confidentially – "I know you'll understand" – how hard it was for her to watch her painfully unilingual husband try to politick in Quebec despite his party's huge majority there, won in 1958 with the aid of the still-powerful Union Nationale machine of Maurice Duplessis.

"*They* are so different from *us*," she said, smiling into my apparently credulous twenty-five-year-old face. Oh God! thought I – and it wasn't the implacable Taskmaster-in-the-Sky of my Presbyterian childhood I was invoking – she thinks we're *alike*. How can I tell this nice woman I find such notions noxiously racist? – a response that was as reflective of my generation's naive one-world idealism as hers was of her generation's sectarian tribalism.

Paradoxically, interviewing Maryon Pearson was a far more difficult task, though superficially we *were* alike, at least in several of our private interests. She had a reputation as "une dame formidable," as the wife of a Quebec Liberal MP warned in advance, advising me to watch out for an ambush.

In the cold light of a November morning, Mrs. Pearson seemed less formidable than I'd feared. She was far more sophisticated in her conversation than Olive Diefenbaker and far less circumspect in bemoaning the problems of political wives, which she described with a wit she had been honing for decades and that by now had achieved a razor-sharp edge. She talked of the ennui she experienced at political events where she had to play the wife of the leader; of the pleasure she took in the work of the Canadian painters David Milne, Lawren Harris and Joe Plaskett; and of her taste in literature (the novels of Muriel Spark, the short stories of Katherine Mansfield, and the poetry of Edna St. Vincent Millay, though she disparaged Millay's verse by saying it reflected the attitudes of "sentimental girls of my generation.")

While Mrs. Diefenbaker had introduced me to her seamstress and her cook, Mrs. Pearson treated her domestic staff as though they were automatons and basked instead in the flattering attentions of the *Maclean's* photographer, a glamorous figure who drove a Jaguar, played the piano with brio, and described his experiences in publishing pictures in *Paris Match* and *Life* while clicking away like mad.

In the wake of the articles' publication, Mrs. Diefenbaker sent me a graceful note, written in a rounded hand on a flowered card. Mrs. Pearson had a secretary ring me up and then came on the line to deliver four or five sarcastic comments in rapid succession, attacking my perfidy in having repeated in print some of her milder dissatisfactions with her lot. In summing up, she said witheringly, "You're just so *young*. Only someone as *young* as you are could be so indiscreet."

Thirty-five years later – in an era of adversarial journalism and confessional celebrity, when revealing the dark secrets of public figures' lives is commonplace – both my article, and Mrs. Pearson's reaction to it, seem to me to be touchingly restrained, redolent of a period when punches were pulled, privacies were respected, and to be called "too young" was considered an insult. At the time, I was first unnerved, then furious and, finally, amused. The "youthquake" was coming and I figured my cohort was on its leading edge.

John Porter-inspired visions of class-based differences between the Pearsons and the Diefenbakers began to bounce around in my busy head. Superficially, the two couples would seem to belong to the same social echelon. Olive Freeman was the adolescent daughter of a Baptist minister in Saskatoon when she met her second husband-to-be, the young lawyer John George Diefenbaker. Maryon Moody was the offspring of a Winnipeg doctor studying at Victoria College when she encountered her future husband, the young history tutor Lester Bowles Pearson. But fate had treated the two women and their husbands very differently.

Widowed in her thirties, Olive had supported herself and her daughter by working as a high school teacher before marrying in late middle age the doughty Dief, who had suffered many reverses both personal and political, which he privately blamed on the fact that his paternal ancestors were German and that his education had been hard-won at raw institutions on the western frontier. Maryon Pearson had danced and dined in embassies around the world, affecting a cigarette holder and engaging in repartee with the great men of her time while her husband had climbed with seeming ease the slippery ladder of international success as a diplomat, leaning only a little on his status as an old Oxonian and a familiar of the internationally well-connected among the central Canadian elite.

Diefenbaker had grown increasingly suspicious as he aged, convinced that this elite was out to sabotage his every effort, and given to refuting criticisms of his government in a desperate bombastic style. Pearson had become ever more urbane, maintaining, even in his darkest travail, his endearing self-deprecatory manner and his habit of showing consideration to all comers.

He phoned me up once after watching a CBC interview I conducted with a specialist on foreign aid and discussed the subject as though he and I were equals, a capacity he had developed as a diplomat when he conversed confidentially with worldly journalists from important British and American newspapers who were eager to hear what had gone on behind closed doors at international meetings.

Remembering that phone call, and one or two other conversations of the same ilk with Pearson, I found his wife's rudeness inexplicable until a Jungian psychoanalyst, with whom I had collaborated on an article on modern marriage, told me she thought that the women were the men's alter egos in both the Diefenbaker and the Pearson partnerships. The saintly, optimistic Olive balanced the dour, pessimistic Diefenbaker, urging him to function according to the tenets of their Baptist youths; the acerbic Maryon acted out the concealed animosities and vented the darker feelings that the always-charming Mike could not let himself express.[4]

In my early years in Ottawa I had viewed the marked differences between Diefenbaker and Pearson as having to do mostly with matters of style. But now I began to see their continuing confrontations – as did so many of my elders and my peers – as embodying a historic struggle between the old inward-turning, backward-facing repressive Canada, refusing to fade away, and a new cosmopolitan, outward-looking, more confident modern country struggling to thrive. Diefenbaker's original freshness of approach to Canada's problems had vanished despite valiant efforts made on his behalf in the early years of his regime by his professional civil service, while Pearson in opposition had become increasingly open to new ideas being expressed by both old and new adherents to Liberalism.

Pearson had gathered around him a remarkable group of policy advisors, political aides and would-be candidates, people who wanted to rebuild the shattered Liberal party as a preliminary step towards putting into effect the legislation necessary to bolster their plans for a transformed Canada more socially generous and more economically independent.

The problems that befell them and their leader as they went about this gargantuan task – the three hard-fought, mind-numbing, body-breaking elections of 1962, 1963, and 1965 that failed to produce a Liberal majority; the series of farcical scandals that exacerbated French-English problems as the Quiet Revolution in Quebec turned noisy; the quarrels over foreign investment and Medicare within the prime minister's office among Pearson's advisors and around the Cabinet table among his ministers, quarrels that were leaked to the press almost as soon as they occurred – diminished Pearson's reputation for composure in the face of crisis and his party's reputation for competence in the management of public affairs.

As his tumultuous prime ministership lurched along, Pearson began to be viewed in much the same way his nemesis Diefenbaker had been in the same job – as a man out of step with his times. When his government's many positive accomplishments were subsumed in the Trudeau phenomenon, Pearson left office in 1968 without being given his due. Louis Robichaud, then the premier of New Brunswick and later a Liberal senator, remembered telephoning the prime minister to protest his resignation as detrimental to Canadian unity, and being told by Pearson that he could not go on in the face of his government's difficulties. He explained that every day he got up and cried a little before he could force himself to go into the office.[5]

It's only in recent years that the achievements of the Pearson era have begun to be recognized – how innovative it was and what far-reaching changes it set in train. Changes in the way the Canadian-American relationship was perceived as a consequence of the impact that the economic nationalist ideas of Pearson's first finance minister, Walter Gordon, had on the public discourse against the background of the Vietnam War; changes in the way social policy developed as a consequence of the influence on Pearson's thinking of his left liberal advisors, Tom Kent and Allan MacEachen; changes in the way the French-English relationship was seen as a result of Pearson's willingness to try to understand the Quebec viewpoint and to accommodate his French lieutenants, from Maurice Lamontage to Guy Favreau, and Jean Marchand to Pierre Trudeau and Marc Lalonde.

These accomplishments – and many others – are being described now in memoirs and detailed scholarly studies of the period. What no analyst has yet taken much note of, as far as I am aware, is the impact of the Pearson era on what's been called the longest revolution: the struggle for greater equality for women.

It's not that Pearson was a secret feminist, a latter-day John Stuart Mill. In their private discourse, a mild misogyny was as endemic among men of his class and generation as their carefully concealed ambitions. But that this civilized, decent human being liked and respected women was apparent in his relationship with his mother and his wife, both of whose opinions he heeded; in his friendships with the intelligent wives of his peers, women like Elizabeth Gordon and Alison Ignatieff, whose views he routinely sought; in his respect for the political savvy of his assistant, Mary Macdonald, who managed his riding of Algoma East; in his often-expressed admiration for the writers Barbara Ward and Barbara Tuchman; and in his treatment of Judy LaMarsh, whom he appointed to the important portfolio of health and welfare, treated with understanding when the male-dominated political system caused her grief, made secretary of state in charge of the Centennial celebrations, and whose demands for a Royal Commission on the Status of Women he acceded to, albeit somewhat reluctantly.

At a seminar comparing the development of feminism in various western democracies that I attended in Italy last year, an English historian asked me whether the roots of the Canadian women's movement were the same as those of American feminism. My spontaneous response was an unequivocal "No, they weren't. American women took to the streets. Canadian women took to the government." And the government we took to, of course, was the government of Lester Pearson.

In this area of women's rights, as in so many other aspects of national life, it was not so much that Pearson turned Canada leftward, as right-wing analysts would have it to this day. It's that he helped consolidate a political culture north of the American border that centred on the value of government, rather than on its venality, entrenching in the Canadian consciousness a view that even in the 1990s accepts deficit-cutting measures only if their main intent is to restore fiscal balance, rather than to attack the state itself.

Decades after I first encountered them in person in the 1960s, Pearson and Diefenbaker still seem to me to have been distinctly dissimilar men. But their individual qualities and ideas were nevertheless historically complementary. In retrospect, their curiously symbiotic regimes can be seen as having generated innovation while assuring continuity. John Diefenbaker's prairie populism was a creative force that challenged the old consociational consensus by confronting the business and bureaucratic elites' hammerlock on government and by calling for better treatment of the disadvantaged. Mike Pearson in office became as catalytic a force domestically in the mid-1960s as he had been internationally in previous decades, filling the policy void left behind by his predecessor with far-reaching initiatives.

Both Diefenbaker and Pearson maintained the federal finance department's prudent postwar Keynesianism which incurred social spending only when it was affordable. (In the 1960s, deficit spending was a temporary budgetary device, not the permanent practice it became in the 1970s and 1980s.) Both men grumbled about American domination while keeping Canada within the North Atlantic alliance, as the western world faced the pervasive fear of a nuclear holocaust that the Soviet threat represented.

The chaotic conditions that these two prime ministers' governing styles produced – and that gleeful journalists made such sport of – have proven in hindsight to be highly productive. Diefenbaker was a populist prophet, Pearson a liberal agent of progress. Both were very Canadian men of their times.

Together they ushered the country into its second century, ready to embrace, for better and for worse, Pierre Trudeau's siren call to create a just society within a bilingual, multicultural state.

Lester B. Pearson
and the Conundrum of
National Unity, 1963–1968

MICHAEL D. BEHIELS

The question of national unity has been at the very heart of Canada's complex and evolving political culture and political institutions. Every prime minister, from John A. Macdonald to Jean Chrétien, has dealt with the conundrum of national unity that must be faced if Canada is to survive as a viable and prosperous nation-state. This is a country, after all, that has had great difficulty in forging its citizenry into a sovereign people with a secure sense of national unity, destiny and identity.[1] Canada, it seems, is still a work in progress.

Looking back on Canada's relatively short history since Confederation in 1867, it is clear that some of our prime ministers have succeeded much better than others in facing and resolving the many and varied challenges to the unity of the country. It is also quite obvious that none of the more important prime ministers escaped the critical judgement of Canadians on how well they understood and managed the more difficult issues that threatened the integrity of the nation-state. Some brief examples will suffice to demonstrate the way national unity has been a double-edged sword that has served both to enhance as well as to damage political fortunes.

Sir John A. Macdonald successfully used the process of nation-building to reinforce national unity. The first prime minister undermined the anti-confederation movement in the Maritime provinces by offering Nova Scotia better terms and drawing its leader, Joseph Howe, into his Cabinet. He then dealt with the Red River uprising of 1869–1870 by assigning George-Étienne Cartier to negotiate with Louis Riel, the French-speaking Métis leader of the community, for the creation of Manitoba. The implementation of the national policy of protective tariffs, a transcontinental railway and settlement of the west – a significant contribution to the economic development of Canada – enhanced Canadians' sense of unity, although virulent opposition to high tariffs emerged in western Canada after the turn of the century.

With Ottawa in a position of strength following the completion of the Canadian Pacific Railway in 1885, Macdonald dealt swiftly and successfully with the Métis/Indian rebellion. Yet his government's ill-fated decision to hang Riel for his role in the rebellion undermined much of what remained of the political capital of the Conservative party in Quebec. Macdonald's successes at stick-handling national unity issues had contributed to his government's popularity and longevity, but socio-economic, cultural, religious and political developments in Quebec, Ontario, and Manitoba altered the nature of the national unity question by the end of his time as prime minister. The issues of minority language and religious rights and the role of the French-Canadian nationality in Confederation were thrust to the forefront of the national political agenda. Macdonald's Conservative successors proved incapable of understanding or dealing with these questions and their party's political fortunes went into sharp decline. Wilfrid Laurier, the French-Canadian and Catholic prime minister, proved far more skilful at resolving francophone/anglophone conflicts and remained in office for 15 years.

According to historians Michael Bliss and J. L. Granatstein, Prime Minister W. L. Mackenzie King was Canada's most successful political architect of unity.[2] He had the good, the bad, and the ugly experiences of Macdonald and his successors to draw upon, and he had a highly tuned sense of personal ambition and political survival, coupled with an innate conservatism and tendency to procrastination, enabling him to avoid the quicksands of unity issues while capitalizing on them for political gain. While at the head of a minority government, he defused, with an astute combination of political cunning and skill, the threat posed to unity by the rise of the western sectional National Progressive movement. In the federal election of 1921, the Progressives won 65 seats, but by 1926 this divisive sectional movement was all but defunct. King followed this feat with the time-honoured tactic of applying the balm of a royal commission to undermine the Maritimes Rights Movement and to restore the political fortunes of the national Liberal party in that region. He also played a significant but understated role in transforming an outmoded British Empire into a decentralized commonwealth of autonomous nation-states in the 1920s, thus calming the fears of French and ethnic Canadians that they would be drawn into Britain's international adventures.

As Blair Neatby demonstrates so well in his biography of King, the political crisis created by the near collapse of industrial capitalism, international trade, and the prairie wheat economy during the 1930s proved far too challenging for King. He failed the test of national unity during the Great Depression until a new generation of Canadian politicians and bureaucrats jolted him into applying Keynesian deficit financing late in the decade. King responded well, however, to the many challenges brought by the Second World War. He ensured that Canada entered the war united on the basis of a promise of limited involvement and no conscription for overseas service. He then manoeuvred to prevent both the anti-conscriptionists in Quebec and the pro-concriptionists in English-speaking Canada from obtaining control of the political agenda. Unlike First World War Prime Minister Sir Robert Borden, King avoided conscription until it was forced upon him at the last possible moment. Unlike Borden, too, King came to understand that the country had to undertake and complete a planned process of comprehensive social and economic postwar reconstruction. His government had the foresight to seek out and appoint the best and brightest minds to undertake that task. As a result, the King government survived the vicissitudes of war and Canadians emerged from the ordeal more united than they had ever been in their past. When given a second opportunity, King compensated superbly for his abysmal performance during the Depression.

When compared with the two great giants of Canadian politics, how does Lester B. Pearson measure up on the issue of national unity? The comparison is a bit unfair since Pearson presided over minority governments during his two hectic, short-lived administrations. Furthermore, Pearson came to the office of prime minister in 1963, just as Canadian society was embarking upon an era of great social, economic, and political transformation – similar to, but perhaps more intense than, the experience of Canadians during the boom years of the early twentieth century. The traditional cleavages of culture, language and region were accentuated by the not-so-quiet revolution taking place in the francophone society of Quebec and by the emergence of a more ebullient and urbane society in Ontario. To these pressures were added new ones arising from the postwar baby boom, the arrival of thousands upon thousands of European immigrants, working-class and new middle-class grievances and aspirations, and the emergence of gender as a social and economic force in Canadian society. The Pearson government's coherent, if perhaps too ambitious and naive, reform agenda was tested severely, and parts of it were derailed, by these old and new forces tearing at the fabric of society.

Partly as a result of the wise counsel of his political advisor, Tom Kent, and his senior mandarin, Gordon Robertson, both of whom were very well attuned to the emerging social, cultural, and economic trends of the 1960s, Pearson met a changing Canada with an impressive range of social and economic reform measures. These included substantially increased funds for post-secondary education and research, the wholesale unionization of predominantly middle-class public sector employees, the passage of a long-overdue, if somewhat flawed, program of health insurance known as Medicare, programs promoting regional economic development and urban renewal, and the expansion of bilingualism throughout the federal bureaucracy and crown corporations. All of these important measures contributed in small and large ways to the maintenance and promotion of social and political cohesion in a society undergoing serious strains at all levels. The defence and promotion of national unity was greatly assisted by the Pearson government's vision and determination to push forward with extensive change. Any full understanding and appreciation of Pearson's legacy on the national unity front must encompass this broader field of vision.

That said, little in Pearson's experience in foreign relations, either as a senior official or as a politician, had prepared him effectively for the world of federal/provincial politics, especially in matters pertaining to the maintenance of the political integrity of the Canadian nation-state. This was especially crucial because no prime minister since Borden had to confront, in such a dramatic and determined fashion, such a serious political challenge to national unity, represented in the 1960s by the rise of neo-nationalist and secessionist sentiments and demands emanating from different factions of Quebec's francophone political and intellectual middle classes. The movement included a miniscule, but highly unpredictable and dangerous, terrorist element. To use the blunt warning of the co-chairs of the Royal Commission on Bilingualism and Biculturalism in their 1965 preliminary report, Canada was passing through the greatest crisis in its history.

Lester Pearson's confidence and judgement would be tried and even shaken by these developments, especially during their initial phase when his government's francophone representatives were wounded by a series of real and apprehended scandals. The learning curve about the new Quebec was very steep and arduous. A great deal of the prime minister's limited time and energy was devoted to "getting up to speed" on the Quebec file, only to find himself confronted with a set of new and even more radical political demands. He found this especially frustrating and unnerving when these emanated from a Liberal Quebec government led by a former colleague and friend, Jean Lesage. When, in 1966, Daniel Johnson became premier as head of a Union Nationale government, Pearson found it easier to confront more forcefully Johnson's neo-nationalist and secessionist rhetoric because he was not having to deal with a fellow Liberal.

The debate surrounding Prime Minister Pearson's handling of francophone-anglophone issues and federal-provincial relations has taken on vigour with the recent emergence of a revisionist school of thought. Initially, Canadian journalists, politicial scientists and historians criticized Pearson for the ham-handed and often belated manner in which his government dealt with the rise of the new Quebec and the increasing demand, led by the government in Quebec City, for a devolution of responsibilities and tax revenues to the provinces. Some of these critics were willing to concede that Pearson's style of quiet domestic diplomacy, which resulted in major concessions in certain areas, bought the Canadian government just enough time to understand the seriousness of these developments to national unity and elaborate a successful counter-attack.

In the wake of the demise of the Meech Lake Constitutional Accord in June 1990 and the defeat of the Charlottetown Consensus Report in the referendum of October 1992, a revisionist interpretation of Pearson's handling of the Quebec question has been proposed by Ken McRoberts, a York University political scientist.[3] In his recent book, *Misconceiving Canada*, McRoberts argues at great length that Pearson, influenced by Maurice Lamontagne, Jean-Luc Pépin, Maurice Sauvé, Tom Kent and Gordon Robertson, became a strong proponent of the two-nations theory of Confederation. Even more importantly, Pearson developed into a supporter of a Canada-Quebec conception of territorial duality because Quebec, in his view, constituted the homeland of the francophone nation. On the basis of limited evidence, McRoberts concludes that the Pearson years constituted a promising golden era in Canada-Quebec relations, and that it was destroyed almost singlehandedly by his successor, Pierre Elliott Trudeau. McRoberts is convinced that the Pearsonian Golden Age has to be restored if Canada is to survive the threat of Quebec secession.

If (according to McRoberts) Pearson's very special formula of "cooperative federalism," created primarily to accommodate Quebec's unique place in Confederation, had been pursued aggressively by succeeding Canadian governments, the Meech Lake Accord would have been ratified very easily. Entrenchment of the accord's five conditions, especially a clause designating Quebec as a distinct society, would have guaranteed the demise of the *Québécois* secessionist movement following Parti Québécois Premier Lévesque's departure from the political scene in 1982. McRoberts contends that the Pearson government made important strides in meeting the new liberal nationalism in Quebec by beginning the process of putting in place an asymmetrical form of bi-national federalism, as symbolized by the Canada-Quebec pension plan and the opting-out of shared-cost programs with complete financial compensation, an offer taken up by Premier Lesage.

Unfortunately, in the McRoberts view, Canada did not continue down Pearson's road because a charismatic francophone intellectual emerged to capture nationalist forces in English-speaking Canada and concentrate opinion against this two-nations model of Canada. Trudeau's panache and intellectual rigour tipped the balance in favour of a one-Canada model based on pan-Canadian official bilingualism. This interpretation has gained the support of most *Québécois nationalistes,* such as Guy Laforest[4] and Stéphane Dion,[5] and left-wing Anglo-Canadian nationalists like Philip Resnick,[6] who champion the entrenchment of an asymmetrical Quebec-Canada federation in order to accommodate Quebec's political and constitutional distinctness.

Which of the two interpretations is a more accurate evaluation of Pearson's conception of Canada and, consequently, of his approach to fostering and maintaining national unity? An analysis of four issues will help shed some light on this debate: the Fulton-Favreau amending formula for the British North America Act, 1867; cooperative federalism and opting-out arrangements; the negotiations leading up to the Canada-Quebec pension plan; and Canada-France relations in the age of French President Charles de Gaulle.

First, the constitution. Pearson's approach to the perennial problem of finding an acceptable amending formula that would allow Canada to bring the British North America Act home from Britain was conditioned by his belief, stated very clearly during the Depression and shared by most of the intellectuals of his generation, that Canada was not a "compact" of provinces. He believed that Canada needed a renewed constitition which would enable a strengthened central government "to provide national leadership for economic management and social justice for Canadians," making Canada better able to retain its independence from the United States.[7]

In the early 1960s, Pearson used his commitment to the Keynesian-inspired, postwar federalism of state social programs and economic intervention to entice Walter Gordon to join his Liberal team. Influenced by his French-Canadian ministers, and by Kent and Robertson, and facing the political crisis created by the rise of nationalist and secessionist pressures from Quebec's political and intellectual classes, Pearson adopted a policy of cooperative federalism in November

1963, thus accepting reluctantly some "decentralization and some asymmetry as well."[8] He clearly believed that a policy of modest accommodations would right the ship of state and help his Liberal friend Lesage to beat back the nationalist tide. He and most Canadians would be sorely disappointed.

Pearson had absolutely no intention of constitutionalizing purely flexible administrative arrangements between Ottawa and the provinces, including Quebec. According to biographer John English, Pearson definitely expected to receive a *quid pro quo* from the Lesage government; that is, the eventual ratification of the crucial constitutional amending formula that had eluded all Canadian prime ministers since 1927 and thus made it impossible to "patriate" the constitution. The Fulton-Favreau formula, named after justice ministers in the Diefenbaker and Pearson governments who were responsible for negotiating it with the provinces, entailed a series of complex procedures for amending various categories of the British North America Act.[9]

Premier Lesage's support for the Fulton-Favreau formula was quite genuine throughout 1963 and 1964 and was expressed forcefully in a speech of 14 October 1964. What Pearson and his closest advisors had not anticipated was that Lesage would experience a veritable nationalist conversion on the road to Damascus during the winter of 1965. Under enormous and relentless pressures from the *Québécois* nationalists in his Cabinet, his caucus, the upper echelons of the bureaucracy, the Union Nationale opposition and, most importantly, the francophone media, Lesage placed conditions on his government's acceptance of patriation of the constitution with an amending formula. He forged an indissoluble link between his acceptance of a formula for changing the constitution and a favourable deal on the renegotiation of the distribution of powers in the constitution. For Lesage and his *nationaliste* colleagues, Confederation was both a "compact" of provinces as well as a "compact" of two nations. Both concepts had to be entrenched in any new constitutional arrangement if it was ever to be ratified by the government of Quebec.[10]

Pearson and Lesage had encountered one another while on their winter vacations in Florida in early 1965. It was then that the Canadian prime minister began to realize that his appeasement gamble had backfired very dramatically. Lesage rejected Pearson's invitation to join his Cabinet and then indicated that he could no longer promise ratification of the Fulton-Favreau amending formula by the Quebec legislature.[11] A vigorous debate over the pros and cons of the Fulton-Favreau amending formula raged throughout Quebec during the later half of 1965. It only started to fizzle out when Lesage indicated in writing to Pearson on 20 January 1966 that his government would no longer pursue ratification of the formula. In his reply, dated 26 February, Pearson expressed his profound disappointment at the Lesage government's refusal to live up to its promise to ratify the formula, which would have resolved a 40-year problem. Jacques-Yvan Morin, a senior Quebec bureaucrat at the time, argued later that Lesage's procrastination before killing the Fulton-Favreau amending formula contributed to his government's defeat in the 1966 election, an indication of the nationalist pressure the premier was under.[12]

Cooperative federalism was the Pearson response to the Lesage government's demands for more taxing powers and administrative responsibility over shared-cost social programs in areas of provincial jurisdiction. This expression was coined by Tom Kent to describe the devolution of programs, together with the necessary fiscal resources, to the provinces. Indeed, in his view, Ottawa had held on to the augmented power and fiscal resources it had acquired during the Second World War long after this concentration at the federal level served a useful purpose. The social and technological revolutions of the 1960s demanded increased spending on education, health, social security, housing, urban transit and recreation, all areas of provincial and municipal responsibility. Since federalism could no longer function in watertight compartments, it was essential for the federal government to work closely with the provinces in order to ensure that federal and provincial economic and social policies reinforced rather than conflicted with one another. In sum, Ottawa's proper role was primarily that of an enlightened overseer and coordinator, while modernized provincial governments would carry out the design, funding and administration of the majority of programs.

Pearson was convinced by Kent's analysis and explained his government's commitment to cooperative federalism at the 1963 federal-provincial conference. Kent maintains in his memoirs that, except for the Canada-Quebec pension scheme and the contracting-out legislation for shared-cost social programs that relinquished control over them to the provinces, the political and bureaucratic obstacles to the implementation of cooperative federalism remained so strong and so deeply entrenched that the Pearson government was unable to transform in any fundamental way the centralist thrust of post-1945 federalism.[13] A debacle over the contracting-out scheme at a 1964 federal-provincial conference resulted when Pearson's ministers remained opposed to an additional transfer of taxing points to the provinces. They feared that this erosion of Ottawa's taxing and spending powers would undermine the federation.

Kent was convinced that Ottawa's continued intransigence would drive both Lesage and Pearson from office and open the door for the more extreme nationalists in the Union Nationale. He and Maurice Sauvé, a Quebec member of the Pearson Cabinet, were able to convince a worried Pearson to offer the provinces additional tax points in 1965–66 and 1966–67, extended family allowances, and a melding of the Canada and Quebec pension plans. Kent and Sauvé were dispatched in early April 1965 to negotiate this package with Lesage and his senior ministers and bureaucrats. They returned with a draft deal which Pearson persuaded his very hesitant senior Cabinet ministers to accept.[14] The minister of health and welfare, Judy LaMarsh, was not included in these crucial negotiations.

As far as Lesage was concerned, his government's political initiatives had paid off in spades. Quebec obtained control over a wide range of social programs, along with the necessary revenues to fund its nationalist-driven social and institutional reforms. At first, Lesage and Pearson believed that this deal would stem the rising tide of neo-nationalist sentiment in Quebec. It was only when Lesage backed out of the Fulton-Favreau deal, and then was defeated in the provincial election of 1966 by his ultra-nationalist rival, Daniel Johnson, that Pearson and some members of his Cabinet came to realize the degree to which cooperative federalism had simply encouraged all the various components of *Québécois* nationalist movement to demand more and bigger concessions from Ottawa.

Some of Kent's contemporaries, such as Mitchell Sharp, offer a different interpretation of what transpired in the area of federal-provincial financial arrangements. Had Sharp been consulted about the Liberal party's 1963 election platform to allow opting-out of joint shared-cost programs, he claims that he would have objected strongly because the process resulted in different federal taxation rates for Canadians living in different provinces. Furthermore, the process undermined the federal government's ability to use its spending powers to regulate the economy and maintain national standards in education, research and health. Finally, the fact that only the Quebec government chose to take advantage of the deal had grave implications for national unity. By 1966, Sharp had joined forces with Trudeau, then the parliamentary secretary to Pearson, and A.W. Johnson, the assistant deputy minister of finance, to "propose some general principles to guide federal-provincial fiscal arrangements in the future, and particularly, to halt the federal retreat from its principal tax fields."[15] This strong federalist team would be reinforced in 1967 when Trudeau's colleague, Marc Lalonde, was appointed as Pearson's policy advisor.

The intense internal debate over what emerged as the Canada-Quebec pension plan belies the McRoberts argument that Pearson's adoption of cooperative federalism was principled rather than primarily strategic. The story, as told in great detail by Kent, illustrates in an ironic way just how badly the Pearson government, including advisors like Kent and Robertson, was outmanoeuvred by the Lesage government and its leading mandarins, such as Claude Morin and Claude Castonguay.

Since 1958, Lester Pearson had been deeply committed to an expanded and universal pension plan for all Canadians, and he made a contributory pension plan the central plank in his 1962 and 1963 election campaigns. It was a promise he intended to keep, no matter what obstacles needed to be overcome. Once in office, he assigned health minister LaMarsh and her deputy, Joe Willard, to work out the details and begin negotiations with the provinces. Kent admits that the government's proposed pension plan was technically flawed because it was not fully funded. He argues, however, that this could have been overcome had the Lesage government, for nationalist and financial reasons, not decided to create an enormous political roadblock when it revealed at the 1963 federal-provincial conference that it was proceeding with a fully funded Quebec pension scheme. The Quebec National Assembly passed an enabling resolution in August 1963 to set this process in motion. Kent realized that the federal scheme was dead in the water. He preferred a strategic retreat based on improving existing programs for the aged, which would avoid a constitutional showdown. This alternative was not politically feasible. Pearson was too committed to his promises of a contributory pension plan and Kent's proposal would have required an unacceptable increase in general taxation. The showdown with Quebec was unvoidable because the Pearson government had been too slow in realizing what the Lesage government had up its sleeve.[16]

Facing a political disaster in the summer of 1963, Pearson decided to assign Kent and Robertson to open negotiations with Lesage to see if some compromise could be reached between his plan and that of the Canadian government. Kent worked out a proposal allowing any province to opt out, in the spirit of cooperative federalism, from the Canada pension plan if it respected certain conditions guaranteeing comparable benefits, universality and portability. Pearson agreed and outlined this proposal to the provinces at the 1963 federal-provincial conference. Little progress was made over the next seven months as Ottawa awaited the re-election of Ontario's Conservative government and Premier John Robarts's confirmation that he would go along with a national pension plan.[17]

Lesage increased his advantage by getting Ottawa to participate in a federal-provincial conference on pensions and contracting-out. This took place in March 1964 at the National Assembly in Quebec City. Lesage upstaged Pearson by divulging to the premiers, behind closed doors, the general features of Quebec's fully funded pension plan. The plan was so attractive to the other provinces that Ottawa's approach was of little interest. The ensuing political crisis served as the catalyst for identical but separate Canada and Quebec pension plans with new features that, in most respects, were marked improvements on the original ideas.[18] In Kent's estimation, Pearson had managed his own Cabinet brilliantly in a tense time, but did not receive the recognition for the achievement. Sauvé spilled some of the internal story to his journalist friends, revealing that Judy LaMarsh had been left out of the negotiations completely by Pearson, who had not even consulted her on the matter. Kent talked LaMarsh out of resigning, but she rightly never forgave the prime minister for his lack of confidence in her.

The confirmed centralist Pearson had "presided over the most rapid and extensive decentralization in Canadian history between 1963 and 1965." During his second administration, however, Pearson turned increasingly to men like Sharp, Trudeau, A.W. Johnson and Lalonde, all of whom advised extreme caution when dealing with the Quebec government's ever-escalating constitutional and fiscal demands.[19]

Another dimension to this analysis of Pearson's handling of national unity issues concerns Canada's evolving relationship with France in the context of Quebec's grandiose international ambitions. The president of France, Charles de Gaulle, had been invited to participate in the Expo 67 celebrations in Montreal. On July 24, 1967, following a tour from Quebec City to Montreal along the Chemin du Roi, de Gaulle uttered emotion-filled phrases comparing his trip along the St. Lawrence with the day France was liberated in the Second World War. He concluded with the explosive declaration, "Vive Montréal! Vive le Québec! Vive le Québec libre! Vive le Canada français et vive la France!"[20] The words reverberated throughout Canada and jolted the indecisive Pearson government into long-overdue action.

Contrary to what was believed at the time, Pearson and his senior ministers and advisors had realized for some time that the Quebec government and de Gaulle were planning to use the occasion of the visit to make a statement about Quebec's position in Canada and the world. This intelligence helps explain why Pearson subsequently reacted with such determination and swiftness. Had he acted on his instincts even earlier, however, this incident might never have occurred. Given a clearly stated, undiplomatic warning by the Canadian government that it would not put up with any interference in its internal affairs, de Gaulle might have chosen not to visit Canada. This warning was never given because of the dispute which raged within the government about how best to deal with the Quebec government's insistence upon its right to act in areas of provincial jurisdiction as an independent international entity capable of signing treaties with foreign governments such as France.

Pearson had in fact endeavoured to develop closer ties with France from the beginning of his first administration. His visit to Paris on 15 January 1964 and the appointment of the respected Jules Léger as ambassador were early steps in this direction. Nevertheless, the emergence of the Gaullist *grand dessin* of a new Europe "from the Atlantic to the Urals" soon spelled trouble. De Gaulle considered Canada to be within the United States sphere of influence; he wanted to curtail American power in Europe by opposing the North Atlantic Treaty Organization (NATO) and developing France's nuclear capability, but with Canada's help if possible. Influenced by the activities of the Quebec mafia in Paris led by Pierre-Louis Mallen, de Gaulle considered closer ties with the emerging modern and technologically oriented Quebec a useful instrument of his grand design. The *Québécois* neo-nationalist political and intellectual elites, led by Daniel Johnson, Claude Morin, Guy Bertrand and André Patry, believed that they had much to gain and little to lose in tying their goal of "equality or independence" for Quebec to President de Gaulle's international ambitions.

Léger and external affairs minister Paul Martin, very much aware of these developments, believed that Canada should give Quebec and France as much leeway as possible, so that Canada could develop a much stronger and more visible presence in the francophone world. Indeed, both wanted to move aspects of Canadian foreign policy closer to policies of France. They invariably cautioned the prime minister not to over-react to the manoeuvres and snubs employed by Quebec and French politicians and officials to establish autonomy for the Quebec government in international affairs. In February 1965, Quebec and France signed a cultural "entente" for French technical and educational assistance to Quebec, despite the clear warnings to Pearson by Marcel Cadieux, the toughly federalist under-secretary of state for external affairs, that this blossoming and potentially very troublesome Franco-Quebec romance ought to be nipped in the bud.

Martin's solution was a Canada-France "accord cadre," signed in the summer of 1965, an arrangement under which French and Quebec officials could develop programs within areas of provincial

jurisdiction as long as Ottawa's primary authority in international relations was recognized and maintained. But the conciliatory approach did not produce the desired results. On the contrary, Canada-
France relations took a turn for the worse when Canada refused to
sell uranium to France without conditions. Implementing his grand
scheme, de Gaulle kicked NATO troops, including Canadians, out of
France in February 1966 and then stubbornly refused to receive a visit
from Canadian Governor General Georges Vanier. In the lead-up to
the 1966 provincial election, Lesage appealed to nationalist voters by
making bold statements about Quebec's right to enter into international agreements in areas of exclusive provincial responsibility. A
fretful Pearson, pressured by his new guard – Trudeau, Lalonde, and
officials Jean Beetz and Alan Gotlieb – accentuated the francophone
dimension of Canadian foreign policy and the expansion of official
bilingualism in the Department of External Affairs. None of this
helped get Lesage's Liberal government re-elected. Quebec nationalists chose the more explicit, even radical, nationalism of Daniel
Johnson and the Union Nationale. In very short order, the Quebec
government's strategy shifted to an aggressive affirmation of Quebec's international personality.[21]

Clearly, the stage was set for a showdown over which government,
Canada's or Quebec's, would determine the agenda for President de
Gaulle's official visit to Expo 67. During the incessant haggling over
the appropriate protocol for the visit, it became increasingly clear to
Pearson that de Gaulle was determined to play his hand in favour of
the nationalist-secessionist Johnson government. The French president, in the words of John English, had become totally infatuated
with the idea of an independent Quebec. He could no longer tolerate
the dominance of the Anglo-Saxon world "over a fragment of the
French people, that fossil that had survived in a pure state from the
centuries of the Valois and the Bourbons, who spoke the language of
Molière's peasants."[22] France treated the Quebec government as Canada's equal and refused to inform Ottawa of its dealings with Quebec. These, as well as several other diplomatic insults, including de
Gaulle's refusal to participate in the fiftieth anniversary of the battle
at Vimy Ridge (the site, on French soil, of Canada's most famous First
World War victory), prompted the Pearson government to launch formal protests with the French ambassador in Ottawa and in Paris.
These were rebuffed derisively. Although some diplomats advised direct confrontation with de Gaulle, the impending visit of Premier
Johnson to France, and of de Gaulle to Expo 67, made the Pearson
government swallow its collective pride, keep silent, and hope that
common sense would prevail.

De Gaulle would let neither Quebec City nor Ottawa decide his itinerary for him. Ottawa agreed that the visit would commence in Quebec City, with a stopover in Montreal, before its conclusion in Ottawa. Everyone assumed, quite wrongly as events proved, that he would refrain from creating any undiplomatic incident because he was culminating his tour in the capital. Little thought was given, except by Ambassador Léger, to what Pearson and de Gaulle would actually talk about. When de Gaulle arrived in Quebec City aboard the cruiser *Colbert,* he was thinking of little else other than renewing France's ties with its long-lost colony of New France. Canada and its interests were simply not part of the picture. Pearson and his entourage had failed to appreciate the degree to which the occasion would illuminate the soul and galvanize the emotions of Quebec's francophone nationality, a community that was undergoing a veritable renaissance and transformation.

Fate and destiny had come together. The imperious de Gaulle seized the moment in the belief that he was reliving his past while simultaneously igniting the future for the French-speaking people of Quebec. No sooner had de Gaulle uttered his impertinent remarks than Pearson knew what he and his government must do. Even a single moment of hesitation would be catastrophic. He disregarded advice from Martin and Léger to ignore the incident in order to salvage what remained of Franco-Canadian relations. Following his keen political instincts in international affairs, and with the support of his Cabinet, Pearson instead issued a tough statement declaring that de Gaulle's remarks were unacceptable. "The people of Canada are free," Pearson declared. "Every province of Canada is free. Canadians do not need to be liberated."[23] The prime minister stressed Canada's special relationship with France and hoped discussions with de Gaulle, who was scheduled to come to Ottawa, would underscore the sense of friendship Canadians had with the French people. Understanding all too clearly the full scope of the terse reprimand, President de Gaulle, perhaps as he had planned all along, cut short his visit to Canada and returned to Paris the following day. Having handled the de Gaulle outburst with brio and panache, Pearson ensured that he left office a few months later on a high note.

Pearson navigated the troubled waters of national unity with considerable skill and aplomb, if not always with dispatch and efficiency. Despite the claims of the revisionists, Pearson did not become a convert to a new form of unity based on the premise of two founding nations, with the province of Quebec as the true and only homeland of Canada's francophone communities. He was not the father of the Meech Lake Accord, the constitutional deal entailing a territorially defined Canada-Quebec dualism and an asymmetrical special status for Quebec.

Under considerable political duress, Pearson accepted reluctantly a fair degree of administrative decentralization for social programs in areas of provincial responsibility. His government accomplished this through the opting-out provision for shared-cost social programs as well as with dual Canada and Quebec pension plans which were identical and portable. At no time did Pearson ever contemplate constitutionalizing this process of administrative devolution or entrenching an asymmetrical federalism. The Pearson government vacillated on the matter of what role, if any, the Quebec government should play in international affairs but, in the end, his instincts enabled his government to step back from the brink with its public rebuke of de Gaulle for his undue meddling in the internal affairs of the nation. This dramatic assertion of Canadian sovereignty did much for Pearson's reputation as an ardent Canadian nationalist, a clear-sighted internationalist, and a defender of national unity.

Pearson's policies and practices in federal-provincial relations must be placed in the larger context of such pan-Canadian achievements as universal and comprehensive Medicare, and that most-cherished symbol of national unity and pride – the bold and beautiful Canadian flag. Given Pearson's conception of Canada and its place in the world, it is not surprising that when it came time to leave centre stage and allow Liberals from all over Canada to choose his successor, his personal although private choice would be for the staunchly federalist intellectual, Pierre Trudeau. This final decision says much about where Pearson should stand in the ranking of prime ministers on the issue of national unity. In giving the nod to Trudeau, Pearson's vision of the future was as prophetic as his understanding of Canada's past was deep.

Lester B. Pearson and Canadian Unity

CLAUDE RYAN

No issue was more important to Lester B. Pearson than Canadian unity. No issue resulted in more initiatives on his part than the relationship between Canada and Quebec, which was then, as it is today, the issue of most concern for national unity.[1]

During the entire time he was prime minister, Pearson always maintained his profound commitment to Canada and its federal system of government. Beyond the ups and downs that marked his time in power, he would repeat constantly that Canada was a country that was "greater than its parts or the sum of its parts."[2] He often emphasized that he believed in a strong central government and equally strong provincial governments. From start to finish, he defined himself as a staunch advocate of the fundamental equality of French- and English-speaking Canadians. While reminding us that, for practical reasons, the country could only have two official languages, he frequently stressed the very important contributions to the development of modern Canada of Canadians whose origins were neither English nor French. Pearson was also convinced that, by giving all Canadians reasonably equal economic and social opportunities, the federal and provincial governments could lay a more solid foundation for Canadian unity. He also believed that this objective could not be achieved without effective leadership from the federal government. Having played a leading role in the development of Canadian diplomacy, Pearson believed that Canada, as long as it remained united, was destined to make an increasing contribution to the cause of peace and cooperation between peoples.

Pearson never deviated from these fundamental beliefs. From the beginning to the end of his two governments, he promoted them in a civilized, courteous manner that was free of dogmatism, open to discussion and respectful of difference, a fact which made him very endearing. Although it began auspiciously, Pearson's time in power ended on a note of incompletion and contradiction. To understand what happened, one must consider in succession each of the Liberal party's two mandates, 1963–65 and 1965–68. From the beginning of the first mandate, in the spring of 1963, to the end of the second, in the spring of 1968, Pearson and his government moved away from the possibilities and potential that shone so brightly at the outset.

1962–1965: MAJOR OPENINGS

Pearson came to power for the first time in April 1963. He had already clearly established his position on the subject of Canadian unity in a speech in the House of Commons, on 17 December 1962. Disregarding the quibbles of lawyers and historians, he maintained that the British North America Act of 1867 resulted from an agreement between the two founding peoples, "on the basis of an acceptable and equal partnership."[3] Noting that the initial agreement often led to opposing interpretations in Quebec and the rest of Canada, he did not hesitate to give English Canada the lion's share of responsibility for the difficult situation the country found itself in near the end of the Diefenbaker government. He also stated that the Canadian unity crisis would not be resolved without equal participation from francophones in the administration of the country's affairs and a realistic acceptance of the new aspirations coming out of Quebec from the Quiet Revolution. In keeping with this view, he made a commitment to establish, as soon as he was elected, a royal commission "into the means of developing the bicultural character of confederation."[4]

In July 1963, a few weeks after he was elected, Pearson created the Royal Commission on Bilingualism and Biculturalism ("B and B"), as he had promised. He gave it a very broad mandate, to "report upon the existing state of bilingualism," but also to "recommend what steps should be taken to develop the Canadian confederation on the basis of an equal partnership between the two founding races, taking into account the contribution made by the other ethnic groups to the cultural enrichment of Canada."[5] This opened the door to a broad examination of all the issues related to bilingualism and biculturalism. The commission interpreted this to include not only language rights and the rights of individuals but also collective aspects and the political dimension of equality. In a preliminary report submitted in 1964, the commission indicated that it intended to deal not only with language issues, but also with the problems arising from the existence in

Canada of two distinct societies, each with its own culture, linguistic majority, and the power to break up the country: French-speaking Quebec and English-speaking Canada. Unless I am mistaken, that was the origin of the term "distinct society." It would appear that, after debating the language to be used, the commission agreed upon this more moderate term, all the while having in mind the emotions which are evoked by the more controversial terms "people" and "nation."

While the commission was carrying out its mandate at a pace that many considered too slow, the prime minister was providing Canada with a national flag, accomplished by a majority vote in the House of Commons obtained in December 1964 after a long and arduous debate. He was also laying a renewed foundation for relations between the federal government and the provinces. In a series of federal-provincial conferences, he proposed a formula for cooperative federalism in which mutual consultation and cooperative relations would characterize the relationship between Ottawa and the provinces. Each would respect the jurisdictions of the other, and both levels of government would receive fiscal resources corresponding to the extent of their responsibilities. These meetings resulted in adjustments that were favourable to the provinces with regard to the division of tax revenues. In addition, they resulted in adjustments to equalization payments that favoured poorer provinces, and a head-on approach to reviewing shared-cost programs.

THE PENSION PLAN AND
THE OPTING-OUT FORMULA

In 1962, Pearson was committed to making joint programs more flexible to accommodate the demands of Quebec, which had suffered major losses as a result of refusing to participate in various programs. In 1964, a plan to create a contributory national pension plan gave Pearson the opportunity to follow through on his commitment. A first draft developed by the federal government was almost aborted because of opposition from Quebec, which wanted to have its own plan and proposed a draft that was very different. After coming close to the breaking point, last-minute negotiations resulted in an agreement that allowed Quebec to have its own plan and the federal government to establish a plan that applied to all the other provinces. However, the provisions of the two drafts were harmonized so that the same benefits were offered to everyone across the country.

Around the same time, the federal government decided to offer the provinces an opting-out formula for some 15 shared-cost programs (out of the 60-odd at the time), in return for financial transfers in the form of tax points based on income and corporate tax revenues. Included were such important programs as hospital insurance and various financial assistance measures for the unemployed, the blind, the handicapped, and people who registered in vocational courses. This proposal resulted in the Established Programs Act, passed in 1964. Quebec was the only province to use the opting-out formula. Moreover, in 1964 and 1965, distinct arrangements for Quebec were made with respect to new measures instituting family allowances for 16- and 17-year-olds, and a bank loan program for post-secondary students. The combined effect of these tax transfers, added to the fact that Quebec was the only province to collect its own corporate and personal income taxes, resulted in a *de facto* particular status for Quebec. Often questioned about this, Pearson stated many times that adjustments to government responsibilities should take into account the distinctiveness of Quebec. In the House of Commons, he specifically stated that: 1) Quebec "as well as being a province is also the home of most of our French-speaking Canadians, the guardian of their language, their traditions and their way of life;"[6] 2) "Quebec in a very real sense is not a province like the others. Therefore its position is bound to introduce special features into federal-provincial relationships;"[7] and 3) it "is not capitulation or betrayal" for "the central government to recognize the special problems arising out of the relationship with Quebec and to seek and find, whenever possible, solutions for them, without prejudicing the position of other provinces."[8]

THE FULTON-FAVREAU FORMULA

In 1964, with the cooperation of the provinces, Pearson set in motion a process that would lead to a constitutional amending formula and the repatriation of the constitution. The Fulton-Favreau formula, named after the two federal justice ministers who co-authored it, one Conservative, the other Liberal, seemed destined to succeed where so many others had failed before. Unveiled in the summer of 1964, it soon ran into strong opposition in Quebec. Faced with such formidable opposition, Quebec Premier Jean Lesage, after having made a commitment to the other premiers to have the formula approved in the National Assembly, had to back-peddle shortly before the November 1965 federal election. This setback must have been distressing for Pearson. I do not remember him expressing any bitterness against Lesage, a fellow Liberal, publicly. He would be remembered for the conciliatory statement he made in the House of Commons at the beginning of 1966: "We have not dropped it [the Fulton-Favreau formula] ... We shall do our best to put it into effect if and when we get the agreement of all the provinces, but without that agreement it cannot be done."[9]

Tired of leading a minority government, after barely two years in power Pearson decided to call a general election in the fall of 1965. Unfortunately for him, he was again to lead a minority government. Moreover, he had to bear the burden of power in a very different environment.

The achievements of the first mandate on the Quebec dossier were largely attributable to the strong influence of Pearson's Quebec colleagues, particularly Lionel Chevrier, Maurice Lamontagne, Guy Favreau, René Tremblay and Maurice Sauvé. Lamontagne and Tremblay were forced to leave the government at the end of 1965 because of a silly scandal over furniture transactions. In April 1964, Guy Favreau was asked to replace Chevrier as Pearson's Quebec lieutenant. He too would be unfairly undone by a scandal, the Rivard affair, in the very first year of the second mandate. At the beginning of 1966, Pearson began a second term with a Quebec team that still included an already-weakened Favreau, but that would soon have Jean Marchand as leader. Marchand insisted on making his entrance into the Liberal party with two friends, Gérard Pelletier and Pierre Elliott Trudeau, who, like him, entered Parliament in 1965.

The achievements of 1963–65 had also been facilitated by the personal relationship that Pearson and Jean Lesage had established while colleagues in the St. Laurent administration in the 1950s. Lesage had already hinted that he would make new demands of the federal government concerning manpower training, social security and regional development when he lost power in June 1966 at the hands of the Union Nationale under the leadership of Daniel Johnson. The new premier had even more ambitious demands and did not hide his affinity for the federal Conservative party.

Among the three new ministers from Quebec in the Pearson government, Trudeau, after a brief breaking-in period, proved to be the most formidable. Completely bilingual, a believer in linguistic equality between francophones and anglophones, determined to promote the constitutional entrenchment of individual rights, Trudeau was deeply suspicious of nationalism and collectivism. He was opposed to increasing the number of particular arrangements with Quebec, reasoning that arrangements negotiated between two governments jeopardized the principle of provincial equality and undermined the role of Quebec's representatives in Parliament.

Several federal initiatives came out of the first two years of the second Pearson mandate, two of which were devised to accommodate Quebec: the Canada Assistance Plan and an improved financial support program to benefit post-secondary education. Quebec had access to the opting-out formula in the first case and to a special tax arrangement in the second. These two initiatives did not raise any controversy in Quebec because they seemed to conform to the spirit of cooperative federalism. This was not the case, however, for other federal proposals having to do with culture and research, which were completely rejected by Quebec.

"NO" TO PARTICULAR STATUS

In September 1966, the provinces were informed that a major policy shift was brewing on tax arrangements. Having presided over the federal-provincial committee on the changes to be made to the tax system, finance minister Mitchell Sharp submitted a report that announced a return to a more rigid and more symmetrical federalism. Each government would increasingly have to take on its own responsibilities. Ottawa proposed to give the provinces responsibility for all shared-cost programs in return for a tax trade-off that was hardly advantageous. Moreover, in the future, the federal government would seek agreements that applied across the board.

The new policy was applied for the first time with the universal Medicare plan. Each province was invited to participate as long as it conformed to the terms defined in the federal legislation. Any province that did not participate did not have the right to the opting-out formula and did not receive the subsidies that came with the program. The policy was then applied to vocational training. As existing agreements expired, the federal government instituted a new grants program for adult students based on a specious distinction between financial assistance for adults, with Ottawa insisting on its power to intervene, and training proper, with Ottawa stating that it wanted in this case to respect provincial jurisdiction. The program was adopted and implemented with no special arrangements with Quebec. It led to major discrepancies in assistance for those looking for work or training, depending on whether assistance came under the federal or provincial program.

At the beginning of his second mandate, Pearson announced the intentions of his government concerning bilingualism in the federal public service. The government planned an intensive bilingualization of the civil service. In addition, as soon as the B and B Commission's recommendations were announced regarding the status of official languages, Pearson committed himself to act promptly upon them. His commitment regarding linguistic equality was constant and unwavering, but Pearson's interest in the collective aspect of equality that the famous "blue pages" had dealt with in the first volume of the B and B report seemed to fade as the second mandate drew to a close. Among other developments that dampened the prime minister's enthusiasm was the growing concern from some anglophone communities about the danger of *de facto* separation that could occur as a result of what some judged to be too many concessions. There was also the visit of General de Gaulle to Quebec in 1967 and, on a larger scale, Quebec's increasing international forays. The General's visit caused a serious diplomatic clash between Canada and France, while Quebec's diplomatic initiatives caused a great deal of nervousness in the federal capital.

Pearson's last major act was to preside over a federal-provincial conference on the constitution in February 1968. The federal government's position paper, "Federalism for the Future: A Statement of Policy by the Government of Canada," did not contain the flexible and welcoming thinking to which Pearson had accustomed Canadians. The priorities of the federal government would now be to introduce a Charter of Rights and Freedoms, entrench language rights, reform central institutions, adopt an amending formula and patriate the constitution. This approach reflected the thinking of Pierre Elliott Trudeau, who had become minister of justice in June 1967, and not the earlier thinking of Lester Pearson. The issue that had always been of uppermost importance to all Quebec governments – the division of powers – was placed on the back burner. Quebec was back to being a province like the others, to the extent that there was no explicit reference to Quebec in the document. Abstract liberal orthodoxy took precedence over Quebec reality, to which Pearson had previously been sympathetic and attuned. Everything that followed, culminating in the unilateral repatriation in 1982, was the logical outcome of the process begun in early 1968, with the results we face today.

PEARSON'S LEGACY

Who was the real Lester Pearson? Was he the Pearson of 1962–65, whose words on relations between Quebec and Canada are surprising even today in their openness and their audacity? Or was he the Pearson of the second government, which was marked by Ottawa's return to conventional thinking that was little favourable to Quebec?

Those who knew Lester Pearson well and the pressures he was under would be better able to respond to these questions. On the basis of my own memories and the public acts that are known to us, I am inclined to believe that he was divided between his sincere desire to accommodate Quebec's distinctiveness and his even stronger attachment to Canadian unity. Towards the end, I think, the second, deep-rooted, sentiment prevailed over the first, which stemmed from his diplomatic experience and his open and generous spirit. He was sometimes well- and sometimes ill-served by an easily influenced and vacillating temperament that made him capable of great flexibility but produced an awkward and unskilful leader incapable of making clear-cut choices.

Some of the lasting effects of the Pearson legacy were the considerable progress on equal language rights, the larger share given to francophones in running the federal government, the selection of a flag and a revamped national anthem, and more flexible relations with the provinces, particularly with respect to shared-cost programs. Thirty years later, the opting-out formula in particular has survived its detractors without the country's unity really suffering from its application. We also have Pearson to thank for adding such major programs as a government pension plan, the Canada Assistance Plan and health insurance to the social safety net that benefits all Canadians.

However, Pearson has to be blamed for the less innovative management of relations between Quebec and Canada during his second term. This issue, which inspired him to launch many groundbreaking initiatives between 1963 and 1966, seemed of relatively little importance by 1968. The unfinished work of the B and B Commission and the 1982 patriation have symbolic value in this respect. The commission hinted that it would deal with the political aspect of the equality plan that was Pearson's dream, but the commission's slow progress, the premature death of co-chair André Laurendeau, the impossibility of an agreement between the commissioners themselves and, finally, the indifference, if not the hostility, of a large part of the English-speaking public, doomed the idea. The much less generous approach of the federal government's paper tabled at the 1968 federal-provincial conference continued when its author, Pierre Trudeau, came to power.

There was a grand ceremony in the spring of 1982 on the grounds of Parliament Hill to celebrate patriation of the constitution. But Quebec was not present, nor is it any more present today. It will never be present as long as it is not recognized as a distinct society – in Pearson's words, a nation "in the historical and linguistic and cultural sense."[10] Quebec will not be present as long as we refuse to accept, as Pearson did on many occasions, the practical consequences of the rebalancing of powers within a federal system without prejudice to democratic principles. To those who now contemptuously and arrogantly reject the very idea of a distinct society, I believe that the Lester Pearson of the first mandate would reply today, as he did one day in the House of Commons, that "a prejudiced and obstinate refusal to recognize that there are special complexities in relations with Quebec, or a failure to appreciate the special sensitiveness of that province as the guardian of the rights of a minority, would soon and finally destroy confederation and make impossible the growth in strength and unity of a Canadian nation."[11]

Prescience, Prudence and Procrastination: National Social Policies in the Pearson Era

P. E. BRYDEN

Slightly more than a month before the opening of the 1958 Liberal leadership convention, and slightly less than a month before Lester Pearson acknowledged that perhaps he might need to do some campaigning, Walter Gordon, his unofficial manager, set down some of the strengths and weaknesses of the leadership hopeful. While generally regarded as possessing an "easy personality," and almost universally acknowledged as a master of diplomacy, Pearson was not without flaws. By far the most serious of these, according to Gordon, was "his reputation for not being interested in or knowing much about domestic affairs."[1] Pearson won the leadership handily over Paul Martin, but from the outset observers recognized that Pearson did not "have as much political moxie as ... Martin ... at least not in the domestic issues that are at the very nub of federal politics."[2]

Nevertheless, throughout the years that the Liberal party spent in opposition, Pearson demonstrated the prescience to embark on a new direction in social policy and surrounded himself with people firmly committed to charting a new course. Soon after achieving power in 1963, however, Pearson's natural inclination for caution began to dominate, and, instead of rushing headlong into social programs whose design was clearly flawed, the Liberals pursued a more prudent course of compromise and conciliation. By the time of the second Pearson minority government, this hesitant approach became more deeply entrenched, with Pearson procrastinating on program implementation dates almost to the extent of causing a Cabinet crisis. There is thus a certain symmetry. The man who began his tenure as leader of the Liberal party in the midst of suggestions that he was feeble in domestic policy ended by providing only reluctant leadership on the question of the timing of universal health insurance legislation. At best, Pearson was the leader who had the foresight to give considerable power to the social policy planners behind the scenes; at worst, his resistance to the implementation of social legislation seriously jeopardized the completion of programs, most particularly national health insurance, that have come to be equated with the Pearson government.

In the years between 1958 and 1963, Pearson wisely left the design of social policy measures to a group of left-leaning Liberals who had congregated around him during the first dark days of opposition. In allowing relative newcomers to the Liberal party to hold important positions in the areas of domestic policy development and campaign strategy, Pearson was not following in the tradition of previous Liberal leaders and not charting a course free of criticism. In this sense, his decisions in opposition and in the early government period marked Pearson as a leader of both considerable foresight and courage, prepared to oversee and encourage the design of innovative social programs despite little background, or interest, in these sorts of public policies. In acknowledging his weakness in understanding social issues, he paved the way for the arrival of the social policy planners.

In the aftermath of the St. Laurent-led defeat of 1957, and the victory of John Diefenbaker's Conservatives, a number of key Liberals offered their prescriptions for regaining power. Most of these people had been influential policy advisors in the St. Laurent government, and some could even trace their lineage back to the King period. In those days of Liberal ascendancy, there was relatively little difference between the front benches and the backrooms; the advisors were, therefore, frequently Cabinet ministers exercising considerable control over their respective regions, and informally charged with the responsibility for translating regional interests into national policies.[3] Many of these people lost their jobs in the 1957 election, and it is not surprising that they blamed the defeat on an electoral strategy that had veered too far from fundamental Liberal principles. Brooke Claxton, a veteran of a number of previous Liberal administrations but retired from active politics since 1953, suggested that the solution lay in producing a "fresh statement" on policy. The party should recognize, he warned, that "studies underway ... go a long way to show that the built-in increases in Canada's social security program have put the economy on a 'collision course' where so large a proportion of the national production will be spent on social services that not enough will be left to meet other costs."[4] Charles Dunning, a former premier of Saskatchewan and federal minister of finance, agreed. An overemphasis on social policy development had lessened "the sense of responsibility on the part of the individual citizen." Surely, he added, "We Liberals must get back to fundamental thinking in terms of principles."[5]

Into the midst of these voices raised in defence of "traditional" liberalism, came a few people who insisted that, instead of being abandoned, social policy goals had to be expanded. Walter Gordon, a Toronto businessman with strong but informal ties to the Liberal party, raised an alternative route to electoral recovery than the one proposed by the old-guard Liberals. "Some people think the main reforms which we have fought for in the past have been accomplished," he wrote, but "there will always be need for reform."[6] Tom Kent, editor of the *Winnipeg Free Press* and a rising Liberal star, agreed with Gordon that the party needed to establish some long-term objectives, whatever the difficulty might be in implementing them. As he explained to an audience of Young Liberals, "There'll always be plenty of other people to give weight enough to expediency. The masters of expediency are often successful in the short run. But it's not too pleasant to wake up from their ministrations and find that the Tories have got into office by putting on our mislaid clothes."[7]

Lester Pearson heard the voices of Gordon and Kent in the weeks and months leading up to his bid for the leadership. Moreover, he had to listen to them in order to present himself as having prime ministerial potential, which meant having a social policy plan. Pearson chose his course quickly, but he chose it well. Gordon managed, and partially financed, the semblance of a leadership campaign which Pearson mounted, and Kent was selected to write the Pearsonian version of "liberal principles" that were unveiled in the new leader's victory address. While clear social policy objectives were missing, Pearson suggested that they were an integral component of the Liberal party platform: "Liberalism is ... freedom from exploitation and injustice and from those crushing forces of insecurity and misfortune against which the individual in our complicated society cannot protect himself. [It is also] freedom of the individual from any kind of state interference which is designed not to expand and liberate his personality but to restrict and reduce it. The reconciliation of freedom and security is perhaps the most important single task of Liberalism and democracy."[8]

Pearson did not quiet the critics of enhanced social programs by moving Gordon and Kent into his inner circle. If anything, he merely heightened calls for their dismissal, particularly after early indications that the new approach was misguided. With a hastily cobbled together "New Statement of Liberal Policy" emanating from the leadership convention, and a neophyte leader, the party struck out on the hustings again in the federal election campaign of 1958. The Liberals were completely routed, and left only with a rump Liberal caucus to face 208 Diefenbaker Conservatives. It was all too clear to the old-guard Liberals that the problem with the Pearson party lay in its advisors. C. D. Howe, the key minister from the Louis St. Laurent days who had been defeated in 1957, advised Pearson "that advice from those who have never been elected to office, and are unwilling to be candidates for office, must be regarded with skepticism." It was a deliberate attack on Gordon: "the team that [Pearson] had with him in the last election were about as inept as could have been gathered together."[9] The problem with the "team," according to Howe, was that it designed a strategy in which "everything was pinned on an attempt to out-promise Diefenbaker."[10] Others, including Saskatchewan's Jimmy Gardiner, agreed that the new advisors were a sorry lot. Pearson seemed committed to "taking advice from the group in Manitoba who ruined Liberalism in the west while Mr. St. Laurent was leader," and the continuation of this practice could only mean that "our route back will be ... a long one."[11]

Although the party warhorses were almost united in their condemnation of the organizational and programmatic approach that Pearson had followed in the 1958 election, the leader remained committed (as Howe had suggested he would) to the team he was beginning to assemble. The most important indications that the social policy planners were at the heart of the Pearsonian Liberal party occurred in late 1960 and early 1961, with his decision to allow a policy conference and the subsequent endorsement of many of the resulting proposals at a general party convention. Pearson had been convinced of the merits of holding a thinkers' conference late in 1959 because it might breathe life into the party and encourage new members to join.[12] If Pearson played only a limited role in the actual events of what was to become known as the Kingston Conference, he was instrumental in both getting it off the ground and establishing the nature of its contribution to policy planning. He insisted that it be a non-partisan affair, and his choice of the long-time civil servant and former deputy minister of trade and commerce, Mitchell Sharp, as the conference coordinator was a reflection of that desire. As Sharp recalled Pearson's invitation to participate, the leader insisted that "if I organize it, it will be far too partisan an affair. People will come if you invite them that wouldn't come if I invited them. And I want it to be an open conference. I want thought; I don't simply want partisan reflections."[13] Thus Pearson was prepared to see the party branch out into new, non-traditional directions, a view that was in stark contrast to that held by the old guard, and in keeping with the views of the new social policy proponents.

The Kingston Conference was four days of formal papers and intense discussion. One of the more important presentations was by Tom Kent on social security, challenging the traditional adherence to discrete social policy measures and advocating a comprehensive and wide-ranging program. His main arguments were outlined in an 11-point scheme that included government-financed medical insurance delivered on a sliding scale according to income, sickness insurance as a means of income maintenance, a restructuring of the unemployment insurance system to provide increased benefits for prolonged unemployment, and enhanced university oppportunities.[14] The response was generally warm, with some commentators applauding Kent's "imaginative proposals in a wide variety of areas."[15]

Despite the favourable opinions of those participating in the Kingston Conference, which included a mixture of academics, journalists and "liberally minded" people from across the country, Liberal politicians were somewhat more guarded in their comments. Former health and welfare minister Paul Martin had wanted it clear from the outset that the conference propositions should be in no way binding "as many of the papers presented ... directly contradicted party policy and revealed little understanding of the political process."[16] Both he and his colleague from Newfoundland, Jack Pickersgill, considered the Kent paper an "embarrassment" and inconsistent with the "mainstream of politics."[17] With obvious reluctance on the part of the old guard to use the Kingston proposals as a basis for a new party platform, neither the thinkers' conference that Pearson had spearheaded, nor the reformers he had moved into positions of power in his opposition team, would be enough to force the Liberal party into adopting a strong social policy agenda. But luck, and careful manipulation on the part of the Kingston participants, ensured that the new social policy proposals were far from forgotten.

Shortly before the opening of the Kingston Conference, the Liberal party announced plans to hold a massive convention of the Liberal faithful and "liberally-minded Canadians in every walk of life," who would be asked to "formulate policy that will intelligently and effectively help us solve our problems."[18] The politicians anticipated what was to become known as the Liberal Rally with enthusiasm, because it would be far more democratic in design than the elite-driven Kingston Conference; Pearson's social policy planners anticipated it as the opportunity to give wider circulation to the ideas they had first put forward at Kingston. Pearson himself explained that the ideas that came out of Kingston would "be combined with suggestions from the constituencies and other organizations, [and] examined by the Rally [from which would] flow the Liberal policies."[19]

Pearson ensured that the Kingston proposals would get a full airing at the Liberal Rally, to be held in Ottawa, by appointing Walter Gordon as the chair of the policy committee.[20] Gordon enlisted Kent to "put forward some specific suggestions as to what should be done about pensions and other forms of social security."[21] The two reform-minded advisors then contrived to redraft the Kingston proposals into language that would be palatable to the grassroots rally participants. Pearson's approval of the policy statements to be voted on at the rally was also secured.[22] In this manner, the resolution drafters produced a "Plan for Health" that became the cornerstone of Liberal social policies and included a commitment to government-sponsored insurance for physician services and prescription drug charges. Although the rally itself, held in early January 1961, left open for discussion the features of each of the policy resolutions, the careful preparation of the planners prior to the opening of the convention ensured that the proposals would be acceptable to all sectors of the Liberal party. Their efforts were well-spent. Despite animated rally debate on the subject of health insurance, the result was virtually unanimous approval for the nine-point "Plan for Health" hammered out by the Gordon-led policy committee.[23]

While a health policy was, in the planners' minds, second in importance only to a plan to decrease unemployment, they also drafted policy statements on scholarships, job training and urban renewal, all of which were to become important elements of the Liberal's social security program. They had not, however, anticipated the delegates' interest in other areas of social policy. The policy committee included a brief statement on the need to reduce the pensionable age for widows and unmarried women from 65 to 60 but, in an effort to limit the range of social programs, it had not included any other statements on pensions. The delegates to the rally pushed for a much more extensive pension policy, and a strong resolution emerged: "The pensions presently available to many older persons are inadequate. This deficiency can be remedied either by a direct increase in monthly payments under the present old age security system or by a new contributory scheme, if this can be worked out with the provinces on a sound actuarial basis. A major objective that should be given high priority is to lower the starting age of old age pensions to 65."[24] The concerns of the rally delegates were to have a profound effect on the focus of the Liberal party's social program. The policy document entitled "Better Pensions for All" was ready for the 1962 election; the Kingston-based proposal, "Health Care As Needed," was unveiled during the 1963 campaign. Both were important features of the "Pearson Plan."

Although Pearson had been instrumental in creating an environment that was conducive to the efforts of the reform-oriented social policy proponents, once charged with the task of bringing the Liberal proposals to the public he began to show his natural tendency to delay. The 1962 campaign was designed to highlight the differences between Conservative inaction and the progressive policies the Liberals intended to pursue once in office.[25] But in the wake of Pearson's second defeat at the polls, Liberal sentiment suggested that "we had succeeded in bringing the Tories to their knees but we failed to move in for the kill – that is, we failed either to be 'specific' or to present a positive alternative."[26] The careful social policy design had not been articulated on the hustings, and the Liberals had come across as more uncertain than the backrooms of the party were. A year later, with a more detailed plan for health under their belts, the Liberals hit the campaign trail ready to make some real promises. Even with a relatively detailed platform position on social issues, Pearson's advisors worried that he was still too hesitant on the hustings. Thus, there was a last-minute pledge for "60 days of decision" once in office. The contributory pension scheme was one of the nine concrete policies Pearson promised would be introduced in Parliament in the first two months.

With the transition to power, the spotlight turned to the prime minister, whose role would be to provide the necessary leadership to secure the passage of pension and health legislation. Yet, unlike those more closely connected with the design of the programs, Pearson was not prepared to rush headlong into new policy directions. He was at once more prudent and more prone to procrastination than his advisors, but the campaign promise to begin work immediately on what would become known as the Canada Pension Plan almost eliminated the possibility of putting things off too long. Although voices in the new Cabinet suggested that "it would be unwise to indicate a target date for the entry into force of the plan in the Speech from the Throne,"[27] the people who had designed the social policies in opposition, and those who supported those efforts, found themselves in positions of considerable power both in Cabinet and the Prime Minister's Office. Support for quick action by finance minister Walter Gordon and policy coordinator Tom Kent served to steel the leader's resolve, and the Canada Pension Plan resolution was announced in Parliament on the 60th day of decision.

In negotiations with the provinces, which began shortly thereafter, Pearson's already shaky commitment to the pension plan began to wobble further, and noticeably so. The first inter-governmental conference, held in September 1963, indicated that the provinces were not about to accept Ottawa's pension design. Quebec premier Jean Lesage rejected the federal proposals outright, and Ontario's John Robarts came very close to doing the same. Both provinces had conducted their own extensive examinations of the question of contributory pensions and were well-positioned to disagree with the skeletal plan advanced by the federal Liberals. The first sign of difficulty shifted pensions immediately into the background, prompting pension advocate and Saskatchewan bureaucrat Al Johnson to warn that "it would be a political catastrophe for the Liberals to back down on this one."[28] While pensions were not dismissed entirely, Pearson was reluctant to commit his government to the policy overhaul necessary before facing the provinces again. The day before the second conference opened in late November, Kent complained to the prime minister that there had been "very little preparation of policy" and the federal delegation had not "thought through our responses to the proposals that we know will come from the Provinces."[29]

The failure on the part of the federal negotiators to revise their pension proposals cost Ottawa dearly. The minister of national health and welfare, Judy LaMarsh, hinted in November that it might be possible for the federal plan to be partially underwritten, but Quebec's announcement in April 1964 of its plan to introduce a fully funded provincial scheme effectively scuttled the federal proposal. Only by admitting that there were certain elements of the original scheme on which Ottawa would not retreat, and by sending Kent to negotiate personally with representatives of the Quebec government, was Pearson able to salvage something of his national contributory pension scheme. The result was a plan which would be compulsory, with funds available for provincial investment, contribution and benefit rates set slightly higher than Ottawa had envisaged; the pension fund was to become fully operational in ten years.[30] Despite all of the planning of the opposition period, the Liberals' failure to respond decisively when provincial stonewalling first became apparent meant that they gave the impression of retreating towards their final agreement. The Pearson team had procrastinated, which is not surprising for a government just getting used to governing, but they eventually followed the prudent course of essentially meeting the provinces half-way. Whether they would be able to apply the lessons of contributory pensions to national health remained to be seen.

The experience of hard negotiations with the provinces over pensions offered certain advantages to the Pearson Liberals. They were made well aware of the pitfalls of introducing social policies that demanded provincial cooperation, and could move decisively to counter the objections they anticipated over health insurance. The first step, as usual, was to convince the prime minister that the government needed to make clear its commitment to introducing a system of comprehensive medical coverage. This was even more difficult than it had been for pensions, because health did not have the push of "60 days of decision" behind it and, moreover, was considered risky after debilitating pension negotiations.

What the health insurance proponents did have in their favour was the July 1964 release of the first volume of the Hall Commission Report, which endorsed a universal, government-sponsored system in line with the program the Liberals had drafted in opposition. Pearson was still hard to convince. In January 1965, in a letter soliciting advice from caucus on what issues should be included in the upcoming Speech from the Throne, the prime minister suggested that he did "not think we can plan to take [Medicare] on, at least in any comprehensive way, in 1965."[31] Walter Gordon disagreed, arguing that it was not an issue the Liberals could afford to ignore any longer.[32] When Pearson ultimately followed Gordon's advice and included health insurance in the throne speech, the finance minister then used the issue to press for an early election call. "As the Throne Speech makes clear," Gordon wrote, "there is a great deal of work to be done – but it will take new elections and a majority government to do most of it."[33]

The constraints within which the federal government had to work were serious enough to convince the officials that the best course would be to wait for a more opportune time to open up the health insurance question. Lesage had already stated categorically that Quebec would no longer participate in any shared-cost programs, and Medicare threatened to be a costly scheme for a federal treasury already stretched to the limit. Added to the mixture was the political volatility of the issue, the general public interest in some sort of health insurance plan, and the legacy of Liberal promises of action. The result was a recipe for disaster. Fortunately, A.W. Johnson, now assistant deputy minister of finance, charted a course through the tangled mess of conditions and expectations, and produced a health insurance proposal which Kent has described as "the kind of solution that, once you have heard it, you kick yourself for having failed to think of."[34]

In a long memo to R.B. Bryce, the deputy minister of finance, Johnson outlined the general features of his plan, and explained how the new approach differed from traditional shared-cost programs. Instead of requiring the provinces to accept legislation devised and announced by the federal government, he proposed, "they would simply have to enact legislation which established a plan in conformity with the principles enunciated by the Federal Government after, and as a consequence of, consultation with the provinces." Johnson was somewhat less clear on the question of financing: he suggested that compensation to participating provinces take the form either of an equal *per capita* payment, or a combination of "the reduction of certain federal taxes to enable the provinces to raise their same taxes by an equivalent amount and ... equalization payments." He preferred the latter approach, since it was "sufficiently dissimilar from present shared cost formulae that Quebec would accept it."[35]

Bryce was the only person aware of the sort of program Johnson was proposing, and while he made a few suggestions and asked a few probing questions, he was not in a position to evaluate the viability of the Johnson plan. Nevertheless, given Bryce's caution about committing the government to expensive social welfare legislation,[36] his overall acceptance of Johnson's plan spoke highly of its merits. With Bryce's knowledge and blessing, Johnson met with Claude Morin, the Quebec deputy minister of intergovernmental affairs, to discuss the possibilities for federal-provincial agreement on national health insurance. The men met for two hours in the Chateau Laurier Hotel bar, and agreed to a procedure under which the national government set the criteria for contributions to provincial health insurance legislation. In essence, Ottawa demanded that provincial schemes be universal, comprehensive, portable and publicly administered. It was only after, and as a result of the meeting with Morin, that Johnson knew that the Medicare scheme would work.[37] Would the other provinces agree?

Breaking with tradition, the four principles for federal Medicare participation were immediately submitted to Cabinet and approved as the definitive national approach at the federal-provincial conference scheduled for 19–23 July 1965. Once its near-foolproof strategy had been determined, the government moved quickly. In his opening statement to the conference, Pearson announced that Medicare demanded merely "a general federal-provincial understanding as to the nature of the health programs which will make a federal fiscal contribution appropriate." The criteria, he explained, were that all services provided by physicians be underwritten (comprehensiveness), that all provincial residents be covered on uniform terms and conditions (universality), that the provincial scheme be administered either directly by the government or by a provincial government agency (public administration), and that all benefits be fully transferable when people were away from their home provinces (portability). Pearson anticipated "general approval" and suggested that a committee of health ministers be established to express the principles "in language sufficiently precise to prevent misconceptions."[38]

With good prospects for provincial agreement, only the Pearson Liberals' own prudence or procrastination could get in the way. Following Gordon's advice, an early election had been called, but the results were not what had been desired. Pearson was returned with only the same minority status as before, and the ensuing Cabinet shuffle turned the balance in favour of those advising caution in implementing national Medicare. While Allan MacEachen, the minister of national health and welfare, supported the scheme, his counterpart in the finance department, Mitchell Sharp, was less enthusiastic. Furthermore, the federal scheme was originally scheduled to go into operation on 1 July 1967, but by the summer of 1966 no provincial government had announced its intention to legislate on full health insurance. Recognizing the need for "greater consensus," Johnson accepted that a delay in legislation was far better than having the "provinces chip away the criteria so as to defeat universal medical care while getting general money for their existing partial plans."[39] Sharp therefore announced that the starting date would be pushed back one year to 1 July 1968.

Even this later date proved difficult. Debates with the provinces, and the uncertainty of achieving a nation-wide program, provoked a new round of stalling and a new round of Cabinet battles. Sharp was warming to the possibility of implementing the scheme "gradually," as a way both to reduce the immediate financial burden and avoid "a direct confrontation with the provinces which could do great damage in many fields, including the constitutional arena."[40] When, on 31 January 1968, the Cabinet finally decided to go ahead with Medicare on 1 July of that year, it was obvious that not all ministers were pleased with the decision. Nor was Pearson pleased with their behaviour, and he reminded them of the need for Cabinet solidarity the next day. Pearson noted "that all members of the government would be expected to support the government's position unequivocally, and that all members of Caucus should support the government's position," but he "expressed regret at the failure of some Ministers to be more flexible with regard to a formula for phasing-in the Medicare program, or for otherwise obtaining more provincial participation."[41] Pearson apparently believed that all of the provinces should have been brought in at once, even at the expense of some of the previously stated national criteria. It was in spite of the prime minister's personal opinion, therefore, that the Cabinet agreed to let the health insurance deadline stand.[42] It would be left to Pearson's successor to ensure that all provinces accepted the criteria and introduced the appropriate health insurance programs.

In his decade as leader of the Liberal party, Lester Pearson wore a variety of hats, sometimes two at a time, when it came to social policy

issues. Certainly in the opposition period, he announced his commitment to social reform by paving the way for reform planners like Tom
Kent and Walter Gordon. By leaving the design of new Liberal programs up to them, Pearson ensured that his party would have a
strong social policy platform. As prime minister, Pearson's personal
role in securing the future of national social policies was even more
determinative than when the Liberals had been in opposition. His
support for these programs, either tacit or explicit, was necessary
throughout the process of negotiation with the provinces and in
achieving Cabinet support for federal involvement. At times, particularly when negotiations became most heated, he encouraged delay
and reassessment; while this may have gone on too long in the pension debates, it nevertheless resulted in a solid agreement. Pearson's
later procrastination on the issue of health insurance, largely a result
of wanting to delay action until unanimous support across levels of
government and within Cabinet could be achieved, left open the opportunity to air other arguments in favour of postponement. Those
who argued for financial prudence, and a delay in the implementation of national health insurance until all the costs involved could be
made clear, were on much more solid ground than the prime minister
in their justification for inaction. Ultimately, however, these were not
persuasive arguments as far as Pearson was concerned, underlining
the fact that his motivations for delay had never been based on financial considerations, and the grudging support he gave to implementing Medicare in July 1968 put a stop to the delaying tactics. Pearson's
legacy, then, is mixed. He created the environment in which social
policy plans could flourish, secured a partial consensus, and then
somewhat reluctantly pushed through the necessary legislation. It is
his foresight in producing the Canada Pension Plan and Medicare
that is remembered more frequently than his caution.

"It Was Walter's View": Lester Pearson, the Liberal Party and Economic Nationalism

STEPHEN AZZI

Lester Pearson's nationalism was central to his attitude towards foreign investment. He was, to use his colleague Jack Pickersgill's phrase, "a status nationalist," concerned with Canada's international standing and the symbols of nationhood, including a distinctive honours system, national anthem, and constitution. Pearson showed his greatest strength and determination in the debate over the Canadian flag, but he was suspicious of other forms of nationalism, and, as Mitchell Sharp has remarked, "He was not an economic nationalist, to put it mildly."[1]

For economic nationalists in the 1950s and 1960s, the main concern was the degree of American investment in Canada. In this period, roughly one-third of Canadian industry was foreign-owned, with higher levels in certain key industries: more than 50 percent in manufacturing, and more than 60 percent in petroleum and natural gas. Approximately 80 percent of the foreign investment in Canada originated in the United States, and most was direct investment, carrying with it control of Canadian companies.[2] Economic nationalists worried that Canada's heavy reliance on foreign sources of capital threatened the country's financial and political independence.

This group was represented in the Liberal party of Pearson's time by Walter Gordon, a prominent Toronto business person, accountant and management consultant. The federal and provincial governments had often retained Gordon to advise on a wide variety of issues, twice appointing him to chair royal commissions. Over the years, he formed strong opinions on public policy, but had no ready means to implement his ideas. Gordon was not content to give speeches and write articles, or even to serve in a minor Cabinet position. He wanted a senior portfolio in the government that would allow him to carry out his proposals.

Although wary of economic nationalism, Pearson initially accepted Gordon's efforts to reduce American ownership in Canada. This was partly because Pearson had a weak understanding of economics. As his son Geoffrey explained, "He didn't have enough knowledge or grasp of monetary and fiscal policy, or wasn't enough interested to develop a coherent view" on foreign investment.[3] Pearson had little confidence in his command of financial issues and relied on those around him, particularly Gordon, whom Pearson said had the best economic mind in the country.[4]

Pearson needed Gordon. He could not have become prime minister without a close associate who could handle the party's organizational and financial needs. He had a weak sense of administration, which he demonstrated when he invited Jim Coutts to work in the prime minister's office. Unable to describe what he wanted Coutts to do, Pearson said, "I have eight empty offices … and I have to fill them up. Would you like to sit in one of them?"[5] By contrast, organization was one of Gordon's strengths. As a founder and senior partner of the management consulting firm of Woods, Gordon & Company, he had been responsible for restructuring many corporations and government departments. To rebuild the party, Pearson required the help of a Liberal who had not been tainted by the defeats of 1957 and 1958, with a proven record as an organizer and strong connections to the business community. In Walter Gordon, he found someone who met all these requirements.

Pearson's relationship with Gordon began in the mid-1930s, when the two men worked for the Royal Commission on Price Spreads. They became friends, though they were not close until after 1948, when Pearson became heavily reliant on Gordon. When Pearson hesitated to surrender his economic security to become external affairs minister, Gordon raised more than $100,000 from his wealthy colleagues to create a trust fund to ensure that the Pearsons would not suffer from the uncertainties of political life. In Pearson's words, Gordon also "had a great deal to do with persuading me to stand" for the party leadership.[6] In late 1957, Gordon organized a giant dinner to celebrate Pearson's Nobel Prize, an event designed to promote Pearson's leadership aspirations. At the party convention in January 1958, Gordon acted as his friend's campaign manager and, discovering that Pearson had no funds, paid the bills himself.[7]

Gordon became a key figure in the Liberal party almost immediately after the shattering election defeat of 1958. He took over the party apparatus, replaced members of the staff with individuals of his own choosing, raised funds to pay off party debts, centralized the campaign structure, and recruited candidates for the upcoming elections. "It was a wonderful unselfish work of political service on his part," Pearson later remembered. "[T]here was no one to whom the party had greater cause for gratitude for the success it achieved ... than Walter."[8]

Before he would run for office or accept an official position in the party, Gordon wanted to know that Pearson shared his views. He had first outlined his ideas on foreign investment in the reports of the Royal Commission on Canada's Economic Prospects, which he had chaired. In its 1956 *Preliminary Report* and its 1957 *Final Report*, the commission recommended that foreign-owned firms include Canadians on their boards of directors, purchase supplies and equipment in Canada, release financial statements to the public, sell 20 to 25 percent of their stock to Canadians, and employ Canadians in senior management, technical and professional positions. The reports suggested tax incentives for Canadian-owned companies, including a special depreciation allowance and a higher withholding tax on dividends paid to non-residents by firms that did not have "an appreciable percentage" of Canadian ownership.[9]

In the early 1960s, Gordon began a series of speeches intended to put his policy ideas on record, including the need to limit foreign investment. In his mind, Canada could not remain a separate country if it did not take steps to halt the gradual amalgamation of the Canadian and American economies, a process he described as "tempting, insidious, considerable and continuous."[10] He insisted that "the loss of our economic independence, which to some extent would follow inevitably from economic integration with the United States, would sooner or later mean the end of our political independence also."[11] These statements are crucial to understanding Gordon because, as he later admitted, his opinions did not change substantially thereafter.[12]

In July 1960, Gordon sent the text of the speeches to Pearson, and told him that he did not wish to become involved with the Liberal party unless he knew that they had similar views on the major policy issues. Together with the royal commission reports, the speeches covered "practically everything on which I have any views that matter." Gordon noted Pearson's response in the margin to one of his letters: "Mike called to say he ... agreed *completely* with my ideas. He repeated this two or three times saying that this is exactly how he feels on these various issues." According to Gordon, "any doubts I may have had about possible differences of opinion about policies were resolved."[13]

Pearson's assurance that he shared Gordon's views demonstrated, to use biographer John English's phrase, "Pearson's tendency to tell people all too often only what they wanted to hear."[14] As a diplomat, he had become successful by delaying decisions, fostering ambiguity and trying to please everyone. He hated being disagreeable and avoided confrontation at almost any cost, often giving the impression that he agreed with people, only to surprise them by acting in an opposite manner. Many observers believed that Pearson was most influenced by the last person with whom he had spoken.[15]

After reassuring Gordon that they had the same opinions on American investment, Pearson spoke publicly on the subject. At the 1960 Study Conference on National Problems, the gathering of liberal thinkers commonly known as the Kingston Conference, Pearson gave an opening speech which must have pleased Gordon. Pearson briefly repeated his friend's argument that economic interdependence threatened political independence, asking "Have we escaped the colonial frying-pan merely to have jumped into the Washington fire? Have we sold our birth-right for a mess of below-par U.S. dollars?" In Pearson's words, foreign investment was "a major problem and I am equally convinced that there is something we, as a Party, can do about it and should – and will."[16]

In addition to Pearson's vague opening remarks, two speakers – Walter Gordon and Michael Barkway of *The Financial Post* – spoke in detail of the need to limit foreign investment. At a session entitled "How Independent Can We Be?" Barkway presented ten complaints about the practices of foreign-owned firms. These included the tendency to ship raw materials elsewhere for processing, to export less than Canadian-owned firms did, to hire consultants from the US, to use research and designs developed abroad, and to favour American suppliers. To deal with these problems, the government should urge foreign companies to improve their performance, a policy "not necessarily involving immediate legislation, but always looking to the possibility of it."[17] As a commentator at this session, Gordon accepted these arguments, mentioning in particular the lack of research and development in Canada, but said that he was not interested in exerting pressure on foreign-owned firms to change their practices. He preferred to restrict the extent of foreign investment in Canada, proposing changes in the tax structure "to encourage U.S. and other foreign owners of Canadian subsidiaries to sell part or all of their companies to Canadians."[18]

The other participants at the Kingston Conference clearly opposed the position advanced by Gordon and Barkway, arguing for the free flow of goods and capital between countries. Economist William Hood believed that Barkway's emphasis was "largely misplaced," asserting that the government could best help Canada's independence

by promoting Canadian business, rather than reducing foreign ownership. Harry Johnson, a commanding figure among professional
economists, attacked Gordon's proposals, saying that measures to
control outside investment and limit trade reflected "not so much the
noble spirit of Canadian independence, as the small, smug mind and
large larcenous hands of Bay Street." Many applauded when historian Frank Underhill commented that the Liberal party had tradition-
ally been close to the US and should leave anti-American preaching
to the Conservatives. These sentiments were summarized by Carleton University president and Ottawa insider Davidson Dunton, who
was called upon to deliver a review of the conference discussions.
"Certainly, there was not much evidence that there were greater dis-
advantages from that capital inflow here than there were advantages."[19] The *Winnipeg Free Press* agreed with this summary: "not a
single voice was raised in support of Mr. Gordon's or Mr. Barkway's
views ... On the contrary both were severely criticized for a form of
economic chauvinism."[20]

There was a similar lack of support for Gordon's views at the Liberal party's 1961 National Rally. The gathering approved a policy
which welcomed outside investment: "Canada has gained enor-
mously from the capital that has come here from abroad, and foreign
investors must always be treated fairly. We should continue to welcome and encourage the inflow of foreign capital in order to promote
the rapid development of the Canadian economy." Although it recognized potential problems, the policy did not include legislation to
limit foreign investment. Instead, "The most desirable way to coun-
teract the tendency towards foreign control of our industry is to encourage greater Canadian participation in the ownership of Canadian
enterprises." Measures to foster domestic investment would consist
of tax incentives, a program to educate Canadians about the importance of investing their savings in Canada, and an amendment to legislation dealing with the investment of pension, trust, and insurance
funds. Although it did say that banks and trust companies should by
law remain under domestic ownership and control, the resolution
never suggested that the government discourage foreign investment
in other sectors.[21]

Gordon continued to push his ideas forward, even though the
party had not adopted his proposals for limiting outside investment.
In the summer of 1961, he wrote *Troubled Canada: The Need for New Domestic Policies*, which he claimed was "a handy guide for many Liberal candidates in the election campaign soon to be upon them."[22]
Published in November, the book outlined Gordon's recommendations for improving the country's social safety net. On American

ownership, Gordon repeated what he had first said in the reports of his royal commission. He still worried that foreign-owned firms were not promoting Canadian managers and executives, and that "technical and scientific personnel are not given sufficient opportunities to use their imagination and skills because the subsidiaries have access to the research being done by the foreign parent company." He was also concerned that American-owned firms would be less likely to export because "it may not be good business for a United States parent company to encourage or even permit its Canadian subsidiary to seek export markets in other countries, possibly in competition with itself." As a solution to these problems, Gordon proposed tax incentives "which would encourage a greater participation by resident Canadians in the ownership and management of Canadian enterprise and resources."[23] The measures focused on supporting Canadian investment, rather than decreasing the level of foreign investment.

At the same time, Pearson continued to speak as though he wished to reduce the level of foreign investment in Canada. When he received letters on the issue, his response sounded a lot like Gordon. "[I]t will be necessary," he argued, "to make a number of changes in our tax laws which will discourage Canadians from selling Canadian resources and Canadian-owned companies to foreigners; and at the same time encourage foreigners and foreign corporations to sell their assets here back to Canadians." As a first step, Pearson proposed that foreign firms should sell a minority of shares to Canadians, "but the ultimate objective must be to buy back Canadian resources and Canadian companies to the maximum possible extent." He concluded by assuring the reader "that if the Liberal Party is called upon to form a government under my Leadership, action along these lines will be taken."[24] This policy went much further than the party resolution, which had not suggested changes in the tax laws to dissuade Canadians from selling their companies to foreigners.

The 1962 and 1963 election campaigns failed to clarify the Liberal position on investment. Indeed, the problem was seldom mentioned, either by Gordon or the other Liberal candidates. According to Tom Kent, Pearson's senior policy advisor, "the nationalist issue as such was simply never faced up to. It didn't feature in all these statements of policy that I drafted and were approved by Mr. Pearson. We really just ignored that issue." Key figures in the party, such as Jack Pickersgill and Mitchell Sharp, did not believe that the party had policies to limit outside investment in the opposition years. Kent agreed: "it was never officially Liberal party policy. It was Walter's view."[25]

When Gordon became minister of finance in April 1963, he immediately acted as though he had a mandate to reduce foreign

investment in Canada. In his first budget, he introduced a 30 percent tax on foreign takeovers of Canadian firms, an increase in the
withholding tax on dividends paid by foreign-owned companies to
non-residents, and favourable changes to the depreciation allowance for firms with at least 25 percent Canadian ownership. He had
not bothered to convince the country or even his fellow ministers
of the dangers of foreign capital. As Cabinet colleague Allan
MacEachen pointed out, Gordon never wanted to discuss his views
on this issue.[26]

The finance minister did review his budget measures with the
prime minister. Gordon later remembered that he "spent a lot of time
with Mike over the budget beforehand including long sessions over
the speech itself. He was as pleased with the Budget as I was."[27] Pearson, in Gordon's words, "expressed great delight" with the budget,
and said "he felt it would put the Liberal Party on the map."[28] Bank
of Canada Governor Louis Rasminsky warned Pearson of potential
problems with the takeover tax and the changes to the withholding
tax on dividends. Although Pearson appeared interested in Rasminsky's arguments, he was not alarmed. He continued to support
Gordon's budget, saying just a few days before its presentation that it
would be "formidable."[29] Indifferent to financial matters, Pearson
had essentially given Gordon *carte blanche*.

The budget was a failure. Faced with widespread opposition from
the financial community, Gordon was compelled to withdraw the
30 percent takeover tax. Perhaps hoping to force Pearson to declare
his confidence in the finance minister and the budget, he offered to
resign. Pearson responded by asking Gordon if he had confidence in
himself, and acted as though the matter was settled with the finance
minister's positive response to this question. Gordon was depressed
by these events, and by what he perceived to be the lack of support
from his Cabinet colleagues, particularly Pearson. "Mike never said a
[public] word in my defence despite the fact it was almost as much
his budget as mine – my ideas but he had bought them."[30]

For the remainder of his term as finance minister, Gordon did little
to reduce the level of American investment in Canada. He advanced
his proposal for a Canada Development Corporation, which would
invest in Canadian businesses, but not with enough vigour to see it
adopted by Cabinet. Although he introduced and secured speedy
passage of bills preventing foreign takeovers of insurance, trust, and
loan companies, he did not obtain approval for a more important bill
dealing with ownership of Canadian banks. After recommending
that Cabinet take no action to protect Canadian magazines from foreign competition, he later reluctantly agreed to measures that would

prevent the production of Canadian editions by American magazines, while exempting *Time* and *Reader's Digest*, periodicals which were already publishing local editions. He also supported the Autopact, which linked the Canadian and American automobile industries. His innocuous 1964 budget had, in the words of journalist Peter Stursberg, "nothing in it – no changes in taxes, no Canadianism, nothing which might not have been drawn up by an official in a caretaker government."[31] His third budget, in 1965, was no different. Gordon had provided the inspiration for many of the government's innovations in social policy, but on the investment issue his actions were essentially the same as those of his predecessors.

After the narrow Liberal victory in the election of 1965, Gordon again offered his resignation. He had pledged that he would resign if the party did not win a majority, but now believed that the prime minister should reject his resignation because Pearson had promised during the campaign that Gordon would stay as finance minister. This time, however, Pearson accepted, knowing that Gordon had angered the Canadian business community and had been a major source of division in the government. Gordon thought that Pearson had betrayed him by allowing him to resign, but expected soon to return to the Cabinet. Certainly, he had no intention of remaining as a back-bench member of Parliament, a job he drily described as "not exactly tolerable."[32]

Pearson's new Cabinet showed how clearly Gordon had lost the fight. Gordon's replacement was the cautious Mitchell Sharp, who, a few days before the election call, had criticized the suggestion that Canada should limit foreign investment. "Anyone who looks objectively at that prescription for national survival is bound to reject it," Sharp maintained. "It could only weaken our economic structure and increase the temptation to join the United States."[33] After assuming the finance portfolio, Sharp continued to speak against measures to curb foreign investment. His policy was "not to penalize or discourage enterprise because it originates outside Canada. For a country like Canada with such a vast stake in non-discriminatory access to capital and to world markets this would be short sighted."[34]

Sharp's replacement as minister of trade and commerce was Robert Winters, a well-known opponent of Gordon's views. During the election campaign, Winters announced that "the less we do to discourage this investment the better. I think we can encourage it without giving away the ownership of Canadian industry."[35] On several occasions after joining Pearson's Cabinet, Winters sharply voiced his opposition to economic nationalism. Like Sharp, he believed that the government should pursue greater Canadian participation in the country's economy, but should not use the tax laws to limit foreign ownership. Rather, Canada should "state the rules of the game," telling foreign-owned firms how they must perform.[36]

Winters demonstrated this approach in March 1966, when he issued 12 "guiding principles of good corporate behaviour for subsidiaries in Canada of foreign companies." The so-called "Winters Guidelines" were a reaction to a similar directive sent by the US government to Canadian branch-plants of American corporations. Designed to improve the country's balance-of-payments position, the American guidelines asked subsidiaries to return more of their earnings to the parent company and to purchase more parts and components in the US. Winters's response urged foreign-owned firms to seek export markets, use Canadian suppliers, develop research facilities in Canada, and retain enough of their profits in Canada to support the growth of their local operations.[37] The Winters Guidelines were not supported by any statute, for "nothing scares money away more quickly than legislation."[38]

Gordon still had supporters in Cabinet, but they either disagreed with his proposals on American ownership or thought that the issue did not merit the importance he attached to it. Judy LaMarsh, for example, criticized the performance of American-owned firms, saying that outside investment "might prove dangerous for Canada in the longer term in regard to our political independence."[39] Aside from giving a speech on the subject, however, she never pursued the matter with much interest or vigour. Similarly, E.J. "Ben" Benson and Jean Marchand both expressed concerns about foreign control, but neither gave the problem the same attention that Gordon did.[40] Benson, indeed, believed that Gordon "worried too much about American influence."[41]

Although his political influence was waning, Gordon continued his efforts to have the party adopt policies to limit foreign investment. Published in May 1966, his second book, *A Choice for Canada: Independence or Colonial Status*, disappointed many of those who expected revelations about Gordon's struggle inside the Pearson Cabinet and found, in the words of one writer, "a rather dull restatement of Gordonism."[42] Gordon again suggested that the tax laws be changed to favour firms with at least 25 percent Canadian ownership, and once more proposed the introduction of a tax on foreign takeovers of Canadian businesses similar to the one he had been forced to withdraw in 1963.[43]

The book appeared at a time when many Canadians were slowly beginning to share Gordon's anxiety about American influence in Canada. The late 1960s were a period of growing criticism of the US, a country that often seemed violent and self-destructive, with racial strife, assassinations, and increasing involvement in the Vietnam war. Canadian television sets vividly portrayed race riots in American cities and carnage in Southeast Asia, events which called American values into question. Because a large number of Canadians now wanted their country to be more independent of its neighbour, Gordon's ideas were having a greater impact. The great irony of Gordon's political life was that he was beginning to win converts on the issue closest to his heart at the precise moment that his influence in the Liberal party was ebbing away.

Although Gordon's book sold more than 12,000 copies within six months, it had little effect on the Liberal government. John Turner, a junior Cabinet minister, said that it did not "represent the main stream of Liberal thinking."[44] Sharp rejected Gordon's emphasis on foreign ownership, insisting that unemployment was a higher priority: "I don't think Canadian independence can be very meaningful or attractive to the unemployed or the under-employed."[45] In a speech in the US, he warned his listeners not to "be misled by [the] occasional burst of what may appear to you to be shrill nationalism."[46] In a subsequent television interview back home, he dismissed Gordon's views as "rather pessimistic."[47]

Gordon provoked a confrontation on the investment issue at the Liberal policy conference in Ottawa in October 1966. Gordon drafted a resolution on foreign control, but did not advocate the discriminatory measures that he had set forth in *A Choice for Canada*, merely suggesting "incentives to Canadians to invest in business enterprises and resources in this country." Gordon urged the government to promote policies, "including tax policies" to "reduce foreign ownership and control of Canadian industry and resources to not more than one-third in the next twenty-five years," an objective which could not likely have been achieved without some action to discourage outside investment.[48]

Gordon's motion was debated in a policy workshop on economic growth and development. Mitchell Sharp spoke against the resolutions, but struck a moderate tone, accepting the existence of a problem while rejecting Gordon's solutions. "We have reason to be concerned about our continued reliance upon massive imports of capital," Sharp acknowledged. In his view, however, "The best way to weaken Canadian independence is to follow narrowly nationalistic policies." Sharp recommended that the party advocate "positive policies, not negative policies," vaguely suggesting that the government should "encourage Canadian industries."[49] Gordon, too, portrayed himself as a moderate, stressing that he and Sharp agreed "on objectives and there is little difference between us on measures to achieve them." His own proposals were a "middle course," and by adopting them the party would "receive a tremendous public response from all parts of the country, particularly from young people."[50] Despite this appeal, Gordon's resolutions were shelved by an overwhelming vote of 650 to 100. Shortly afterward, Gordon's representatives arranged a meeting in a small back room with Sharp, Manitoba Liberal Leader Gildas Molgat, and other senior delegates from western Canada. The group hammered out a compromise statement which was approved unanimously in the plenary session later that day. According to the new resolution, "the government should take steps to encourage greater Canadian ownership of the economy, without discouraging foreign investment."[51] It did not include Gordon's stipulation that the government should reduce foreign ownership to one-third in 25 years.

According to journalist Bruce Hutchison, the conference "was the final destruction of Walter Gordon."[52] Gordon was "disappointed in the Convention and particularly in the fact that a good majority of the delegates made it quite clear they are not interested in doing anything about the increasing foreign control of our economy."[53] He recognized his growing powerlessness in the Liberal party: "Quite frankly, I am not at all sure that I can accomplish very much in the position I am in at present."[54]

After the conference, Gordon told Pearson that he would resign from the party and would publicly criticize the government's policies. Gordon's friends in caucus may not have fully accepted the former finance minister's ideas on foreign ownership, but they were still loyal to him because of his personal and political support, and because they shared his progressive views on social policy. They urged Pearson to bring Gordon back into the Cabinet. Eventually, Pearson succumbed.

Gordon responded that he would only take a Cabinet post if the prime minister fulfilled stringent conditions. With the title of deputy prime minister or president of the privy council, Gordon would have wide-ranging powers that would make him *de facto* co-prime minister. He would take over the privy council office, which functioned as the prime minister's department, and would supervise the work of Cabinet, controlling the agenda and ensuring that decisions were implemented. Gordon also wanted a key political role, and the power to plan political tactics, chair a party policy committee, and act as liaison between Cabinet and caucus, and between Cabinet and the Liberal party. He wished to chair a Cabinet committee that would draft a white paper outlining measures to limit foreign investment, and wanted assurances that the government would not back down on its amendments to the Bank Act dealing with foreign ownership of Canadian banks.

Pearson could not possibly agree to these conditions, but gave Gordon the impression that he did, preferring to avoid public criticism from Gordon and the internal dissent generated by Gordon's friends in caucus. Gordon became president of the privy council and directed a task force on foreign investment, but never gained the other powers and duties he had been promised. Again he felt betrayed, and was angry when Sharp proposed changes to the Bank Act bill that would have given the American-owned Citibank more time to reduce its ownership of the Mercantile Bank.

After Gordon's return to Cabinet, several ministers gave speeches demonstrating that government policy on foreign investment had not changed. In January 1967, external affairs minister Paul Martin said that the government would not introduce measures to discourage foreign investment.[55] A few days later, Winters maintained that Canada welcomed foreign investment, "regardless of doubt-provoking rumours to the contrary." The government had no plans to adopt "negative or punitive legislation affecting foreign interests."[56]

Faced with increasing press speculation of a major rift in Cabinet, the prime minister dealt with the issue in a national television address on 1 February 1967. Echoing Sharp and Winters, Pearson announced clearly that Canada welcomed foreign capital, and he warned that Canadians "must avoid discriminatory or unfair treatment which would create the kind of atmosphere that discourages necessary foreign investment." The government's objective was that "Canadians should own and control as much of our industry as is possible," but it would achieve this goal "not by action which is unfair to foreign interests, but by positive action which will marshall and encourage Canadian capital to invest increasingly in Canadian enterprise." This position, Pearson claimed, was "accepted by all the present government, and by all its members, as the basis for the formulation and application of foreign economic policy, and, in particular, of our economic and financial relations with the United States."[57]

In well-publicized speeches over the next few months, several Cabinet ministers attacked Gordon's views on foreign control, though they never mentioned him by name. Maurice Sauvé and Robert Winters rejected the contention that foreign-owned firms were less likely to employ Canadians in senior management positions or to seek export markets. Winters told an audience that foreign-owned firms generally "conduct themselves as good corporate Canadian citizens," and were often better behaved than their Canadian counterparts because they felt particularly vulnerable to criticism from Canadians. There might be problems with a few companies, but he did not believe that "there is validity to the charge that foreign-ownership *per se* acts against our national interests." In a comment clearly aimed at Gordon, Sauvé declared, "In our acute sensitivity to the imagined effects of foreign ownership on the performance of our economy I believe we have allowed ourselves to be distracted from more important problems facing us." The fundamental question was not the origin of investment capital, but rather how to manage it. Sharp echoed the comments he made at the 1966 policy conference, saying that government policies "should be positive, not negative, directed not against foreign capital but in favour of Canadian capital." He preferred "to see as much of Canadian industry owned and controlled by Canadians as is possible," but the first priority was "to see Canada grow and develop," and this meant that Canada would continue to require considerable levels of foreign investment.[58]

Despite opposition in Cabinet, Gordon succeeded in setting up the Task Force on the Structure of Canadian Industry, with economist Mel Watkins as chair. Some ministers, however, did not want the task force to publish its report, even with a disclaimer saying that it did not represent official policy. In February 1968, Gordon won his fight to have the report published, largely because Watkins had leaked the document to the *Toronto Star*, and had told officials that the newspaper planned to publish it if the government refused.[59]

The report's recommendations were mild – much milder than Gordon's own proposals on foreign investment. The task force never suggested that the government stop or even discourage takeovers of Canadian companies by foreign firms. Its very reasonable recommendations included greater disclosure of information by corporations, steps to foster competition and increase the efficiency of Canadian industry, a reduction in the tariff, and measures to limit the extraterritorial application of foreign laws. Despite these moderate suggestions, Cabinet refused to endorse the report and, a few days after it was tabled, Gordon resigned from the ministry.

In the end, Walter Gordon's concerns about foreign control had little influence in the Pearson government. Having few strong opinions on economic matters, the prime minister had initially allowed Gordon to believe that he agreed with him, but over time Pearson began to side more and more with Mitchell Sharp. Even Cabinet colleagues such as Ben Benson and Judy LaMarsh, who were sympathetic to Gordon, thought he was putting far too much emphasis on the issue. Gordon's ideas would only begin to make an impact in the years after he and Pearson left the political scene.

"A Good Man for the Middle Innings": Lester Pearson and the Media, 1963–1968

PATRICK H. BRENNAN

Voters often defeat governments rather than elect them. In April 1963, however, Canadians elected a Liberal government as much as they defeated a discredited and widely unpopular Conservative one. Most pundits deemed the miserable relations "enjoyed" with the media by the outgoing regime, and especially its leader, John Diefenbaker, to have contributed mightily to his government's fall from grace. The media, many argued, had been alternately the making, in 1957–58, and then the unmaking of "The Chief." As for the victorious Liberals, led by L.B. Pearson, they had returned to their normal state as the "government party," not the least, as they acknowledged themselves, because they had successfully conveyed to the voters their Kennedyesque vision of a "Camelot of the North." The "political" media, overwhelmingly favourable to the Liberals and their leader, had been essential to their success.

During the next five years, the same media would be anything but kind to both Pearson and his party. This can be attributed to controversies on the policy front and manifest political administrative failures, but also to a pronounced shift to a more adversarial journalism, already underway as Pearson and his ministers were being sworn in by the governor general. Under intense media scrutiny, Mike Pearson and the new Liberal team, for whom expectations were practically boundless, were found wanting. Pearson's own leadership image, all but unquestioned in that moment of triumph in the spring of 1963, was quickly discredited.

More than any of the mandarins who dominated Canadian government during the era of grey but highly competent Liberal wartime and postwar governments, diplomat Lester Pearson had understood how to get along with and make profitable use of the fourth estate. His effortless transition to minister of external affairs in 1948 established him as one of the media darlings of the St. Laurent government and the *beau idéal* of the Ottawa establishment, including its journalistic component. Selling Canadian diplomatic initiatives to the public during the Golden Age of Canadian foreign policy, it is true, proved relatively easy – the substance of the policies and widespread sympathy for them ensured that. But Pearson's unmatched rapport with the leading editors and reporters of the day greatly aided him and the government, all the while further embellishing the reputations of both.

These were the heyday years of the "Ottawa editors" like Grant Dexter, Ken Wilson and Blair Fraser, who, along with such other journalistic lights of the period as George Ferguson and Bruce Hutchison, were themselves committed internationalists. Pearson's marvelous combination of intellect, affability and self-effacing wit bewitched them. The intimacy of this "responsible, civilized" relationship enhanced ordinary Canadians' understanding of complex foreign policy issues and Pearson's celebrity in almost equal measure.[1] Thanks to his assistance, these journalistic "insiders" usually managed to avoid "creating [any] wrong impressions," as Bruce Hutchison once coyly phrased it.[2] Not surprisingly, for most of the "establishment" journalists, this seductive mixture of affection and admiration spilled over into unabashed support for Pearson's thinly disguised ambitions to succeed Louis St. Laurent as Liberal leader and prime minister.

When St. Laurent resigned after the Liberal defeat in 1957, there seemed little reason to doubt that Mike Pearson's obvious brains, competence and smooth facility with the media would carry him far politically.[3] Yet, accomplished diplomat though he was, and despite nine years on the Liberal front benches, Pearson was a rank amateur as a politician. This deficiency would soon be clear to all, cruelly exposed within a matter of weeks by his nemesis, John Diefenbaker, whose revitalized Progressive Conservatives, so long the butt of Liberal jokes, buried the Grits in the spring 1958 general election. The Pearson political reputation was more gold-plated than golden.

Nevertheless, to most Liberals and a great many Canadians, he was still Mike Pearson "the pure heart," a man "above politics" who deserved no blame for the disasters which had befallen his party.[4] With the Diefenbaker government's antics making voters ever more desirous of an alternative, it was enough that the Liberals offered one. The party's march back to power was marked by a steady drift to the political left and, after the American presidential election of 1960, an equally determined effort to duplicate the "Kennedy magic" of new, inspiring ideas and dynamic leadership. The Liberals, who had taken journalists for granted and badly fumbled the advent of television in Canadian politics, now took on both with a passion as the keys to resurrecting their party's electoral fortunes. Essential in this respect, the party's new operatives recognized, was the transformation of their leader's media image. While the idea of a "new Mike" and the leftward lurch of policy alarmed some of the more conservatively minded of Pearson's and the party's loyal journalist allies – Hutchison, Dexter and the old *Winnipeg Free Press* crowd in particular – the "Camelot" Liberals, with Keith Davey, Richard O'Hagan and Tom Kent in the forefront, disregarded the grumbling and plunged ahead.[5] Central to the reshaping of Pearson's media image, beginning in 1961, were the organizing whiz Davey and the equally able and innovative press secretary, O'Hagan. The former combined backgrounds in both radio and backroom politics, while the latter had worked as a journalist and advertising executive. Both were strong advocates of the new Kennedy-style politics of image and passion, both knew how to "work" the media to get a story "right," and both appreciated, as O'Hagan stressed to the leader, the "incalculable importance of television as a force in modern politics."[6] When the Diefenbaker government began to unravel, and the Chief's honeymoon with the press turned sour, their task would become considerably easier.

Pearson was enthusiastically and unanimously endorsed by the Canadian media – and Canadian elites – when the 1963 election returned his party to office, albeit with a minority status in the House of Commons. Even the Montreal *Gazette* and Toronto *Telegram*, paragons of Tory press virtue, had come out for the Grits. Virtually every element of the Canadian intellectual community, including the great majority of working journalists, personally welcomed the result. Indeed, affection and respect for Pearson the man, by those who, like political journalists, regularly saw him in the intimate circumstances in which he had always shone, was universal. "Probably the most distinctive development in Canadian journalism during 1963," media observer Wilfred Kesterton observed at the time, "was a sharp improvement in relations between press and government."[7] Pearson and his advisors, having witnessed the role which the media had played in destroying their predecessors, were wisely committed to ushering in a new era in press-government relations. Appropriately, then, the new prime minister's first public address was made at the annual meeting of the Canadian Press in Toronto, at the end of April, where he promised an amicable relationship without coziness and invited vigilance and criticism from journalists. Pearson seemed sincerely to appreciate the fundamental dilemma of media-government relations in a democratic society, that the government would have to accept a balance between its own proper need for secrecy and the right of the public, facilitated by the media, to know what was happening.[8] The display of such an understanding seemed to augur well for the new government's and prime minister's relations with the media. Certainly many of the journalists were impressed.[9]

There had been much of the "new politics" in the Liberals' 1963 campaign, epitomized by the extensive use of television image-making and the promise of "60 days of decision." In fact the Camelot of the North seemed to have everything – ideas, style, and a blizzard of "forward looking" policies – everything, as it turned out, but a Kennedy. Pearson had promised to set the tone for his government with a burst of energetic, innovative and competent administration; but, instead of great expectations fulfilled, Walter Gordon's budget fiasco shattered the illusion for all but the truest of the true believers. Media loyalists such as Fraser, Ferguson and Hutchison still wanted to believe in their man's promise, but even they were disappointed by the early signs of disarray.[10] For most journalists, the first "60 days" were a revelation with lasting implications, planting seeds of doubt in their minds and hence in the minds of their readers and listeners that perhaps the unthinkable was possible – perhaps Mike Pearson did not have the "right stuff" after all.

The opening stumble need not have been fatal and, indeed, it was not. As one Conservative insider correctly pointed out, the press would continue "treating Pearson kindly because the alternative continues to be seen as more horrendous than Pearson's vacillating and fumbling."[11] This was undoubtedly reinforced in reporters' and editors' minds by the relentless accusations hurled in their direction by Diefenbaker and his caucus that the press were performing as little more than publicity "flacks" for the new government. Still, repairing the damage and getting the media back on Pearson's side was not going to be easy. Relations between the government and the media were undergoing radical change in Canada and, from the perspective of the politicians, not for the better. Instead of the 1950s group of intimates Pearson could trust (and charm), and who sincerely wanted to help him,[12] the press gallery had swollen to well over a hundred members and was growing rapidly. Many of the newcomers represented the electronic media. Television, soon to dominate the reporting and analysis of public affairs, would not be especially kind to Pearson's personality. The warmth, sincerity, candour and humility which won over all but the most hardened opponents in intimate encounters went missing on television, and he only rarely exhibited the now requisite passion and charisma. Try as his handlers might, no amount of coaching and manipulation could bring about more than a modest change in this state of affairs.[13] Instead, there was the bland and sometimes snobbish intellectual, well-intentioned but none too practical and, increasingly, a weak and muddling figure.[14]

Just as importantly, the very philosophy of journalists and the nature of journalism were changing too. By the mid-1960s, the press tended to be a lot more cranky, suspicious and disrespectful of government and politicians. In part this was Diefenbaker's legacy, five years of increasingly poisonous press-government relations which had served to entrench reporters' view that they were the political system's "unofficial" opposition. But it went deeper than that. By and large, the new generation of journalists covering national affairs embraced the "libertarian" cat-among-the-pigeons philosophy that the media were the guardians of the citizens' rights and it was their duty to uncover and expose ineptitude and hypocrisy in government wherever and whenever they found it. This view was rooted in an underlying assumption "that the politicians were always motivated by personal or partisan self-interest, at odds with the public interest," and it was soon apparent that "the assumption proved an all too convenient way of explaining just about everything happening in Ottawa."[15]

This would have been hard enough on any political leader. It was all the harder for one who had become perfectly attuned to the requirements of the journalistic *ancien régime*, with its healthy component of "social responsibility" journalism, predicated on the view that individual reporters and editors should make informed and balanced decisions on what the public in practice needed to know, thus permitting a considerably greater measure of cooperation between the journalist on one side and the politician or bureaucrat on the other.[16] A significant number of adherents to this approach remained, among them Blair Fraser of *Maclean's*, Anthony Westell of the *Globe and Mail*, Bill Wilson of the Montreal *Star*, and that paper's editor, George Ferguson, as well as the redoubtable Hutchison. But, for most in the press gallery and in the editorial offices and newsrooms across the country, adversarialism and "independence" were in the ascendant. Television in particular was having an enormous impact on political perceptions. As media historian Paul Rutherford has observed: "The newscasts and the public-affairs shows of television reached so many people, [and] the influence of its images seemed so compelling, that it had altered the nature of the political game. The news media, print as well as television journalists, were bent on establishing their own brand of authority over political life. The twin notions of investigative and adversary journalism had gained increasing favour in press circles."[17]

Television's more critical and more visceral approach was coming to print journalism as well, as epitomized by the emergence of Peter Newman as English Canada's foremost national political commentator. By 1964, his columns in the Toronto *Star* were reaching an audience of two million. Newman, who had once been Fraser's understudy, was no practitioner of the "responsible, civilized relationship," as the publication of his best-selling exposé of the Diefenbaker government's inner goings-on, *Renegade in Power*, made obvious. The book brought full-blown investigative journalism to Ottawa. Newman wrote publicly the way everyone in Ottawa talked privately. Watching from the editorial offices of Newman's sometimes-employer, *Maclean's*, Robert Fulford was perfectly placed to see the impact. "His frankness changed Canadian journalism, and helped change the way Canadians saw their government," Fulford concluded, and "by the time *Renegade in Power* finished its run on the best seller lists, the era in journalism exemplified by Fraser was over and the Newman era had begun."[18] Fraser, the most influential political commentator in English Canada during the 1950s, had written *from* Ottawa, both physically and, more to the point, spiritually, and that had given him credibility.

Newman wrote *about* Ottawa, but not as an "Ottawa man" wearing that badge proudly, and that gave him credibility. Henceforth, most younger journalists followed the lead of "non-partisans" like Newman or the *Globe*'s George Bain, and Charles Lynch of Southams, who defended their personal "independence" and tended to view all politicians with suspicion. In this environment, the pressure to write critically became intense. As Lynch, one of the few who operated successfully in both print and television, remembered it: "I'd sit down many a time and say to myself, 'it's be kind to Pearson week' – I loved the guy. Half-way through the piece the monkey on my back would get there and the piece would end up another critique. I was almost incapable of writing a sustained positive piece about policy."[19]

For Pearson, who favoured politically sympathetic journalistic friends and discreet, off-the-record discussions, the aggressive and adversarial style of the "new" press gallery was unwelcome, undignified and distasteful. It was difficult to tell who could be confided in when the rules of engagement changed.[20] When possible, the prime minister fell back on those whom he could trust, and who trusted him, and avoided contact or was at least increasingly reticent with the others, only to be accused of being too secretive and reverting to the favouritism that had so frustrated press outsiders during the bad old Diefenbaker days.[21] As early as the autumn of 1963, Douglas Fisher, the former MP who was another of the new-style Ottawa reporters and a most definite outsider to the Liberals, began to complain that the government was not delivering the much touted "openness." The only openness Fisher could see was the open granting of special treatment to favoured journalists.[22]

Media scrums, replete with TV cameras and tape recorders that rendered off-the-cuff remarks so dangerous, scared Pearson. Leaks were another curse, and the Pearson Cabinets and caucus proved a veritable Niagara of leaks. It was more than ironic, and infuriating to Pearson, that Newman, whose insider reports had so tormented Diefenbaker, now laid bare the divisions and blunders of his own government.[23] After government spokesmen righteously complained that the press were publishing caucus secrets, the respected George Bain acidly dismissed the accusations by suggesting that the Liberals punish the miscreant MPs instead of harassing journalists.[24] It was hard to meet the media's expectations. They probably could not be met. When Pearson was decisive, he was dismissed as "opportunistic," and when he compromised, he was accused of being "indecisive."

This media criticism took its toll on Pearson's morale and his good intentions to improve the media-government relationship. Blair Fraser, an intellectual admirer of the prime minister and most of his agenda and no practitioner of the new-style journalism, was quick to notice this. Commenting on the annual spring press gallery dinner in his regular "Backstage at Ottawa" column in *Maclean's*, he observed the surprising fact that the prime minister had displayed as much asperity in his remarks to the assembled reporters as had Diefenbaker. "The Liberals' resentment is almost as strong as the Conservatives'," Fraser pointed out, "and is based on the same ground." Political reporting had become "biased, opinionated and presumptuous."[25] Attacks on the press, as the Liberals were learning, were not necessarily bad politics but, as Fraser and a few of his other colleagues shrewdly concluded, this tactic was only serving to arouse the media's growing sensitivity to criticism and in turn leading to more criticism of the politicians.

By 1964, it was clear that the Liberals were actively pursuing "new management" strategies, particularly with the print media. These efforts, while not on the scale attempted by the Diefenbaker government, nonetheless rendered the earlier promises of candour and fairness hollow to many reporters, and were much resented. Kite-flying became the norm, with some ministers becoming accomplished at making impromptu announcements of important policies in casual surroundings, sometimes the very day they could have released the same news to Parliament, and thus the entire gallery. The prime minister, for instance, revealed to eight pre-selected journalists his plans for a new national flag and his intention to speak about it at an upcoming Royal Canadian Legion convention. Complaints of favouritism only mounted, as did accusations of undue influence over reporting and commentary on CBC television news programs. The network's cancellation of the broadcast of *Mr. Pearson*, a much ballyhooed frank television program based on a day in the life of the prime minister, raised eyebrows. Many journalists simply assumed the Liberals had arranged its demise, and the fumbling of "official" explanations did not reassure the doubters.[26]

"In politics," Keith Davey's political maxim maintained, "perception is reality."[27] Beginning with the Gordon budget *faux pas*, reality for the Pearson Liberals became progressively more grim. Much of the criticism focused on the ministerial scandals and administrative confusion which seemed to plague the government. A good deal of it, as befitted the new journalistic priorities, took Pearson personally to task, and specifically his leadership capabilities and style: in the environment fostered by the "new" journalism of the mid-1960s, the leader now *was* the party. While the prime minister himself was apparently never overly concerned with press and public fault-finding over his style, the ceaseless criticism of intentions and actions took its toll. After all, "to a nation in trouble," as Newman later pointed out, "the *appearance* of poised, responsible political leadership was not a factor of marginal consequence." Indeed, "to look wise was nearly as essential as to be wise." Television had made the average citizen much more aware of the process of government and hence of leadership. Pearson's methods, even if they achieved some of the government's objectives, were "undignified, creating the impression of a bumbling, incompetent administration making the worst of each bad situation [and] not so much governing Canada as presiding over its survival ..."[28] In the 1960s, to be a government of missed opportunities was a damning indictment.

When it came to dealing with the media, Pearson was hamstrung. On a philosophical level, he believed in open and honest government, which he recognized would entail a well-informed press. As a politician, he was conscious of the natural conflict between the government and the media, and yet he accepted that in a democracy the public's right to know should rarely be impeded. Both ministers and journalists had important responsibilities: journalists to use their judgement in exercising the public's right to know in *carte blanche* fashion, and politicians in not denying information to journalists – and therefore to the public – simply out of self-interest.[29] Pearson felt the former was too often being discarded in the pursuit of sensationalism, and the rationalizations of the media seemed to him simply pious hypocrisy. There was too much speculative analysis and too little of the "factual, responsible" reporting he had grown used to during his days as a diplomat and minister, when the press had practically constituted a personal cheering section, but also when the best, like Blair Fraser, had done their homework and given the government the benefit of the doubt. Hurt by the "inadequacy" as much as the "unfairness" of the coverage he received, Pearson liked to lecture journalists on the problem as he saw it: "Newspaper editors are always bleating about the refusal of politicians to produce mature and responsible discussion of the issues. The fact is, when we do discuss policies seriously, we are not reported at all or reported very inadequately. Reporters do not appear even to listen, until we say something controversial or personal, charged with what they regard as news value."[30] The lectures from the erstwhile history professor were to little avail.

From the perspective of the journalists who covered the Pearson administration on a day-to-day basis, too often there was little but infighting, poor judgement, and inappropriate behaviour to report. As Newman wrote in *The Distemper of Our Times*, his unflattering account of the Pearson prime ministership: "It was a time of national distemper, a time when the political affairs of the country were in such a state of disorder that there was something faintly absurdist about their unfolding, a time when many Canadians were left with the feeling that much of what was happening had no meaning and that all they could do was ask themselves a series of unanswerable questions: Is the country being governed by fools? Or is it ungovernable?"[31]

Apart from a consensus leadership style in Cabinet and caucus that left more than a few of his colleagues exasperated, [32] Pearson had some built-in difficulties which contributed to his media woes. There was always Diefenbaker, the opposition leader *sans pareil* and, of course, the government's perpetual minority status. The gulf between ideas and personalities became more pronounced as the years passed. The issues themselves were complex and divisive, running the gamut from national unity and "cooperative federalism" to the flag, the social safety net, and Vietnam.[33]

The 1965 election marked a turning point in Pearson's relationship with the media and, consequently, his relationship with Canadians. The government's motives in calling the election, the country's fifth in barely over eight years, were transparent and roundly criticized in the press. Asked by a Toronto *Telegram* reporter early in the campaign why he had called the election, Pearson replied opaquely: "I have my reasons. And my reasons are good."[34] Walter Gordon, Pearson's soon-to-be-discredited policy *éminence grise*, was more candid, referring to the Liberals' need for "a comfortable majority" and, in the process, reminding many voters of Liberal arrogance in the not-too-distant past. Half the metropolitan dailies that had supported the Liberals in 1963 switched to the Tories, including the influential *Globe and Mail*, while many others withdrew their support though remaining "neutral." Liberal insiders, who seemed to have forgotten the negative role the press could play in an election campaign, were re-educated.

Few Canadians saw the necessity of an election that was likely to produce the same arrangement in Parliament already governing the country, and press commentary reflected that conclusion. Fewer still wanted this Liberal gang to operate unchecked. The hard-fought struggle for a national flag, "Pearson's pennant" to the unconvinced, seemed to have worn out Pearson both physically and emotionally and clouded his judgement so that he seemed more indecisive and less in control of his colleagues than ever. The endless scandals of the previous year had eroded "the repute of the Government as a whole and in particular the reputation of Pearson himself."[35] The man who had been the youthful "golden boy" until he was nearly 60 was now an "old" 68.

Revealingly, many of the journalists covering the 1965 campaign expressed – and privately now felt – little admiration for "poor old pooper Pearson," as they derisively nicknamed him, while sympathizing with the old war horse Diefenbaker's determination and energy, if not his policies or personality. Certainly, the Chief's last hurrah contrasted all too graphically with still another slick, Kennedy-style campaign mounted by the Grits, which added to the resentment, even cynicism, felt by many journalists and clearly a lot of voters.[36] At the same time, journalists were noticeably divided on how to deal with the steady stream of scandal revelations that formed the grist of the Diefenbaker campaign (and, in the two years preceding, the Diefenbaker opposition, too). Senior and respected adherents of the "social responsibility" school, including Anthony Westell, Bill Wilson and Blair Fraser, found their role as accomplices in transmitting Diefenbaker's claims to be distasteful. They considered many of the claims to be distortions, or patently untrue, and refused to play the Tories' game.[37] Not surprisingly, the growing number of "libertarians" in the press and electronic media believed this attitude smacked of arrogance and old-style favouritism. As far as they were concerned, the public could decide who was telling the truth and Diefenbaker's charges, no matter how wild and thinly substantiated, should be reported. The voters could do the "editing."

In the end, Pearson's media image, shaped for a more sophisticated metropolitan Toronto and Montreal audience, alienated rural and, to use the Liberals' condescending phrase, "outer" Canada. The Liberals were returned to power, but with only two more seats and another minority to show for their exertions. In the aftermath of the election, most in the media saw the government slipping and its leader as having failed.[38] Although the Liberals continued to deal with important matters and were certainly an activist government by any standard other than their own exceptional first term in office, little of this seemed to get across. The Toronto *Star*, as sympathetic a major daily as the government could find, lamented the party's failure to renew itself at its 1996 policy conference. "We were hoping for a new vision of Liberalism which would inspire Canadians in the years ahead [but] all that emerged was a dull grey ghost of a once-great party."[39] The prevailing perception between the election of 1965 and the end of Pearson's prime ministership was that Parliament, as Peter Newman later described it, became a kind of "Disneyland-on-the-Rideau." A *fin de siècle* mood pervaded the government.

Pearson seemed to have lost interest in governing, dejected by his inability to master the office. Or so one would have concluded from his portrayal in the media. Few journalists now considered him a well-meaning innocent, though some, like Fraser and Hutchison, felt sympathy and even harboured some measure of guilt that perhaps they had personally "let him down."[40] Liberals, and a great many ordinary Canadians, continued to admire Pearson for his past achievements, his avuncular style, and his support of progressive policies no matter how much he bumbled. He was a lame-duck, however, and rivals for the mantle of Liberal leadership operated openly.[41] Combating the perception of drift and confusion was not made easier by the fact that Pearson's post-1965 Cabinet did not act like a team, nor did it feel like one. During its second term, the vaunted "Pearson team," in the assessment of one historian, "deteriorated into a herd of quarreling, petulant individualists, more disorganized than the Diefenbaker cabinet had been."[42]

The press and television preyed on such pathos and disarray, and none were more eager than the promoters of the CBC's revolutionary public affairs program *This Hour Has Seven Days*. With new-style journalists Douglas Leiterman, Patrick Watson, Laurier LaPierre, Warner Troyer and Roy Faibish, *Seven Days* had burst onto the scene in 1964. Successfully marrying television drama and adversarial journalism, the program was endlessly controversial and astonishingly successful. Naturally, it begged imitation and, along with Newman's *Renegade*, went far in establishing adversarial journalism as the Canadian norm. As Ron Haggart of the Toronto *Star* wrote, the *Seven Days* style dictated that "journalists themselves [would] decide which are the issues of concern and importance." In effect, Pearson would be the first victim of "a journalism in which [the public agenda was] established not by politicians, but by those who watch them with pencil and film."[43] The pursuit of sensationalism, of course, could always be conveniently rationalized as the pursuit of truth and justice.[44] Pearson despised (and feared) the "aggressively controversial" tone of *Seven Days*, refused to cooperate with the program, and ordered his Cabinet to do the same.[45] But to no avail. Liberal "counter-scandals," like the Munsinger affair of 1966, were designed to exact revenge for scandal-mongering by the Diefenbaker Tories; this backfired on the Liberals once *Seven Days* and its print imitators were finished with their treatment. In the end, it only served to make Parliament itself look shabby, a *Seven Days* specialty.[46]

The work of political cartoonists measured the steady deterioration of Pearson's public image. In 1963, Pearson was the smiling relief pitcher, cap jauntily askew, confidently taking over on the mound from a shell-shocked Diefenbaker. Through his first year in office, he was boyish and bow-tied, the well-intentioned if somewhat disorganized boy scout. Scandals and unfulfilled expectations took their toll, however, and it was not long before another Pearson began to appear with regularity – this one overwhelmed, confused, the befuddled political juggler "beaned" on the noggin by his own juggling pins labelled "Rivard" and "Dorion Inquiry." Cartoonists apparently found it hard, though, to caricature Pearson with anything approaching the cruelty reserved for Diefenbaker, doubtless a reflection of the perception of his inherent decency and unpretentiousness.

The last year of Pearson's administration celebrated the centenary of Confederation but saw few important legislative achievements and contributed to the general image of drift. Pearson's obsession with national unity earned him few kudos. With so many conflicting interests within and without the government, governing was not easy. Especially among younger, better-educated Canadians, the Pearson-Diefenbaker generation's leadership was increasingly found wanting.[47] Duncan Macpherson, the brilliant political cartoonist of the Toronto *Star*, captured this sentiment perfectly by portraying a decrepit Diefenbaker and Pearson, wheelchair-bound and flailing away at one another with cane and crutch, yelling "resign! resign!" Many Canadians, furthermore, began to doubt the country's most pressing problems, starting with Quebec, had political solutions at all.

The long-awaited replacement of Diefenbaker as Conservative leader in 1967 made Pearson's retirement only a matter of timing. His announcement in December of that year that he wished to step down as leader was received with relief, not the least by his friends. The accidental "defeat" of his government in the House of Commons two months later offered Pearson a last encounter with the media. Grasping television's power to reach ordinary Canadians quickly, he articulately and convincingly made the case against his government's resignation. Most observers concluded that it was the most effective broadcasting performance of his political career.[48] Too late, apparently, he had gotten the knack.

In his first attempt, Pearson's successor, the suave, charismatic and unorthodox Pierre Trudeau, captured what had eluded Pearson in 1962, 1963 and 1965 – the hearts of Canadians and a majority government. Trudeau would prove no compromiser, whether it was with journalism's self-proclaimed needs or much else. Having witnessed firsthand the damage done to the Pearson government by uncontrolled leaks to the media and generally haphazard media relations, he was intent on cutting the informal channels of communication and talked vaguely (but ominously) about "centralizing" and "reorganizing" the official ones. Moreover, in personal terms, he tended to be distant from and dismissive toward journalists as a group. Evidence of the media's disenchantment with the new order under Trudeau was apparent from the outset but, as Christina Newman shrewdly observed, "Trudeau can afford to be cool to the press so long as he has the public's adoration and the ability to maintain it through TV."[49] It was an advantage that Mike Pearson had never been able to claim.

"Politics is [a] people business [and] if you fail to communicate, you perish," Keith Davey, the political conjurer *par excellence* observed in his memoirs. Throughout the 1960s, Pearson had been one of Davey's principal projects, with mixed results.[50] Despite numerous public relations operatives scattered through the Prime Minister's Office, government departments and the Liberal party organization, not to mention some shrewd media heads, the Liberals had failed to get their message across to journalists or the people.[51] In a television age, with so much emphasis on the leader, much of the blame had to fall on Pearson, whose personality, so endearing in intimate company, simply never made the leap to the family television screen. Clearly, another strike against his image as leader came from the fact that, while his government initiated much useful legislation, from Medicare and the Canada Pension Plan to the maple leaf flag, the impact of each accomplishment "was obscured by yet another spectacular failure of spirit or method" ensuring that he had "the misfortune to appear during most of his tenure in office as a confused and inept politician" stumbling from one crisis to the next.[52] Canadians, led in this direction by the media, came to wonder if Pearson had any real plan or any vision to inspire, or whether it was just endless compromise and muddling. The gap between expectations, which were so high in 1963 as to be unattainable, and the somehow insufficient accomplishments thereafter, made Canadians question his suitability for the office. In the end, drawing an analogy from the game of baseball so near to his heart, Mike Pearson proved to be "a good man for the middle innings"[53] who, despite having less than outstanding talent, could keep his team in the game with grit. Too many in the Liberal party and too many Canadians wanted a Kennedy or the mythic Pearson of Nobel Prize fame. Faced with having to settle for the "real" Pearson, itself an artifact of the new age of television and adversarial journalism, disappointment was inevitable. It is little wonder he frequently seemed so exasperated and perplexed.

Minding the Minister: Pearson, Martin and American Policy in Asia, 1963–1967

GREG DONAGHY

For many Canadians, perhaps the single most enduring image of Pearsonian diplomacy in the 1960s was captured in the work of one of Canada's leading editorial cartoonists: an oversized Texan, President Lyndon Johnson, is shown holding a much smaller Canadian prime minister several feet from the ground and scolding him vigorously for daring, however mildly, to criticize the American bombing campaign in Vietnam. This image, with its implication that the seasoned and successful diplomat of the 1940s and 1950s had somehow lost his touch, was a harsh and unfair caricature.

As prime minister, Pearson retained his interest in international affairs, although there were now real limitations on his ability to conduct foreign policy. He was continually occupied with any number of domestic concerns. He was also constrained by the complicated nature of his relationship with Paul Martin, the secretary of state for external affairs. Friends and rivals for many years, they respected one another's abilities. Yet Pearson did not completely trust Martin's political instincts; in turn, the prime minister's successes were sometimes resented by his foreign minister. The reserve which characterized their uncertain partnership, and a reluctance to undermine his minister's authority, obliged Pearson to tread carefully when he entered Martin's domain.[1]

Despite these limitations, Pearson actively pursued a number of foreign policy initiatives. Some of these – his role in trying to resolve the Rhodesian crisis or his interest in increased economic aid to the West Indies – arose naturally from his participation in Commonwealth heads of government meetings. His interest in the North Atlantic Treaty Organization (NATO) and the United Nations (UN) grew out of his long association with these international institutions. Largely freed here from the constraints placed on Martin and the professional diplomats in the Department of External Affairs, Pearson could explore some of these issues in fresh and innovative ways that occasionally annoyed his former colleagues.[2]

No single foreign policy issue preoccupied Pearson as much as Canada's relations with the United States. Significantly, he hurried off to Massachusetts, just after his election, to meet with President John F. Kennedy and slice through the backlog of business that had been allowed to accumulate under Prime Minister John G. Diefenbaker. Unfortunately for Pearson, the quintessential "North Atlantic man," the American decision in July 1965 to escalate the war in Vietnam placed that conflict, and western relations with the People's Republic of China, at the centre of domestic politics in both the US and Canada. Growing public opposition to the war in Vietnam, and Washington's irrational determination to continue excluding Peking from the international community, raised questions about the very nature of American society and Canada's relationship with it. Pearson's government was caught between domestic demands for a response to the Asian crisis that reflected Canadians' evolving self-image as a peacemaker and Washington's expectations of a close and loyal ally.

By the time that Pearson's government assumed office in the spring of 1963, the continuing crisis in Southeast Asia had already become a fixture on the Canada-US bilateral agenda. For almost a decade, the two countries had worked closely together in the uneasy peace that followed the signing of the Geneva Accords in 1954. As the western representative on the three ineffectual international commissions established to oversee the provisions of the cease-fire agreements in Laos, Cambodia and Vietnam, Canada had watched, with mounting frustration, as communist insurgents operated with impunity to undermine the Geneva settlements in Indochina. For just as long, the US had sought, with an array of military assistance programs and an ever-growing number of military advisors, to create a stable and independent South Vietnam. Exposed to the same influences, and exchanging information regularly, Canada and the US shared the view that the Viet Cong insurgency in South Vietnam was inspired and supported by communist Hanoi.

Washington's inability to convince Hanoi that it was determined not to permit a communist victory in South Vietnam led to Ottawa's increasingly direct involvement in Southeast Asia in the spring of 1964. In a late April meeting with Pearson and Martin, the American secretary of state, Dean Rusk, asked for Canada's help in ensuring that Hanoi understood the US position. Rusk stressed that the US was not anxious to escalate the war, but wished simply to tell Hanoi "that it would be wrong ... to expect that the United States were getting discouraged and were thinking of pulling out. It was important for them to realize that if they didn't put a stop to their operations they would be in deep trouble." Rusk asked that Blair Seaborn, who was soon to become Canada's representative on the International Commission for Supervision and Control (ICSC) for Vietnam, act as an intermediary between Washington and Hanoi. Pearson and Martin readily agreed.[3]

Despite the accommodating position adopted by the two Canadians, Rusk suspected that Ottawa would place clearly defined limits on its cooperation. He was right. In late May, Pearson met secretly with President Johnson in New York to review Seaborn's mission. The prime minister backed the president's determination to avoid withdrawing from Vietnam and endorsed the use of conventional bombing "if [the] action could be carefully limited and directed [to] the interdiction of supply lines from North to South." He cautioned Johnson against the use of tactical nuclear weapons, an idea then being touted by Republican presidential candidate Senator Barry Goldwater, and warned "that any drastic escalation would give great problems both in Canada and internationally."[4]

Simultaneously, Martin met in Ottawa with William Sullivan, head of the State Department's Vietnamese Coordinating Committee. The ground rules that would govern Seaborn's employment were quickly worked out; not unexpectedly, Martin insisted that all communications with Seaborn pass through Ottawa, while Sullivan stressed the importance of transmitting American messages as faithfully as possible. However, Martin was irritated and suspicious at the lapse in time between Rusk's initial approach in April and Sullivan's visit to brief Seaborn. He wondered whether the mission had already been left too late, and emphasized the domestic problems that would be created by an American decision to escalate the war. "[T]he Opposition tended to be suspicious of United States policy in Indochina," Martin explained, warning that "he would find it difficult to condone ... direct [US] intervention."[5] Like Pearson, Martin used the Seaborn exercise as an opportunity to establish the limits of Canadian support for a direct US military role in Vietnam.

The results of Seaborn's first trip to North Vietnam calmed some of the Canadian fears. In a meeting with the North Vietnamese prime minister, Pham Van Dong, Seaborn delivered the American message, which underscored the administration's determination to defend South Vietnam, the consequences that would follow continued aggression, and the material benefits that would flow to Hanoi from a peaceful settlement. Although the message resulted in no change in Hanoi's position, Ottawa was pleased that Pham Van Dong was ready to meet Seaborn again and that a channel had been successfully established between Washington and Hanoi.[6]

For different reasons, Washington was also grimly satisfied with these results. By mid-summer, the administration had forged a "scenario" according to which the president, after securing a Congressional resolution authorizing him to act, would launch a series of graduated air strikes against targets in North Vietnam. Seaborn's report confirmed the American view of an intransigent North Vietnam and the need to carry the war northward.[7] In August 1964, the US was given cause for action when the administration alleged that North Vietnamese torpedo boats had attacked the USS *Maddox* in international waters off the coast of North Vietnam.

From the Canadian perspective, the American reaction to this apparent aggression in the Gulf of Tonkin was measured and reassuring. Rusk, on Johnson's instructions, informed Pearson personally of the attack. The US intended to respond, "but would ensure that the retaliation was relevant to the provocation and to the attack."[8] Canada's ambassador to the US, Charles Ritchie, found the same considered tones echoed in discussions with members of the administration. "My impression ... is that the USA is fully aware of the gravity of the steps it has felt forced to take."[9] Well within the limits established by Pearson and Martin in the spring of that year, US bombing strikes in the fall of 1964 had little immediate impact on official Canadian attitudes. If anything, by signalling the American intention to respond militarily to North Vietnamese aggression, the crisis reinforced Ottawa's inclination to lend Washington a helping hand. Nowhere, perhaps, was this more apparent than on the ground in Vietnam, where the Canadian representative to the ICSC redoubled his efforts to have the commission "take account of communist infringements of [the] Geneva Agreement, and build up a record of meaningful findings."[10] At the same time, Ottawa announced that it would substantially increase its non-military aid to South Vietnam.[11]

Even as it brought Canada's public posture more closely into line with Washington's more pugnacious attitude toward North Vietnam, Ottawa was becoming a little worried about the course of American policy. In the aftermath of the Gulf of Tonkin crisis, Canadian observers had watched Washington's interest in using the Seaborn channel evaporate, but had remained hopeful that the US might become more forthcoming after the November presidential election. By early December, however, it was clear that the re-election of Johnson had changed little. Only after repeated Canadian prompting did the US agree in mid-December to send another message to Hanoi through Seaborn. Washington added nothing new to this communication and even diminished its significance by insisting that Seaborn deliver it as his own personal estimate of American determination. Canadian officials were deeply disappointed at Washington's insincerity and resented its patronizing attitude about the Canadian channel. These sentiments were accompanied by a growing sense that American officials were less than frank in discussing the nature of US policy in Vietnam.

Pearson was much more uneasy than Martin. His January 1965 meeting with Johnson at the LBJ Ranch in Texas stripped away the veneer of correctness that had defined their first two meetings and exposed their profound differences in outlook and temperament. Dressed in a formal black suit and diplomat's homburg, Pearson was discomfited on arriving at the ranch to discover the president in a cowboy suit. A barrage of television cameras awaited the two men, whose meeting began poorly when Johnson introduced Pearson as "Prime Minister Wilson." There was no time during the two-day meeting for the kind of leisurely, wide-ranging discussion of international developments that Pearson enjoyed. Instead, loaded into three cars, Johnson, Pearson, the "press" and the "ladies" embarked on a whirlwind tour of the ranch. The president dispensed drinks liberally and swore loudly.[12] Dinner was a hurried and informal affair: steak and catfish on the same plate. Throughout, aides and valets bustled about and telephones rang. "General MacArthur would not have approved," Pearson observed, "nor, I suspect, John Kennedy."[13] The visit left him feeling deeply disturbed.

In early February 1965, the war in South Vietnam entered a new and more dangerous phase. Washington responded to a raid on the American base at Pleiku with limited air strikes against North Vietnam. Within days, gradually intensifying bombing signalled the start of "Operation Rolling Thunder." Pearson tried to discuss the crisis with Johnson over the telephone but was rebuffed. The prime minister feared "escalation" and thought that the South Vietnamese "were the first to want to get rid of the Americans, and that a compromise would have to be reached."[14]

Pearson was given an opportunity to voice some of his apprehensions in early February, when India appealed for an unconditional halt in hostilities and a Geneva-type conference. The Department of External Affairs gave the prime minister a draft statement which endorsed New Delhi's call for a negotiated settlement, marking a small but distinct shift in Canadian policy. Although hedged with conditions designed to secure the US position in Indochina, the proposal for a Geneva-style conference clearly represented a retreat from the steadfast support accorded American policy thus far in Vietnam. Pearson went even further than Martin expected when he delivered this speech to the Canadian Club in Ottawa. With one eye on the increasing number of domestic critics of the bombing, he hinted at Canada's growing disagreement with the US over the militarization of American policy. The prime minister carefully presented his criticism of American policy as a defence of "quiet diplomacy." Acknowledging that Canada's security depended on American support, Pearson warned his audience that "official doubts about certain United States foreign policies often should be expressed in private, through the channels of diplomacy." He dutifully acknowledged the role of North Vietnamese aggression in expanding the war, but went on to observe that "we cannot overlook the fact that U.S. policies in Vietnam seem to have found no solid basis of support through a South Vietnam government of strength and popularity."[15]

The difference in view between Pearson and Martin grew wider as the bombing intensified, and as rumours concerning the use of napalm and nerve gas surfaced in early March. International pressure on Pearson, who was widely assumed to have Washington's ear, to do something to stop the bombing grew steadily. During a meeting with the prime minister, U Thant, the UN secretary general, begged Pearson to use his influence "to convince [the] Americans that no lasting settlement in Vietnam could be achieved by [the] use of force alone."[16] Canadian missions in the Soviet Union and Eastern Europe, where the bombing seemed likely to complicate Sino-Soviet relations further by driving North Vietnam into closer alignment with Peking, reported that their interlocutors hoped that Canada would help reduce Washington's enthusiasm for bombing.[17]

The bombing helped the various elements of the now vocal Canadian anti-war movement to coalesce. Disproportionate among their numbers were the intellectuals and younger members of Canadian society whom Pearson wished to attract to the Liberal party. Pearson was also influenced by the views of his wife, Maryon, and his son, Geoffrey, who both thought that the American policy was dangerous.[18] Escott Reid, an old friend and colleague who had served under Pearson in the Department of External Affairs, joined them in urging the prime minister to speak out.[19] Gradually, Pearson moved toward the idea of making public his concern.

Still very much undecided on his next step, the prime minister asked Marcel Cadieux, the under-secretary of state for external affairs, to include in a speech Pearson was scheduled to deliver at Temple University in Philadelphia the idea of using a pause in the bombing to test Hanoi's willingness to talk. Martin tried to dissuade the prime minister and then cautioned "that a proposal of this kind would be more effective if it were put forward, in the first instance, privately to President Johnson."[20] Ritchie recommended that Pearson give the White House an advance copy of his speech. Pearson agreed, and a meeting with Johnson at the White House was immediately arranged.

On 30 March 1965, Pearson met with Marquis Childs, the chief Washington correspondent of the *St. Louis Post-Dispatch*, whom he had known since his first posting to the American capital in the 1940s. Drawing upon information picked up in Washington, Childs warned Pearson "that President Johnson was embarked upon a course which, in the next three or four weeks, would bring the United States perilously close to war with Communist China and the u.s.s.r."[21] Isolated and encircled by a small group of like-minded advisors, Johnson needed to hear a different point of view. Childs reassured Pearson that the general line of his speech " 'would not be resented' in Washington." The prime minister decided to go ahead. Worried lest Johnson persuade him not to give the speech, Pearson cancelled his meeting with the president and informed Martin that he planned to go ahead with the public call for a brief halt in the bombing.

Martin threatened to resign, but quickly withdrew his threat when he saw that it would not dissuade the prime minister. On 2 April, Pearson addressed the graduating class of Temple University. The suggestion for a bombing pause was decidedly understated and firmly placed within the context of continued Canadian support for American objectives in Vietnam: "After about two months of air strikes, the message should now have been received loud and clear. The authorities in Hanoi must know that the United States with its massive military power can mete out even greater punishment. They must also know that, for this reason, the cost of their continued aggression against South Vietnam could be incalculable ... There are many factors which I am not in a position to weigh or even know. But there does appear to be at least the possibility that a suspension of such air strikes against North Vietnam, at the right time, might provide the Hanoi authorities with an opportunity, if they wish to take it, to inject some flexibility into their policy without appearing to do so as the direct result of military pressure."[22]

The president's reaction was immediate. Pearson had violated one of Johnson's rudimentary but sacrosanct political precepts – "you don't piss on your neighbor's rug."[23] Moreover, the prime minister's timing could not have been worse. Johnson had just helped Pearson secure an exemption for Canada from harmful economic measures designed to improve the American balance of payments, and was struggling to get the Autopact through Congress, a battle he had reluctantly undertaken at the prime minister's behest. The Canadian's transgression occurred in the midst of an internal debate over the direction of American policy, a discussion in which Johnson perceived himself as the moderate, resisting hardline demands for a greater American role in Vietnam. The president, worried that his own position had been undercut, invited the prime minister and Ambassador Ritchie for lunch at Camp David. After a tense meal, during which he spent most of the time on the phone, Johnson led Pearson into the garden for a frank exposition of his position. From a distance, Ritchie watched the pantomime as the two men talked. The president "strode the terrace, he sawed the air with his arms, with upraised fist he drove home the verbal hammer blows ... From time to time Mike [Pearson] attempted a sentence – only to have it swept away on the tide."[24] "We are confident," the under-secretary of state, George Ball, observed later with deliberate under-statement, that "Pearson sensed [the] President's displeasure over import of speech at April 3 meeting."[25]

Once back in Ottawa, Pearson tried to undo some of the damage. In a lengthy and detailed letter to Johnson, he explained why he had made the speech. He assured Johnson that Canada was anxious to give "all possible support, difficult and thankless ... [of] aiding South Vietnam to resist aggression." But there was "a quite genuine feeling [in Canada] that current u.s. policy in Vietnam is wrong and heading for trouble ... [which] a minority Government cannot merely brush off ... as unimportant." It was against this background that he felt compelled to suggest that the us might at some point suspend the bombing. Pearson continued to explain exactly how limited his suggestion really was:

In my proposal for a "suspension" or "pause" in the series of "increasingly powerful retaliatory strikes," I did not argue it should be done now but might be considered "at the right time"; that it would be "for a limited time" ...

My point is that, once the destructive effects of air strikes are really being felt by the Hanoi Government, they might wish to "cry quits" but without being accused of doing so in the face of continued air action. In other words, this "pause" would give them an opportunity to stop the fighting in the South – if they wished to use it for that purpose. If they didn't, then their aggressive intransigence would have been exposed and it would be made very clear who was preventing a negotiated solution. I should have thought that this would have strengthened your position diplomatically, without weakening it militarily, because the suspension would only be for a short time; long enough for Northern Communist intentions to be made clear.[26]

In Washington, Pearson's letter was acknowledged as suitably repentant. Nevertheless, the relationship between Pearson and Johnson, never close, was seriously strained.

Despite the unpleasant American reaction to the Temple speech, both Pearson and Martin remained anxious to find some means of helping the US escape from Southeast Asia. This was especially true following Johnson's decision in July 1965 to send large numbers of American troops to Vietnam. This step, which fundamentally changed the nature of the conflict, meant that the war could no longer be treated as just a struggle for the freedom of South Vietnam. It had become part of the American effort to contain Communist China and heightened the risk of a confrontation with China, the Soviet Union, or both.[27] Pearson and Martin differed, however – and this difference would grow over the course of the following year – on the right approach to take toward helping the US extricate itself from Vietnam.

Pearson was increasingly sensitive to the risks associated with meddling in "Johnson's war," and was much more inclined to wait and take his cue from Washington. By the end of 1965, however, Pearson's "quiet diplomacy" was no longer enough for Martin, who was convinced that the seriousness of the international situation demanded extraordinary efforts to get talks underway.[28] Martin was also anxious to respond to growing public doubts about American policy in Vietnam. He wondered whether "we could stick with the United States in defence of its basic purpose, if we did not show that we were taking extraordinary steps towards getting negotiations started." Moreover, and quite legitimately, he sought the kind of personal diplomatic triumph that would secure his position as the front-runner in the undeclared race to succeed Pearson. In early 1966, Martin approached Pearson with a proposal to send Chester Ronning, a retired Canadian diplomat and "old China hand," to Peking and Hanoi. Ronning was to resolve the question of Chinese admission to the UN, while seeking to determine whether North Vietnamese views had shifted under the impact of the American bombing campaign. Pearson was sceptical but allowed Martin his head.

As the prime minister suspected, American officials greeted the projected mission with undisguised hostility. In so far as Martin's scheme was presented in the context of the president's declared interest in peace, American policy-makers felt that they had no option but to fall in with Martin's plans. In addition, most American officials viewed Ronning, who was widely known to be critical of American policy in Asia, with unfriendly suspicion.[29]

Martin's sponsorship of the mission was also a problem. American officials were uncomfortable with his tendency to "politicize everything" and were inclined to discount him and his diplomacy.[30] The American assistant secretary of state for Far Eastern affairs, William Bundy, dismissed him as "pas serieux."[31] Rusk tended to treat the foreign minister, a little indulgently perhaps, as a "nuisance."[32] Any chance that the scheme had of achieving some sort of standing in Washington disappeared in late January, when Pearson (perhaps to protect his own fragile standing among American policy-makers) pulled away the ground on which his minister stood. In a conversation with Walton Butterworth, the American ambassador to Canada, "Pearson confirmed Ronning mission was Martin's idea, that it entailed greater dangers than Martin had perhaps appreciated and that he had 'scared the hell out of Paul last night' " by saying that "if anything went wrong, his government would disavow any involvement in the Ronning mission."[33] Not surprisingly, Rusk wrote off the Canadian initiative. "Quite frankly," he assured the American ambassador to Saigon, Henry Cabot Lodge Jr., "I attach no importance to his [Ronning's] trip and expect nothing out of it."[34]

The Ronning missions failed to produce a breakthrough either in China, where he was refused admittance, or in Vietnam. Ronning returned from his first visit to Hanoi in March 1966 with an uncertain suggestion from North Vietnamese Prime Minister Pham that a bombing halt might result in direct negotiations. Under persistent questioning, Pham admitted to Ronning that North Vietnam would be prepared to undertake preliminary talks in exchange for "an official declaration that it [the US] will unconditionally stop for good all military operations against [the] territory of NVN [North Vietnam]."[35] Ronning was delighted, although Pham's meaning was not entirely clear for he also told Ronning that North Vietnam "had already suggested a similar offer in the January 4th [1966] foreign ministry statement."[36] In this proclamation, Hanoi insisted that: "[A] political settlement of the Vietnam problem can be envisaged only when the USG[overnment] has accepted the 4-point stand of the DRV [Democratic Republic of Vietnam], has proved this by actual deeds, has stopped unconditionally and for good its air raids and all other acts of war against the DRV."[37] In linking his offer to Ronning with the foreign ministry's statement, Pham introduced a dangerous element of uncertainty.

In Washington, where Ronning arrived on 20 March 1966 to de-brief State Department officials, the discussion turned on the question of the relationship between Pham's offer and the January declaration. Neither Martin nor Ronning had anticipated this. During the talks which followed his presentation, Ronning admitted that Pham had "started to hedge ... [and] had implied that his statement was nothing more than had already been said in the DRVN [Democratic Republic of Vietnam] foreign ministry statement of 4 January."[38] Bundy seized on this remark and quickly pointed out "that the link between the DRVN's 4 points and the declaration of cessation of bombing was ambiguous in the January 4th statement ... it could conceivably be argued, if certain punctuation was accepted, that there was a hint that issuance of declaration on bombing would imply an acceptance of the 4 points." Confronted by Bundy, Ronning's certainty wilted: "[H]e might be entirely wrong in concluding that DRVN was separating bombing from the Four Points but this was undoubtedly the impression that Pham Van Dong wished to create." Not surprisingly, Washington interpreted this to mean that "on balance, [Ronning] frankly did not himself think anything significant had emerged from his visit."[39] The question was closed as far as Bundy and his American colleagues were concerned.

Martin was disappointed and angry at Bundy's lack of enthusiasm. Telephoning the American official, he upbraided him for Washington's failure to respond in a more forthcoming manner and pressed him to mount a second mission.[40] The Americans were anxious to defuse Martin's anger and reluctantly gave in, but made it clear that their position remained unchanged. Washington's second message for Ronning to deliver to Hanoi categorically rejected Pham's proposal and simply reiterated the US willingness either to talk unconditionally or to agree to a reciprocal reduction in military activity.

By the middle of May 1966, this second mission (which would take place a month later) had become the source of further tension. In order to emphasize the Canadian nature of the initiative and preserve Ottawa's standing in Vietnam, Martin insisted on briefing the South Vietnamese government about the mission.[41] American officials in both Washington and Saigon were "disturbed" by Canada's effort to interfere in a relationship that they regarded with proprietary interest.[42] On the other hand, Canadian officials were distressed to learn from published reports in early June that the US had conveyed the sense of the second Ronning message to Chinese officials at the regular monthly Sino-American meetings held in Poland. Indeed, American representatives had gone much further and had explained that the US would stop the bombing in exchange for a halt in the infiltration of North Vietnamese troops and equipment.[43]

Having over-estimated the American commitment to the second Ronning exercise, Canadian officials were surprised at the apparent

American effort to sabotage the mission: "While this is not something you will wish to say to Rusk, we find it difficult to comprehend why a message on these lines should be conveyed to Hanoi through the intermediary [Peking] which is known to be most vehemently opposed to any form of accommodation in Vietnam."[44] They urged Martin, then in Paris for a NATO ministerial meeting, to explore with Rusk the relationship between the Canadian and Chinese messages. Rusk declined to answer the minister's question directly and explained that there could be no end to the bombing without a stop to the infiltration. This, Martin remarked plaintively, was not the message that Ronning was carrying.[45]

Canada's representative in Saigon observed that Ronning's message now lacked any new elements and that the mission was destined to fail. Washington, he asserted perceptively, had already reached this conclusion and had adjusted its strategy accordingly. "The Americans appear to be putting Hanoi behind the eight-ball again and to be escalating what was allegedly a serious and practical cease-fire overture into a peace offensive reminiscent of their campaign last January."[46] Pearson was distraught. "It would be a sad ending to our initiative in this matter," he telegraphed Martin, "if we became merely an instrument of USA propaganda or for putting the DRVN on the spot."[47] Martin insisted that the mission proceed.

By early June, there were further indications that American motives had changed. After a long debate, US Secretary of Defense Robert Mac-Namara had decided to authorize bombing strikes against petroleum-oil-lubricant (POL) facilities in Hanoi and Haiphong. He now began to press Rusk for support. Rusk counselled delay and suggested that the US wait for the results of Ronning's second message. These would almost certainly reveal Hanoi's continued intransigence and justify the bombing in the eyes of those allies, like Pearson and British Prime Minister Harold Wilson, who questioned American policy. In the meantime, Rusk promised MacNamara that he would ask to receive an early report on the Ronning mission.[48] Bundy made no effort to hide the American intention to link the scale of hostilities in Vietnam with the results of the Ronning mission. The request was made, he explained, "so that USA authorities could receive info on situation as soon as possible in case some prompt USA response, such as a change in the scale of USA activities, appeared desirable."[49] Martin was concerned at this latest development, but agreed that Ronning would reveal the "general flavour" of the exchange if he considered that this might have an "immediate" bearing on American deliberations.[50]

Ronning discovered no flexibility in the North Vietnamese position. While Martin considered how to interpret this negative result in

Washington, he asked Rusk to ensure that the US did not step up its bombing operations in the immediate aftermath of Ronning's visit. He did not, however, divulge Hanoi's response to Ronning. On 20 June, the minister called in officials from the American embassy and repeated the request that the US not jeopardize the Canadian channel by increased bombing so soon after Ronning's return from Hanoi. Again, he refused to reveal the results of Ronning's visit. This tight-lipped approach was resented in Washington as an effort "to keep us hemmed in on the grounds that the channel is still open."[51] When the results of the mission were at last given to Bundy on the afternoon of 21 June, Martin interpreted the North Vietnamese rejection in the best light possible and underlined Hanoi's declared interest in using the Canadian channel again. Bundy was not fooled, bluntly concluding that "[b]asically, Hanoi turned Ronning down cold on their paying any price whatever for the cessation of bombing."[52]

Over dinner that evening, Martin and Bundy went over the exchange with Hanoi. Martin was obviously upset with the failure of the Ronning missions and complained bitterly that the American position "had not been forthcoming enough."[53] Within a week, he had grounds for further recriminations. In late June, news of the Ronning mission was leaked. On the respected television program *Meet the Press*, the American under-secretary of state explained that "there was nothing in what Ambassador Ronning brought back which gives any encouragement that Hanoi was prepared to come to a conference table. In fact, the line that they have been taking seems to us to be quite as hard as it has been at any time." Martin quickly called the American ambassador, Walton Butterworth, to express his outrage.[54] A few days later, Martin was distressed to learn that the US had begun to bomb POL facilities near Hanoi and Haiphong. Again, Butterworth was quickly made aware of the minister's displeasure.[55]

The Ronning missions and the unseemly bickering between Bundy and Martin that accompanied them had two important consequences. In Ottawa, they undermined Pearson's confidence in Martin's judgement. The prime minister's unhappiness with Martin had been growing since early 1966 and he did not try to hide his distress.[56] In the fall, he told Walter Gordon that Martin's views on foreign policy no longer mattered.[57] A few months later, he remarked to Paul Hellyer, the minister of national defence, that he "wanted to get Paul Martin out of External Affairs ... [he] is getting too involved in the Vietnam thing to the exclusion of our overall relations with the U.S."[58]

In Washington, the Ronning experience fuelled concerns in the White House and the State Department about the decline in public support in Canada for American policy in Vietnam and the effect that this might have on bilateral relations. In early 1966, Butterworth had warned Washington how hard it was becoming to maintain Canadian support for American policies in Asia: "We wrung from Pearson and Martin fulsome official statements of support for U.S. policy in Vietnam, but the Prime Minister in particular and the Government in general continued to have grave misgivings about the conflict's escalation, were prone to be oversensitive to criticism from Canadian Vietniks, and still had difficulty relating Vietminh/Vietcong aggression to their own and Western security. If and as the war worsens, we can expect to find that whatever lip-service they give to our effort will be extracted from them in future, as in the past, against their emotional predilection. A by-product will be their restraint from doing what they are fully inclined to do, such as recognizing Red China and voting for its admission to the UN."[59] Polling conducted in April and May showed that Canadian support for Washington's "handling" of the war had declined sharply; although 35 percent still approved of the American effort in Southeast Asia, 34 percent disapproved.[60] Johnson demanded to know if there is "anything constructive we can do in relation to Canada at the present time."[61] The secretary of state recommended a presidential visit to help dispel the widespread popular doubt in Canada about Washington's Asian policies: "[T]he political and psychological climate in Canada suggests that a visit by you could have a tremendous impact in focusing the attention of Canadians upon the 'enduring common interests between our countries and in redirecting their fixation away from such problem issues between us as Vietnam and China, which they persistently view so astigmatically.' "[62] Throughout the summer, Rusk and his department continued to press Johnson to visit Canada. After all, as the veteran American diplomat Robert McClintock reported to Ball in May 1966, Pearson, "despite his harsh criticism, particularly over Viet Nam … is still one of the best friends the United States has."[63]

Increasingly reluctant to leave Washington and the business of running the war in Vietnam, Johnson hesitated before deciding impetuously in early August to pay a brief visit to New Brunswick, where Canada and the US were transforming Franklin D. Roosevelt's summer home into an international park. The president arrived in a good mood, and his private talks with Pearson "took place in the most friendly atmosphere throughout."[64] American officials were gratified by the results of the meeting. When Pearson hinted that his government might drop its opposition to Chinese representation at the UN, Johnson made clear his disagreement and insisted that the two allies approach this problem together: "He thought that the two governments should keep in close touch on the issue and that the relationship [being] what it is between our two countries we could always work out any differences between us."[65] The implication for Canadian officials was clear: "[H]is intention to talk to us later on the matter seems to presage at least the possibility of pressure on us to support the United States position as the vote draws near. It would, therefore, appear that, if the Canadian Government wishes to change its vote, the timing and tactics to use vis-à-vis the United States will be important and delicate."[66]

The president's views, which were expressed in the midst of a debate in Ottawa over how far Canada should go toward seeking a resolution to the problem of Peking's exclusion from the UN, almost certainly reinforced Pearson's inclination to proceed cautiously in this matter. Martin, however, remained anxious to press on with the second part of his two-pronged approach to resolving the conflict in Vietnam and to admit Peking to the UN. Ronning, whom the Chinese had refused to see on his way to Hanoi in March, had failed to advance this project. Martin was consequently inclined to try a more direct approach. He endorsed a proposal that Canada abandon its opposition to the habitual Albanian resolution, which called on the UN to expel Taiwan from the international organization and assign the Chinese seat to Peking. Instead, Canada would abstain and support a simple resolution that gave Peking a seat in the UN without explicitly mentioning Taiwan.[67]

Pearson was doubtful. He rejected the minister's assertion that an abstention would have a minimal impact on Canada's relations with the US. Washington, he noted, would consider an abstention a "radical departure" from Canada's established position and no less irritating than a decision to take an active role in the expulsion of Taiwan. He objected to Martin's reluctance to pursue a "two-Chinas" resolution, arguing that "we are too emphatic *against* delaying tactics – they may turn out to be the best of evils." To bolster his case, he enlisted the support of Norman Robertson, a widely respected former under-secretary of state for external affairs. He shared Pearson's view that developments in Vietnam made it "unwise ... for Canada to contemplate a shift [in policy] this year."[68] The prime minister decided to defer his decision until the probable American reaction could be explored more fully.

During the course of the following few weeks, Martin had ample opportunity to learn how the US would respond to a Canadian initiative. Rusk made it perfectly clear in late September that he considered any move to legitimize Peking's international status to be inimical to western interests in Southeast Asia.[69] Confirmation of the prime minister's fears made it difficult for Martin to sell Pearson on a China initiative. The foreign minister was therefore obliged to adopt Pearson's view that Canada should promote a " 'one-China, one-Taiwan resolution' which would seat representatives of both governments in the General Assembly."[70]

Significantly, the position that Pearson forced on Martin was not all that different from the policy Washington was preparing to adopt. Washington did not minimize the importance of Canada's decision to adopt a more forthright China policy on the American strategy of containing Peking: "The Canadian shift makes a crucial difference. If we lose the support of these friends, it is probable that the Albanian resolution will obtain a simple majority for the first time [and] ... we will have suffered an important defeat." Convinced that Canada was not to be dissuaded from an initiative, and might even attract the support of Belgium and Italy, Rusk and Johnson were inclined to compromise and support a resolution which would establish a "study committee" to examine the issue before the next General Assembly. As the US would neither control the membership of this committee nor its terms of reference, Rusk was not sanguine in anticipating the exercise's results: "At a minimum, I would expect that this Committee would recommend some form of 'two-Chinas' solution."[71] In effect, Canada and the US differed, and only marginally, over a question of timing.

After discussing the problem with Johnson, the secretary of state wrote Pearson, reiterating the familiar American position. A move forward now would simply encourage Peking's belligerent policies in Southeast Asia and Vietnam. In addition, Rusk outlined a number of problems with the specific wording of the Canadian resolution. There was only one possible American response to the Canadian initiative as it now stood: "we would have to oppose your resolution in its present form, if it were introduced, and indeed, would have to exert every ounce of our influence to defeat it by the heaviest possible margin. I need not underscore the seriousness of such a split between our two nations." As an alternative course, Rusk proposed, Canada might join with one or two other countries in sponsoring a resolution to establish a study committee that would examine the question of Chinese representation at the UN.[72]

Pearson was disturbed by the American and international reaction, but Martin was determined. Canada was prepared to discuss the American suggestion for a study committee without any implicit or explicit commitment, using the possibility of a Canadian abstention on the Albanian resolution as a threat "to induce the USA and Italians to move to [a] position which is in closer accord with our own resolution."[73] Over the next few days, George Ignatieff, Canada's permanent representative to the UN, reached an agreed text in discussions with the Belgian and Italian delegations. Although quite different from the original Canadian resolution, the tripartite draft did contain an important reference to "the conflicting territorial claims of the two governments [of China] and the need to seek an appropriate solution taking into account ... the political realities of the area." But the Italians retreated the next day and, with Chile's support, began to solicit support for a resolution establishing a study committee.[74]

With debate on the Chinese question scheduled to begin shortly in the General Assembly, Martin turned to the Cabinet for advice. The government would need to decide whether the Italian-Canadian-Belgian draft represented the minimum Canada could accept and, if so, whether Canada should disassociate itself publicly from the Italian initiative. In addition, the government needed to consider how Canada would vote on the Italian and the Albanian resolutions. Martin hoped that "the Canadian delegation [would] be left free to vote in the negative or to abstain from voting" on an Albanian-inspired resolution.[75] Cabinet endorsed most of Martin's recommendations: it agreed that the government could go no further than the tripartite compromise resolution and should make a full statement explaining its position and its unsuccessful efforts to advance Chinese representation. Pearson refused to allow Martin to abstain on an Albanian resolution without prior consultation, effectively retaining control over Canadian policy.

The prime minister's reluctance forced Martin to return to New York in search of a compromise. On his arrival, he was met by the US ambassador to the UN, Arthur Goldberg. Martin explained to him that the government could not support a study committee without appearing to retreat from its stated policy. The Canadian suggested that Ottawa's position might be met if the Italian resolution could be amended to include a brief reference to the competing claims of Peking and Taiwan. While Goldberg undertook to consult Rusk and Johnson, Martin telephoned Pearson, who agreed that Canada would co-sponsor an amended resolution.[76] Washington, however, rejected the amendment and the following day, in a meeting of interested delegations, Italy announced its determination to proceed with its own resolution.

During the following week, Martin was faced with conflicting advice from the members of the Canadian delegation to the General Assembly. Officials from the Department of External Affairs, convinced that Canada had achieved all it could with its forceful advocacy of its original resolution, urged the minister to oppose the Albanian resolution. Other members of the delegation, including Pierre Trudeau, vigorously pressed Martin to abstain. Pearson meanwhile hoped that Canada would support the Italian resolution for a study committee.[77] On 23 November 1966, Martin intervened in the General Assembly debate on the question of Chinese representation and carefully explained why the Canadian government found both the Italian and the Albanian resolutions unsatisfactory. While indicating that Canada would support the proposal for a study committee, he did not reveal how Canada would vote on the Albanian resolution.

During a meeting with Rusk, two days prior to the vote, the question was not addressed. Instead, the Americans simply asked the minister to inform their allies in Asia that Canada had been pursuing its own policy during the preceding months and was not acting as an American stalking horse.[78] On the morning of 29 November 1966, Martin telephoned the prime minister and discussed how Canada might cast its vote. The minister contended that an abstention would disarm the government's domestic critics and lend weight to the idea of an independent Canadian policy. He reassured the prime minister that an abstention would not greatly anger the Americans.

There was something in these assertions. Martin, directed by Pearson, had come so close to reaching a compromise with the US that the differences between the two countries could be safely disregarded. When Pearson agreed that Canada would abstain, the Americans said nothing. Indeed, after discussing the question with leading members of the US delegation, J.G. Hadwen, the prime minister's special assistant, concluded: "The general tenor of our exchanges ... was satisfactory. I would take it as the kind of exchange which Canadian and u.s. officials have on points on which their governments disagree ... I don't see, to judge from this conversation, that we will likely get any serious Washington fallout."[79]

Pearson's relations with Martin, however, never fully recovered from the stresses and tensions that resulted from the Ronning mission and the abortive China initiative. For Pearson, it was crucial to ensure that Canada's approach to Asia took proper account of the country's partnership with Washington. When Martin overlooked this, the prime minister intervened, quietly but decisively, to restore an element of balance in Canada's Far Eastern policy. During Pearson's final year in office, Canada's approach to the crisis in Southeast Asia reflected the prime minister's cautious determination to maintain harmonious relations with Washington. In the face of pressure from the Canadian public and Cabinet, Pearson refused to condemn American policy. He vigorously defended the sale of Canadian military equipment to the US, despite strident opposition by university faculty, and defended the activities of Canada's representatives on the

ICSC in support of American efforts in Vietnam. When Walter Gordon urged Martin and Pearson to press the US to halt the bombing in May 1967, Pearson rebuked him in public.

Only in private did Pearson press Johnson to stop the bombing in Vietnam. This moderate posture won few friends on either side of the border. However, in smoothly deflecting Martin's unwise efforts to pursue a course in the Pacific independent of American interests in the region, Pearson demonstrated that, despite the constraints imposed by his office and his relationship with Martin, he still understood the fundamental realities that determined Canada's approach to the world.

LEGACIES

Pearsonianism

ANDREW COHEN

Legacy, in its literal sense, means something handed from one generation to another. In politics, it has come to mean a tradition, an example, a lesson. In thinking of Lester Pearson and foreign policy, this is particularly apt. For it is in the realm of international relations that Pearson left us an intellectual and moral legacy, a rich bequest which endures today in spirit, if not in practice.

It has been more than 100 years since the birth of Lester Pearson. More pointedly, it has been over a quarter century since his death. That isn't a long time in the breadth of history, but it is long enough to draw some conclusions about Pearson's internationalism and how his successors interpreted and adapted it.

By the time he came to office in 1963, Pearson was one of the great diplomats of his time. He was the winner of the Nobel Prize for Peace for his mediation in the Sinai. He had been secretary of state for external affairs. He had been president of the United Nations (UN) General Assembly. In the postwar years and before, there was scarcely a major international issue that he did not witness or did not influence.

It was here that he established the philosophy and the style which came to be known as Pearsonian diplomacy. The elements of the style were conciliation, moderation, patience, and creative ambiguity. The elements of the philosophy were Canada as honest broker and helpful fixer – the middle power as negotiator, peacekeeper, donor, humanitarian. It was Canada's belief in collective security, freer trade and multilateralism, through the Commonwealth and the UN. If Pearson did not invent that role, he certainly embraced it enthusiastically. In the bipolar world of the 1940s and 1950s, he knew that it gave Canada an influence beyond its size or stature, allowing it to punch above its weight.

This, then, was the philosophy and style which Pearson brought to office. But his legacy does not necessarily flow from any one achievement in foreign policy as prime minister. In fact, for the most part, his foreign policy was undistinguished. As Peter Newman argues, Canada's posture in external affairs was not altered in any imaginative way during those years: "The failure of his government to pioneer a single dramatic new approach to world problems must rank as one of the great disappointments of Lester Pearson's time in office."[1]

On the key items of his agenda – the recognition of China, membership in the Organization of American States (OAS), leadership of the reform of the UN and a closer relationship with the West Indies – there was little progress. Canada did take a stand, and made a difference, on Rhodesia, where Pearson brokered a settlement between black and white members of the Commonwealth. He took a stand, albeit muted, on the Vietnam War, which ruptured Canadian-American relations. He dispatched Canadians to Cyprus, though he never thought they would stay almost 30 years. Significantly, he increased foreign aid by 280 per cent between 1964 and 1967.

Thus, when we think of his legacy today, we think of his belief in peacekeeping, in multilateralism, in humanitarian assistance. He thought Canada could be the successful mediator, the builder of institutions, the exemplar of humanitarian assistance. He also thought that Canada must be sovereign and independent, particularly as against the United States, though he would never be as independent and assertive as the New Democrats and others wanted him to be.

It is crucial, though, to understand how clearly he saw the national interest. As he wrote in retirement in 1970, "Surely a far better foreign policy is that which is based on a national interest which expresses itself in cooperation with others; in the building of international institutions and the development of international policies and agreements, leading to a world order which promotes freedom, well-being and security for all."[2]

If these are the elements of liberal internationalism, we ask ourselves today, how have they fared in the years since? How did his successors see them? Allowing for a different world, we can argue, by and large, that they have fared well. In fact, what is most flattering about the diplomacy and world view of Lester Pearson is that it has been adopted or imitated, in one form or another, by every prime minister since. Fundamentally, the practices and principles of Lester Pearson, which have governed Canadian foreign policy since the war, survive today.

Under the governments of Pierre Trudeau and Brian Mulroney, and to a lesser degree, Jean Chrétien, Canada has had an engaged, activist foreign policy, most of which Pearson could have embraced, which isn't to say that he would have agreed with everything.

In fact, when Trudeau took office in 1968, he thought Canada had not a foreign policy but a defence policy. As he saw it, Canada would no longer be the world's boy scout; Canada would he shrewd, hard-headed and rational. Foreign policy would be more measured and more modest; it would be seen less in terms of what it could do for others than what it could do for us.

But Pearsonian values could be found even in the narrow definition of the national interest as described in *Foreign Policy for Canadians*, the government' s foreign policy review of 1970: the importance of foreign aid, the preservation of the environment, the pursuit of social justice. Still, Pearson was deeply hurt by what he saw as a repudiation of his world, which is what prompted his 1970 comments on the national interest.

Of course, we know what happened over the course of Trudeau's mandate. Canada stayed in the North Atlantic Treaty Organization (NATO), despite the debate over withdrawal. It recognized China. It took an initiative in the Caribbean Basin. It maintained its role in peacekeeping. It increased foreign aid and pushed the North-South dialogue. Most telling, Trudeau adopted Pearson's personal diplomacy. Having scorned the helpful fixer and the honest broker, ultimately he played precisely that role himself. When he launched his quixotic peace crusade in his last days in office, he turned to the professionals in external affairs, becoming as Pearsonian as Pearson himself. No wonder historians J.L. Granatstein and Robert Bothwell called their account of Trudeau's foreign policy *Pirouette*. Canada had come full circle and, for all the illusion of change, had returned to the values of Pearsonian diplomacy. When Pierre Trudeau left office, the legacy of Lester Pearson lived.

Brian Mulroney, for his part, had less international experience than either of his two immediate predecessors. But he, too, accepted Pearsonian principles of Canadian foreign policy. Although he distrusted the Department of External Affairs, politicized the foreign service and folded a government-supported foreign policy think-tank, his government showed that, in its essentials, foreign policy didn't necessarily have to change when governments did. In other words, there was a consensus in Canadian foreign policy, and it was based on Pearsonianism.

Under Mulroney, Canada expanded peacekeeping in 1988, joined the OAS, and embraced a greater role in *la francophonie* – all of which Pearson would have supported. We saw New Democrat Stephen Lewis as Canadian ambassador at the UN, surely an expression of

Canada's support for the organization. We saw the government isolate South Africa and support, however modestly, the struggle for human rights in China, Indonesia, and Kenya. We saw Mulroney push the rights of children. In his way, he had made Pearson's work his own.

Pearson would have parted company with Mulroney on his continentalism. Pearson was for free trade, but in the context of multilateralism. He probably would have approached the Canadian-American free-trade omnibus agreement with grave reservations, and he would have held out for a better deal. He would have thought Mulroney too close, incapable of putting any moral distance between our two societies, as he had done, at some cost, during the war in Vietnam. In handling the United States, the country's most important relationship then and now, his legacy would have demanded more ambivalence and more caution. Mike would recite baseball batting averages with Jack Kennedy at Hyannisport, but he wouldn't have sung a duet with Ronald Reagan.

On the other hand, as former Prime Minister John Turner has perceptively argued, Pearson would have joined the allied coalition in the Gulf War. He might have sought more time for sanctions to take effect and he might have tried to intensify the search for peace. At the end of the day, though, he would have seen Saddam Hussein as the threat to peace that he was, and he would have backed multilateral military intervention. Indeed, Pearson's gritty fingerprints are all over the Conservative foreign policy. Thus, when Brian Mulroney left office, the legacy of Lester Pearson lived.

That brings us to the present. Ironically, it is Jean Chrétien's government which has probably moved farthest from the Pearsonian ideal. While he hasn't wholly abandoned it, he has severely tested it.

In the foreign policy review in 1995, the government retreated from the principles which have long governed foreign policy. If Mike Pearson worried about Pierre Trudeau's view of the national interest, he would have been apoplectic about Jean Chrétien's. Here the national interest is expressed wholly in economic terms. Mr. Chrétien's foreign policy is less engaged, less idealistic, less empathetic. Foreign policy is a matter of what we can afford, and we can't afford to be so generous or involved.

What drives the government first is the promotion of prosperity and employment, then the protection of security, then the projection of Canadian values. This is no small point. Under Pearson, and his successors, the pillars of foreign policy were sovereignty, independence, collective security, national unity, democracy, human rights, and international aid.

Not now. As the white paper explains, what counts today is economic growth and job creation. Everything else is a distraction. Were he around today, Pearson would look at this foreign policy and look away. He would recognize only some of himself here, surely less than he would have in the previous governments that succeeded him.

On trade, yes, he would see a government which still supports the World Trade Organization. He would like that, as he would like regional free trade, but he would worry about its impact on our independence. He probably would have endorsed the North American Free Trade Agreement (NAFTA) as a bridge between North and South, however much he would have been suspicious of some elements.

In other areas of foreign policy, he would see his legacy fraying. Consider three.

As the man who recommended in 1970 that countries should give one percent of their gross domestic product to foreign aid, he would be dismayed that Canada has abandoned this field. Its percentage has now dropped to 0.29, not much above the average of the countries of the Organization of Economic Co-operation and Development (OECD).

The man who believed in multilateralism and the integrity of international institutions would be appalled at Canada's handling of the fishery crisis in 1995. Pearson knew too much about the integrity of international law. He would have been uncomfortable seizing Spanish trawlers. His way would have been the International Court at The Hague.

Lastly, the man who believed in human rights, and the efficacy of collective action, would be disappointed in Canada's lack of courage here. As a pragmatist, he would know the limits of threats, cries and laments, and the limits of quiet diplomacy. As an idealist, he would also understand the need to lend moral support, however careful, to democrats and dissidents everywhere. Mike Pearson knew the power of gesture to assert moral authority. On China, Nigeria and Burma, he would have striven for consensus and, if he had not found it, he would have found a way to assert a distinctly Canadian view.

But for all the departures, there is strong continuity. It would be easy to declare our foreign policy neo-isolationist, selfish and parochial, and send Pearson back to Heaven in despair, bow-tie askew, homburg in hand. We could, but we wouldn't be right.

The legacy survives, however threadbare it may seem at times. Canada still remains a peacekeeper in Bosnia and Haiti, and Pearson would applaud Canada's establishment of a centre of peacekeeping studies and training (bearing his name). Canada tried to lead the rescue mission in Zaire and, however fitful the execution, Pearson would have applauded the motive. Canada remains a champion of reform at the UN, a supporter of a rapid reaction peacekeeping force and collective action, a supporter of the global warming treaty, and a member of every international club going, and he would applaud that, too. As a Nobel Laureate, he would be pleased that it was Canada, under foreign minister Lloyd Axworthy, that championed the International Campaign to Ban Landmines. That group, and its coordinator, Jody Williams, was recognized with the Nobel Peace Prize in 1997.

Canada remains in NATO, even if it is virtually out of Europe, and he would have too much proprietary pride to want to leave it. If our foreign policy isn't as interventionist and altruistic as Pearson would have liked, it is less isolationist and self-centred than he might have feared, particularly at a time when the United States has slipped into a neo-isolationism.

Of course, Pearson lived in a different world, and would allow for differences in this one. He would understand that the special relationship with Washington matters more than it did, largely because the relationship with Great Britain and Europe matters less. Sentimental as he was, this transition might bother him but would not paralyze him.

He would recognize the collapse of communism and the end of the cold war. As his son Geoffrey says, he would seize the opportunities that have opened for more creative diplomacy. And while he would understand that in a unipolar world, where everyone talks to everyone else, the purpose and style of our diplomacy would change of necessity, he would not lament the decline of traditional diplomacy or the disappearance of the helpful fixer. He would simply get on with it.

Instead of Europe, he would look to Asia and Latin America. Instead of promoting disarmament in the councils of the world, he would press an agenda of anti-terrorism, drug interdiction, the environment, and the dissemination of information. If there was to be a new regional focus, there would be the new collective security, and there would still be the old obligation of compassion. In Lester Pearson, all would find a champion, an innovator, a clear and moral voice.

The legacy today is not so much a cluster of policies as a concentration of principle. It does not belong to one party, but to Canada itself. Those who doubt this might examine the Conservative party's foreign policy, as expressed in its platform during the 1997 federal election. Jean Charest was often more Pearsonian than Jean Chrétien.

It is not about shirking responsibility but accepting it. It is a matter of seeing foreign policy as an instrument of pan-Canadian unity, one of those great national endeavours which transcends language and region. It is not only what should be done but what might be done. That is the legacy of Lester Pearson, and that is what he leaves us today.

Pragmatism

ROSS CAMPBELL

The word "peace" in contemporary Canadian usage has become synonymous with the name "Pearson." Be it his Nobel Peace Prize or Canada's international peacekeeping activities, L.B. Pearson's name is inseparably linked with the concept of peace – not just the avoidance of war through diplomatic means (although Pearson was a past master at that art) – but the active pursuit by international means of measures, both military and political, to create conditions in which the settlement of disputes by negotiation could take place. The Pearsonian vision of a postwar world was one in which armed conflict would be progressively replaced by an enforceable international rule of law.

In pursuit of that noble goal, however, Pearson the idealistic visionary always marched hand in hand with Pearson the pragmatist. Witness his support for clauses in the draft United Nations (UN) Charter which would permit collective security arrangements between likeminded nations to reinforce the fledgling international regime then rising Phoenix-like from the ashes of the Second World War. It was as well that Pearsonian caution helped to lay the groundwork for a back-up strategy for keeping the postwar peace, for the Utopian vision of the UN as a powerful security organization was soon to be placed in jeopardy in the second half of the 1940s by the falling-out of the victorious wartime allies and the emergence of a hostile Soviet Union determined not only to consolidate its wartime military gains but to test repeatedly the resolve of the western powers to uphold the territorial limits set by the terms of the armistice.

Few Canadians now recall that it was Prime Minister Louis St. Laurent, on the advice of Pearson (by then secretary of state for external affairs), who was among the first to spell out the need for an Atlantic partnership to contain the rising militancy of the Soviet Union. Out of this was born in 1949 the alliance known as the North Atlantic Treaty Organization (NATO) which, despite repeated Soviet-inspired crises over the next four decades, managed to keep the peace and preserve the territorial integrity of its members while at the same time developing its governing council's global disarmament measures and peaceful solutions to difficult East-West issues. This latter function of NATO as a unique political forum in which all collective western policies for peace were developed – another little known fact or at least little publicized in Canada – was one particularly prized by Pearson. He believed not only in collective security measures but in collective and continuous political consultation as practiced in the Permanent Council of NATO under guidance from members' capitals and refined and endorsed as policy at periodic meetings of ministers.

Still fewer Canadians today remember that Pearson steadfastly upheld throughout his tenure of office Canada's commitment to collective security arrangements with our Atlantic partners, seeing it as the only tenable policy for a country of our vast size and small population, and that the commitment, to be effective and credible, had to involve a substantial contribution of combat-capable forces. Mr. Pearson's administration was the last in Canada fully to observe and preserve this prudent sense of balance in international security affairs.

My point in re-tracing these historical facts is simply to illustrate that Pearson the pragmatist was no less in evidence than Pearson the idealist when it came to practical issues of national and international security. Despite his personal aversion to military solutions, he did not hesitate to support collective military measures when international peace was under threat.

My further point is gently to deplore the extent to which Pearson the pragmatist has been forgotten by the public and, to some extent, by successor Canadian governments in their zeal to promote exclusively the image of Pearson the UN protagonist. This in turn has led to an unbalanced emphasis on peacekeeping under UN auspices as a comprehensive answer to Canadian security needs. It is not, and I believe that Pearson would be upset, even dismayed, to discover that his pioneering efforts in UN peacekeeping had been distorted to arrive at such a conclusion. The simple fact is that we were in the 1950s and 1960s, and we are still today, at the stage where peacemaking must precede successful peacekeeping. Nations are not yet ready to entrust peacemaking to a military force under direct UN control, nor is the UN structured for such a role.

If he were alive today, I am sure Pearson would agree with that assessment. He would be continuing to pursue the more Utopian goal, but at the gradual pace that improving but still uneasy great-power relations dictate, while in the meantime supporting coalitions for collective security. He would have applauded the recent demonstration in ex-Yugoslavia of the rightness of his own twin-pronged approach to security. There, as we all know, it was only after four frustrating years of UN attempts to resolve the internecine strife by traditional peacekeeping methods that NATO was called in and, by applying its practised military professionalism, managed within a few weeks to halt the fighting and to set the stage for a political solution. Canada was an active participant in both phases of the operation – the UN phase, as part of a largely unsuccessful and sometimes humiliating peacekeeping operation – and the NATO phase, as part of a rapidly successful peacemaking operation.

We should draw the right lessons for today's world from the experience of the past. We should recognize that Pearson was a pioneer half-a-century ago of an effective mix of peacekeeping and peacemaking – peacekeeping as exemplified by his pioneering effort in creating the UN Emergency Force in Egypt at the time of the Suez Crisis, and peacemaking through his active sponsorship of collective security in the shape of NATO. Mr. Pearson knew that both were indispensable elements in the quest for a stable world order on which ultimately our own national security rests.

Continuity

MONIQUE BÉGIN

I became a member of the Liberal party of Canada late in the spring of 1972, and I was elected to the House of Commons on 30 October of the same year, a few weeks before Lester B. Pearson's death on 27 December. I never met him, nor even saw him in person, and so my memory of him is that of an ordinary citizen who gets a feeling for one's political leaders through television and the other media. The Right Honourable Lester B. Pearson, for a young French-Canadian woman in her thirties like myself at the time, had always been a most honourable political figure, a man of total integrity, both a humanist and a humanitarian, and a man of peace. He was "a wise elder," to borrow an expression from our native cultures, but he was not someone from my generation to whom I could relate spontaneously.

I was astounded by the *Maclean's* survey of the 25 scholars of Canadian political history, which ranked Mackenzie King as the greatest prime minister to lead the country.[1] He never represented much for me or for the people around me, I am sorry to say. This perception has nothing to do with age or generation, nor has it to do with party politics. Sir Wilfrid Laurier has been, for the longest time, an important presence in my *musée imaginaire* of political leaders. Over and above specific events or decisions, some historical figures count for individuals in a special way; they are positive figures with a significance. Their actions convey meaning which, in turn, nurtures a relationship of the mind and heart with a historical character, a person we may never know, someone dead or far away. These people are symbols.

When I was first elected, and when Parliament started sitting the following January, the Right Honourable Pierre Trudeau's minority government (his second government as prime minister) seemed to me in complete continuity, in terms of values, with those of Mr. Pearson. Granted, the times had changed; we were in the immediate aftermath of the California counter-culture, and society's sensitivity was still evolving rapidly. Many of the actors had changed, both in elected politics and behind the scenes. The style had certainly changed. So had the structure of Cabinet committees and of the machinery of the Privy Council and of the Prime Minister's Office. The economic challenges were changing, although we were acting as if we were still in the era of the "Affluent Society." But the deep beliefs and commitments remained the same.

When studying the Liberal party, its history and its public policy platforms, as a newcomer to it and a newly elected member of Parliament, I did not sense at the time any disruption in the threads running through the successive party resolutions between the early 1960s up to what was to be "my" first national convention, one I co-chaired with Judd Buchanan in mid-September 1973. The themes of the famous January 1961 Kingston Conference – universal government-financed Medicare, income maintenance programs, regional economic development, vocational training, and other progressive measures – were still there. So was some measure of nationalist economics. So were the concerns about the place and power of Quebec in Canada, about bilingualism and about the separatist movement. I had joined a party where French Canadians – Quebeckers in particular – felt at home, and where minorities in general, be they women, newcomers to the country (immigrants, refugees and draft dodgers) or aboriginal peoples, shared a sense of belonging.

Mr. Pearson's role, his talents, and his views in matters of foreign policy and defence were well established, even before he became party leader. He had already given Canada a greater prominence on the world map by winning the Nobel Peace Prize. After all, up until January 1958, when he was elected leader of the Liberal party, most of Mr. Pearson's public service employment or public role had been as a diplomat, not as a domestic policy-maker. His apprenticeship on the domestic front was arduous and varied, from the creation of the historic Royal Commission on Bilingualism and Biculturalism (1963) to the no less historic and emotional Canadian flag legislation (1965), and including the troubled times of Quebec's emerging extremist separatist groups and the first bombings by the *Front de libération du Québec* (*FLQ*).[2]

Although he may not have been the best of elected politicians, his years in government corresponded to the Affluent Society decade and its extraordinary dynamism. His governments brought us a host of social policy initiatives in the broad sense of the term: the Canada

Pension Plan, the Medical Care Act, a major expansion of post-secondary education federal funding, manpower training initiatives, the community and regional development program (the Fund for Rural Economic Development (FRED) and the Agricultural and Rural Development Agency (ARDA)), the Company of Young Canadians, the Royal Commission on the Status of Women, and a divorce act. In these initiatives, Pearson brought Canadians into the modern era, an exercise later to be completed by Trudeau's election as Liberal leader and prime minister in 1968. After the years of war economy and of industrial development of Mackenzie King and Louis St. Laurent, the Pearson years of social policies brought the federal government closer to its citizens and their daily concerns. As two public policy analysts have concluded, "it is clear that Pearson strongly supported and preferred these largely social policy initiatives."[3]

When I inherited the portfolio of national health and welfare in 1977, all the major programs falling under my department, with the exception of family allowances and old-age pensions, had been created by Mr. Pearson's government. In addition to those I have named, there were also the Canada Assistance Plan, a major reform of social assistance to individuals and of social services delivered by the provinces, the Guaranteed Income Supplement (1966) to the old-age pensions, and the Health Resources Fund (1967) for building and developing medical schools and other health facilities. His legacy in social and health matters is so significant that the recent report of the National Forum on Health found it natural and appropriate to quote Mr. Pearson at a First Ministers' conference in 1965 on "Medicare": "The scope of benefits should be, broadly speaking, all the services provided by physicians, both general practitioners and specialists. A complete health plan would include dental treatment, prescribed drugs, and other important services, and there is nothing in the approach we propose to prevent these being included, from the start or later, if this were the general wish. We regard comprehensive physicians' services as the initial minimum."[4]

Some people in government may not want to hear these words in today's squeezing down of the welfare state, and I am conscious that they belong to an era where ongoing, continuous growth was the creed. But they attest to the generosity and openness of the 1960s.

At the time that I was appointed minister of national health and welfare, Prime Minister Trudeau did not give me any mandate; the meeting with him lasted some ten minutes. Such was the man; it was as if he knew he could count on his candidate to do a good job, whatever the challenges. Nor did he, or any of his senior players, ever indicate to me any change in orientation at any point in time during my seven years in that portfolio. Thus, when two senior "economic" ministers were reported in the media as suggesting the end of universal family allowances and old-age pensions two weeks after I had been sworn in, I simply fought back. Most of the years to come were to be devoted to saving the universality (and budgets) of social programs, including Medicare, usually behind the scenes. I was accused by some Cabinet colleagues of fighting a rear-guard action, of not having understood the times we found ourselves in and the need for monetarist policies. What I had understood very well was that we had no mandate to undo the "safety net," and that I could not see what superior good was to be achieved by others with all the billions of the social programs entrusted to me. Towards the last years of my term, I could see that the economy was changing, and changing for good. Had there been valid proposals for "real" job creation programs – through tax credits to business and industry, for example – I would have taken my share of responsibility to convince Canadians of the need to reduce somehow the safety net in a collective effort of social solidarity.

Let me recreate the ideological environment of the times. The winds of economic neo-conservatism and its moral innuendos had started blowing hard in Canada. I had the impression that most of Canada's elites had read Milton Friedman and loved his message. Cuts in social programs were favoured to fix all these abuses; a pure market economy was the panacea and absolute competition was the rule. In that way of thinking, the private sector was the only functional approach and health care was a market commodity. My personal objective as a new minister was to carry on the Pearson legacy by bringing about the guaranteed annual income for Canadians. I was quickly crushed, however, by the new environment which surrounded me. After four months in office, I realized that, instead of playing a glorious and historical role, I would be lucky if I could simply save for my fellow citizens the best acquisitions of the past.

What I found particularly difficult during all these years was the fact that, in the field of health and social policies, all major ideological and financial battles at the federal government level took place in a covert way. The attacks were sly, even deceitful. Nothing was clear and direct. The caucus or the party had no idea of what was really going on. My other major problem was the absence of any articulate counter-ideology to the powerful neo-conservatism. I recall discussing with my friend Kalmen Kaplansky, a Co-operative Commonwealth Federation-New Democratic Party colleague of David Lewis, the arguments for universality when pensions and family allowances had been created, hoping to capture a line of reasoning and arguments that I could in turn use. But the times had changed!

Since Mr. Trudeau had not given me any particular mandate, I hung on to the Pearson legacy. Whatever senior civil servants, political strategists or colleagues told me of "the prime minister's wishes," I knew that Trudeau supported my work. I always assumed, rightly so I am convinced, that Trudeau wanted me to save social programs and Medicare, the social philosophy he subscribed to when he himself was recruited by Pearson to join the ranks of the Liberal party and the government. It was therefore Mr. Pearson's legacy, personified by a few key players around the Cabinet table, Allan J. MacEachen among them, that enabled me to carry on.

On the world stage, Pearson spoke and acted in a manner in which Canadians recognized themselves – our fellow citizens, whom officials so often underestimate as naïve and unsophisticated, our fellow citizens, who do not easily and publicly discuss foreign affairs and international relations, but have clear views that are not easy to turn around. International peace and security, development and equal partnership among nations remain issues of tremendous importance to Canadians.

Pearson was a significant reference point for all Canadians, a symbol. Both Pearson's "war on poverty" and Trudeau's later "just society" not only touched the heart and made us dream; they also nurtured the best in us, the sense of generosity and tolerance in Canadians. Mr. Pearson embodies in our collective memory what Northrop Frye so aptly labelled "our quest for the peaceable kingdom."[5]

Reformism

TOM KENT

I want to discuss three issues: why the Pearson government was the way it was; why its achievements are now in disrepair; and whether, nevertheless, we can build on them.

The distinction of the Pearson government is clear: in no other five years was so much done to improve the circumstances of life for Canadians with average and lower incomes. Medicare, pensions, social assistance, and post-secondary education stand out in newspaper accounts, but there was much else: the federal labour code (the first of Allan MacEachen's lasting legislative achievements), employment services, training, family allowances extended to age 18 for those staying at school, student loans, the guaranteed income supplement, full equalization of expanded provincial tax points, industrial and rural development. Above all, economic growth and virtually full employment were restored, after a recession that may seem small now but at the time had been severely felt. All this was achieved without deficits, indeed with declining indebtedness over the 1965–74 decade. It was not until six years after the end of the Pearson government that our economy and finances began to go seriously astray.

What drove the Pearson burst of equality-directed reformism? I suggest three factors, in a summary historical analysis, because that fits the bent of L.B. Pearson's mind.

First, the Pearson reforms were a delayed response to the postwar mood. In all democracies, people were determined not to return to the social conditions of the Great Depression. Wartime experience of what government could do had destroyed, for a generation, the old dogma that private is good, public is bad. Ottawa quickly responded to this mood with extensive welfare-state proposals, but the war had

had less impact on provincial governments. In face of their opposition, Ottawa had retreated to a few, though important, reforms, and the apparent security in office during the 1950s bred Liberal complacency. C.D. Howe was at the controls and all was well with Canada.

We come to the second factor that led to the Pearson reform government: the dynamics of politics. Since it was getting nowhere by being more conservative than the Liberals, the official opposition shifted to the leadership of a maverick Prairie Tory, John Diefenbaker. That worked. One consequence was to raise pensions by $14 a month, in place of the measly six bucks of the Liberals. However, the Diefenbaker government was too divided, and too ineptly led, to maintain much impetus. The disappointment of expectations opened a new opportunity for Liberal reformers. A national political party is necessarily an alliance of shifting elements. When it had been long in office, the Liberal party was dominated by its establishment and managerial elements. With the crushing defeat in 1958, apparently beyond early recovery, they faded into the background. The organization based on being the government party was moribund. The faint torch was passed to those activists who saw the electoral defeat as the penalty of having run out of reform ideas.

At this point, the new leader had no choice. If the Liberal party was to be revived within four years, he had to rely chiefly on reformist elements, existing and new. Fortunately, that chimed with his inclinations. There were hesitations on the way, but in the end the Liberal party went into the 1962 and 1963 elections with a strongly reformist platform. The document was slighter than the Liberal party's Red Book of 30 years later. It was not verbose enough to be open to much selective reinterpretation. It was mostly a precise and definite statement of measures that a Pearson government would undertake.

That, however, was not the end of the affair. We come to the third factor, the "distinctively Pearson" factor. Politicians in office do not necessarily do what they promised in opposition. That is not entirely because of cynicism or miscalculation. Partly, it is because power shifts. Influential Liberals who had stepped back in 1958 returned in force in 1963. They joined others who had been unable to combat reformism in opposition, but consoled themselves that in office much of it could be set aside. They misunderstood Mike Pearson.

One of his outstanding qualities as a politician was his deep respect for the democratic processes of representative government. His international experience of other sorts of government had reinforced his moral conviction that in office he owed it to the people to do, as nearly as possible, what he had said he would do. He agonized over resistance within the Cabinet and in influential circles outside it. He was aged by that and by the other trials and tribulations – some self-made – of his government. At times he hesitated. Yet in the end he almost always led his Cabinet to implement the promised agenda.

That was why and how Canada became, with a late but remarkable burst of speed, a moderately developed welfare state. That was the legacy of L.B. Pearson's prime ministership.

Was it wise? Could the social commitments be afforded, then and since?

The validity of a "yes" answer depends on economic policy. In this, the Pearson government was not innovative. It reverted to a proven formula. In the great period of postwar prosperity, Ottawa managed the economy with a fairly tight fiscal policy and a fairly easy monetary policy. The formula was somewhat breached in the Diefenbaker years. The Pearson government returned to it, and again it worked.

The Trudeau government soon embarked on the opposite course, and the Mulroney government followed it. For 20 years we had a lax fiscal policy, at times very lax, and a tight monetary policy, at times very tight indeed. There is no need to recite the consequences in strangled economic growth, unemployment, increased social costs and accumulated debt.

It is true that the world had become a less kindly place for the Canadian economy. No policy would have restored the extraordinary growth rate of the early postwar years. A sensible policy would have required us to accept a lower exchange rate sooner than we did, but there was no irresistible force compelling us to accept severe unemployment and declining real incomes. That was the choice, no less real for being muddled in motive, of governments. It led to the degree of indebtedness at which nearly 40 percent of federal taxes went not to provide people with services but to pay interest to bond-holders, many of them outside Canada. At that point everything became difficult to afford. However, it was not because the social programs inherited from the Pearson era had dragged us down. The blame for our financial crisis lies squarely with bad economic policy, policy entirely different from that of the Pearson and earlier years. A little better economic performance over the past 25 years would have been sufficient to sustain our welfare state; with significantly better performance, it could have been improved.

To diagnose the cause does not remove its results. The fiscal stringency arising from accumulated debt had to be dealt with, and the present government deserves its credit for doing so. Here I come to my third topic: how to preserve and to build on the Pearson legacy. To do so, we have to recognise its vulnerable feature: a vulnerability not of purpose, not of scale, but of method.

The main method was cost-sharing. Ottawa induced the provinces to undertake reasonably consistent social programs by promising to reimburse them for half of the cost. In that way, nation-wide social security was built despite the constitutional allocation of responsibilities. But it required federal politicians to collect taxes for provincial politicians to spend. The governments of the 1950s and 1960s were remarkable for such generosity. Later governments, beginning in 1977, have retreated further and further from it.

Perhaps I am showing a little surviving bias, but I cannot believe that the present government was motivated by a desire to destroy the Pearson legacy. Social programs have borne the brunt of expenditure-cutting, not because they are social but because they are provincial. Downloading is more politically palatable for federal politicians than either tax increases or deeper cuts in direct federal programs. That is understandable. We have to recognize that the 1960s instrument of social policy is outworn. Even if Ottawa became miraculously willing to revert to large-scale cost-sharing, the provinces would not trust it again. To restore the purpose of the Pearson period requires other methods less politically vulnerable.

It is entirely possible. The methods are available and can be made financially viable over the term of a government.[1] L.B. Pearson's legacy, though shaken, is not yet lost. His path, the path of equality-directed reforms to our society and our economy, is now even more needed than it was when he became the leader of the Liberal party 40 years ago. We can take that path again. Or we could take it if there were a sufficient shock to political complacency to revive, again, the reformist embers within the Liberal party.

Consistency

A. W. JOHNSON

Mr. Pearson was a simply splendid prime minister to serve. I didn't work for him directly, I must say. Walter Gordon was my minister, and then Mitchell Sharp, during my time in the Department of Finance, and the great Bob Bryce was my deputy. It was my good fortune, however, to have been assigned to many of Mr. Pearson's priorities and, therefore, to have seen a good deal of him.

I came to the Public Service of Canada early on in the Pearson government, almost straight from Tommy Douglas's bureaucracy in Saskatchewan, and I felt right at home. Mr. Pearson said to me more than once: "That is because we're both sons of the manse." I would agree: much of his value system stemmed from the church. But his values stemmed, too, from the social liberal philosophy of the likes of L.T. Hobhouse and T.H. Green, the branch of liberal philosophy that has had such an impact on the humanization of the market economy. These were the values that lay at the root of Mr. Pearson's policies. I'm not so sure, by the way, that the economic liberals had a similar hold on Mr. Pearson – Adam Smith, John Stuart Mill and the rest!

Mr. Pearson's policies had a remarkable thread of consistency. Consistently humane, consistently concerned with fairness, consistently related to governance that would unite Canada through serving all its inhabitants.

I cannot get over the great sweep of the social reform he introduced in four years. The equalization of provincial revenues, for example, was a sea change from the past. So much so that, during negotiations at the official level, provincial public servants like Jacques Parizeau and Claude Morin came to me privately to argue that Quebec would benefit so much from the proposed equalization formula, in aggregate dollar terms, that it would never get through the federal Cabinet. "Jiggle the formula to direct more money to the Atlantic provinces," they said. I said "no," that the formula was designed to be fair, and was fair in *per capita* terms to all provinces; that it was designed to be totally objective and politically tamper-proof; and, moreover, that it was for the prime minister to decide what would or would not get through Cabinet. I had no doubt in *my* mind: Mr. Pearson's values were such that he would be bound to support a program designed to ensure to all Canadians a reasonably even level of provincial public services – and which would in the process contribute to national unity.

The same was true of Medicare. The story is well known. By the time Medicare came onto the government's policy agenda, Mr. Pearson was already committed to the Canada Pension Plan, or the Canada Pension Plan/Quebec Pension Plan as it came to be, plus the equalization of provincial revenues – a huge increase in expenditures. He also faced a substantial review of federal support to Canada's universities and colleges. So the treasury was by this time a bit strained. Moreover, Quebec's Premier Lesage had announced that his province would never again agree to a shared-cost program, and that was the only vehicle the federal government had to fashion a national, universal medical care program.

But Mr. Pearson persisted. It was obvious the prime minister was insistent that a Medicare package in one form or another must be designed and at least put on the federal-provincial table. At almost every meeting of the small and unofficial committee on Medicare, Tom Kent would say, "well, if we can't afford full Medicare, what about partial or phased-in measures – kiddie-care, or gericare for example?" Finally, however, we came up with a comprehensive plan that *would* bring Quebec in, based not on a conditional grant agreement for any premier to sign, but instead on a set of principles in national legislation to which the provinces would have to adhere. The Medicare program would be founded on the right values – equal access for all Canadians, and bringing the provinces on side through the enunciation of principles, not arid conditions.

Thus Mr. Pearson announced Medicare in 1965. Then, after giving the finance department some fiscal breathing space, he legislated it into being in 1968.

It was the same with the federal financing of universities and colleges. A huge new program was introduced under which the federal government undertook to pay to the provinces 50 percent of the operating costs of universities and colleges. Again, the same just and humane Pearsonian values and principles were brought to bear: making higher education possible, financially, for most students (with the help of the Canada Student Loan Plan, also started in the early Pearson years), and extending federal support to both categories of higher education, universities and the more technically oriented community colleges. The program increased hugely the participation rate in universities and colleges of the young people of Canada.

There are legions of people who now say, "But all that was so easy in the 1960s, when Canada's growth rate was closer to four percent per annum, compared with today's two percent." They are missing the point: the Pearson government devoted a significant part of the dividends from that four-percent growth rate to human well-being and the dignity of individual Canadians. And that was a great achievement.

It was in that climate the public service of the middle 1960s worked. Small wonder that we found the Pearson years inspiring.

Duality

H. BLAIR NEATBY

Pearson's years as prime minister were the period when Ottawa began to respond to the Quiet Revolution. Nobody at the time knew what Quebec wanted, or would want – and that included French-Canadian as well as English-Canadian political leaders. Pearson was as bemused as any but, to his credit, he was one of the first among the English-Canadian leaders to recognize that what was happening to Quebec was a threat to national unity.

It is important to analyze his various responses to the challenge. As a preliminary, however, we might well ask how it was that Lester B. Pearson was sensitive to, and even sympathetic to, the radical aspirations of the minority.

The answer will not be found in his early years. An Irish-Protestant background and a Methodist upbringing were almost designed to undermine any potential sympathy for Roman Catholics, and the imperial sympathies of small-town Ontario fostered dark suspicions of the French Canadians, who failed to share the same enthusiasm for the British Empire. Indeed, even in 1917, at the age of 20, for all the potentially broadening experience of wartime service and travel abroad, Mike Pearson was denouncing those traitors back in Canada who were not going to vote for conscription. The war may have made Pearson less colonial but his definition of Canada was still a very English-Canadian one.

Historians might also note with some concern that the study of history at Toronto, and then at Oxford, did little to modify this perspective. Nor did his years in the Department of External Affairs, where English Canadians were the dominant group and where it was taken for granted that English was the only appropriate language of communication.

How, then, did Pearson become aware of bilingualism and biculturalism and their central importance for national unity?

Personalities form part of the explanation. Louis St. Laurent was a crucial figure. Pearson worked for him when St. Laurent was minister for external affairs and entered politics as a member of St. Laurent's government. St. Laurent was a French Canadian and a Roman Catholic who combined exceptional intelligence and a commitment to public service with an engaging patrician charm. He was also an internationalist. Jean Lesage was another influence, in this case as a protégé of Pearson's in Ottawa and, later, when he shifted to provincial politics, as a French-Canadian leader whose loyalty to Canada was, for Pearson, beyond question. Allan MacEachen has reminded me that Maurice Lamontagne also deserves mention. Lamontagne was an advisor to Pearson during the opposition years and drafted the speech of December 1962 which first outlined the Liberal party policy on bilingualism and biculturalism.

Personal relations are important, but they can only be understood in a broader context. If Pearson's religious and political perspectives had not evolved, it is unlikely that he would ever have appreciated, much less admired, these men. His Methodism, like that of many of his contemporaries, had given way to a secular commitment to public service. For Pearson, however, the specific context which seems to have altered his perspective was his increasing involvement in politics and with the Liberal party.

Pearson was an internationalist, hoping to shape the international institutions of the postwar world. That meant influencing Canadian government policy. But this was the 1940s, when the Canadian government was a Liberal government and, what was more, it was widely assumed that it should be. The Liberal party had become "the government party" in the minds of Liberals, of course, but also in the minds of many who saw national unity as a prerequisite for winning the war and winning the peace; this blurred the distinction between government policy and Liberal party policy.

It must also be remembered that in the 1940s the Liberal party was a political institution with a distinctive character. Under Laurier and, even more so, under Mackenzie King, the Liberal party depended on a solid bloc of Quebec voters for its majority at Ottawa. Anybody concerned with Canadian leadership in the international sphere had to be preoccupied with national unity as the Liberal party defined it, underlining the importance – even the necessity – of winning significant support for government policies among both French and English Canadians.

It was in this context that the influence of Pearson's French-Canadian colleagues must be assessed. National unity at its worst could mean no more than bribing French Canadians, retaining their votes by a careful distribution of loaves and fishes. Men like St. Laurent and Lesage, however, seemed to share Pearson's commitment to cooperative federalism and peaceful internationalism. Thus, as a senior diplomat and then as a politician, Pearson's definition of Canada came not only to include French Canada, but to include it as a potentially creative partner. By the 1960s, this meant that Pearson could even accept a commitment to an undefined bilingualism and biculturalism. He had travelled a long way from southern Ontario and the early Department of External Affairs.

That did not mean that the Liberal party's view of national unity was a reliable compass in the gyrating world of the 1960s. As prime minister, for example, Pearson was constantly searching for a French-Canadian lieutenant, an equivalent to an Ernest Lapointe, who would bring to his government the support of the Quebec members of Parliament and the Quebec voters. He never realized that in the new Quebec that was emerging no one man could speak for the entire province. But at least Pearson had learned that national unity required listening to Quebec. In the 1960s that meant listening to many strident and contradictory voices, but his listening surely contributed to holding the country together.

Unity

GORDON ROBERTSON

In volume three of his memoirs, Lester B. Pearson says: "My passionate interest when I was in government, apart from the ultimate question of peace and war, was in the national unity of our country."[1] My job as clerk of the Privy Council and secretary to the Cabinet for all of Mr. Pearson's time as prime minister, except the first problem-ridden "60 days of decision," would have made it inevitable that I become his principal instrument in whatever area he decided was to be his principal concern. The secretary to the Cabinet is the prime minister's deputy minister, responsible for whatever the head of government wants him to handle. This tendency is particularly pronounced when the area of prime ministerial concern does not fall clearly within the responsibility of any one minister or department.

"National unity" is an amorphous, undefinable question. As Mr. Pearson rightly said, it was "a problem of many facets embracing, among other factors, the constitution, federal-provincial relations, and the bread-and-butter issues of tax-sharing and equalization grants." This was not all: he was convinced that "the problems of culture and language are pre-eminent."[2] If he was here today, he would encompass constitution, culture and language in the words "recognition of the distinct society of Quebec." There is no question where Mr. Pearson would stand on that.

Apart from the non-departmental nature of "national unity" as a problem, there was another factor that brought it into my bailiwick. "National unity" in 1963 and 1964 did not centre on the separation of Quebec from Canada. The Parti Québécois did not exist. It came into being only in 1968 and did not gain power in Quebec until 1976. The problem of the Pearson years was finding accommodations with the Quiet Revolution in Quebec, led by a federalist Premier Jean Lesage, within the federal system. As the Royal Commission on Bilingualism and Biculturalism warned in its preliminary report in 1965, the Confederation pact established in 1867, and never since seriously challenged, was now for the first time being rejected by the francophone population of Quebec.

Jean Lesage was an intelligent, dynamic, impatient, and proud man. He was also hard-pressed by more extreme people within his Liberal party, such as René Lévesque. Jean and I were good friends. Prime Minister St. Laurent had appointed us to be, respectively, minister and deputy minister on the same day, 15 November 1953, in the same department. He charged us personally to produce a new policy for the Canadian North. There was to be no more of the "absence of mind" which had produced national embarrassment during the war and in the postwar years, as the Americans had to do things in our North that Canada, as owner, ought to have done but couldn't. Jean and I worked closely together until the defeat of the St. Laurent government in 1957.

The impatient Premier Lesage wanted decisions and action. He and the prime minister had good relations, but Mr. Pearson had other things to worry about than Quebec. Jean made it clear that, when he could not reach the prime minister, he would deal with Tom Kent or Gordon Robertson. No one else.

From 1963 to 1966 the efforts to staunch the Quiet Revolution were by non-constitutional means: Quebec's opting-out of shared-cost programs and receiving compensation in cash or equalized tax points; adjusting the Canada Pension Plan to fit with a separate plan for Quebec (an arrangement that would not have happened without Tom Kent); and adopting a policy of cooperative federalism under which Quebec (and other provinces, if they wanted) could exercise more control in policies and programs of concern to them.

In 1964 an effort was made to agree on an amending procedure for the constitution – the Fulton-Favreau formula – but it was dropped when the Lesage government became worried about its rigidity. Some of the constitutional changes Quebec might want could be blocked. But it was only in 1967, shortly before Ontario Premier Robarts's Confederation of Tomorrow Conference, that Pearson decided that *de facto* adjustments to the operation of Confederation would not be enough to solve the Quebec problem. Constitutional change became not simply desirable but necessary. Thus Pearson opened, in February 1968, the first of the series of constitutional conferences from which we have yet, 29 years later, to emerge.

Mike Pearson's minister of justice, Pierre Trudeau, said the constitution was a "panier de crabes" – a can of worms. René Lévesque claimed it was hopeless. Canada could not change to meet Quebec's needs: separation was the only answer. Yet Pearson was undoubtedly right to launch the effort. Constitutional reform had to be attempted or the field was abandoned to the separatists, who were beginning to grow in strength.

An intriguing question is whether constitutional change could have succeeded if Mr. Pearson had been able to remain prime minister long enough to handle it. He was a superb diplomat. There probably would not have been the solution to the Suez Crisis in 1956 without him. The Nobel Peace Prize was not awarded for nothing.

One can identify at least three critical points in our long constitutional saga since 1968 when Mr. Pearson would almost certainly have taken a different tack than was in fact taken. One was at the Victoria Conference of 1971. Pearson probably would have agreed to paramountcy for a province in the area of social policy, as had been provided for old-age pensions in 1964, and as Premier Robert Bourassa of Quebec belatedly sought at Victoria. The Victoria Charter was an excellent plan with a much better amending formula than the mess we have now. We might have changed the whole unity picture 26 years ago.

The second crucial decision was the "agreement without Quebec" in 1981, which has caused so deep a wound, and which still is bedevilling the federalist cause in Quebec. Pearson would never have done that.

The third opportunity missed was the handling of Meech Lake in the fatal last days in Manitoba and Newfoundland. Meech could almost certainly have been saved with Pearson's diplomacy and skill. There would have been no rolls of the dice, no attempt to strong-arm Newfoundland Premier Clyde Wells. Instead, there would probably have been a reference to the Supreme Court to test whether there really was a time limit to kill the whole effort.

These are tantalizing "might-have-beens," but they do make a point: there is nothing inevitable about history. People of genius can and do make a difference. We might not now be at the edge of the abyss if we had had Pearson's healing talents for a few years longer.

Notes

INTRODUCTION

1 Geoffrey A.H. Pearson, *Seize the Day: Lester B. Pearson and Crisis Diplomacy* (Ottawa, 1993), 5.
2 J.L. Granatstein, *Canada 1957–1967: The Years of Uncertainty and Innovation* (Toronto, 1986), 202.
3 Compare Barbara Ward, " 'That Shrewd Yet Visionary Voice,' " in Michael Fry, ed., *Freedom and Change: Essays in Honour of Lester B. Pearson* (Toronto, 1975), 244, and Robert Bothwell, below, 19–20.
4 Richard Gwyn, *The Shape of Scandal: A Study of a Government Crisis* (Toronto, 1965), 153.
5 Peter C. Newman, *The Distemper of Our Times: Canadian Politics in Transition, 1963–1968* (Toronto, 1968), 36–7.
6 Robert Fulford, "The Puzzling – to Almost Everybody – Personality of Lester B. Pearson," *Maclean's*, 6 April 1963, 13–15, 50–56. See also Bruce Hutchison, *The Far Side of the Street* (Toronto, 1976), 248, 355.
7 Fulford, "Puzzling," 52.
8 John English, *The Worldly Years: The Life of Lester Pearson*, Vol. II: *1949–1972* (Toronto, 1992), 393. See also 267.
9 Grattan O'Leary, *Recollections of People, Press and Politics* (Toronto, 1977), 137.
10 John A. Munro and Alex I. Inglis, eds., *Mike: The Memoirs of the Rt. Hon. Lester B. Pearson*, Vol. III: *1957–1968* (Toronto, 1975), 109.
11 Ibid., 186–7.
12 Denis Stairs, "The Pedagogics of John Holmes," in Kim Richard Nossal, ed., *An Acceptance of Paradox: Essays on Canadian Diplomacy in Honour of John W. Holmes* (Toronto, 1982), 4.

13 John English, *Shadow of Heaven: The Life of Lester Pearson*, Vol. I: *1897–1948* (Toronto, 1989), 333–4.

14 For example, James Eayrs, "Sunny Side Up," *Weekend Magazine,* 17 December 1977, 5.

15 Interviews with L. B. Pearson, Lord Garner of Chiddingly and Alastair Buchan, Windsor Great Park, England, September 1971.

16 James Eayrs, *In Defence of Canada: Peacemaking and Deterrence* (Toronto, 1972), 33–4 note.

17 English, *Shadow of Heaven*, 137–40.

18 National Archives of Canada, O.D. Skelton Papers, vol. 12, Diary, 9 and 23 October 1931.

19 National Archives of Canada, L.B. Pearson Papers, vol. 1, Diary, 1 January 1936.

20 Charles Ritchie, *The Siren Years: A Canadian Diplomat Abroad, 1937–1945* (Toronto, 1974), 54.

21 Interview, Carleton University, September 1972.

22 James Eayrs, "Sunny Side Up," 4–5.

23 Geoffrey Pearson, "The Diplomacy of L. B. Pearson," *bout de papier* 13, no. 3 (1996), 19.

24 Charles Ritchie, *Diplomatic Passport: More Undiplomatic Diaries, 1946–1962* (Toronto, 1981), 54; English, *Shadow of Heaven*, 297.

25 John A. Munro and Alex I. Inglis, eds., *Mike: The Memoirs of the Rt. Hon. Lester B. Pearson*, Vol. I: *1897–1948* (Toronto, 1972), 293.

26 Christina McCall, "Men of an Age," *Saturday Night*, December 1997/January 1998, 17–23.

27 Greg Donaghy, "Hegemonic Hug: Canada and the Reordering of North American Relations, 1963–1968" (Ph.D. thesis, University of Waterloo, 1998), ch. 1.

28 Hutchison, *Far Side of the Street*, 355. For fresh material on the evolution of the Pearson-Gordon friendship, see Stephen Azzi, *Walter Gordon and the Rise of Canadian Nationalism* (Montreal and Kingston: McGill-Queen's University Press, 1999).

29 Newman, *Distemper*, 44–5.

30 Ibid.

31 Norman Hillmer and J.L. Granatstein, "Historians Rank the Best and Worst Canadian Prime Ministers,"*Maclean's,* 21 April 1997, 34–9, and two of the questionnaires for that study: Neatby to Hillmer, 4 February 1997, and Smith to Hillmer, 11 February 1997.

32 Donaghy, "Hegemonic Hug," 371, and passim.

33 P. E. Bryden, *Planners and Politicians: Liberal Politics and Social Policy, 1957–1968* (Montreal and Kingston, 1997).

34 Bryden to J.L. Granatstein, 17 February 1997, for the Hillmer-Granatstein prime ministers' study.

35 See also "Social Policy Godfather Blasts Liberals," *Ottawa Citizen*, 23 December 1997.
36 English, *The Worldly Years*, 259; Pearson, *Mike*, III, 237–8; Stairs, below, 49.
37 "Grading the Ministers From A to F," *Globe and Mail*, 1 January 1998.
38 "Lester Would Be Ashamed," *The Ottawa Sun*, 1 November 1997.
39 "Flag Flap Reflects Our Failure To Make Our Country Work," *Financial Post*, 21 March 1998.
40 Addresses at the Lester B. Pearson Centennial Symposium, Ottawa-Hull, 22–23 April 1997; on the symposium, see Kevin Spooner, "Reflecting on Lester Pearson," *Literary Review of Canada* 7 (January/February 1998): 8.

CANADA'S MOMENT

1 Barbara Ward, " 'That Shrewd Yet Visionary Voice,' " in Michael Fry, ed., *Freedom and Change: Essays in Honour of Lester B. Pearson* (Toronto, 1975), 247–9.
2 John English, *Shadow of Heaven: The Life of Lester Pearson*, Vol. I: *1897–1948* (Toronto, 1989), ch. 4.
3 A point well made by John English in ibid., 168–70.
4 Lester B. Pearson, *Mike: The Memoirs of the Rt. Hon. Lester B. Pearson*, Vol. I: *1897–1948* (Toronto, 1972), ch. 17.
5 He considered himself qualified to be O.D. Skelton's successor when Skelton died suddenly in 1941. King appointed, instead, a younger man, Norman Robertson.
6 There are other resemblances between Pearson and Acheson. Both men stood by individuals victimized by the anti-communist fervour of the time. In Pearson's case, it was Herbert Norman, and in Acheson's, Alger Hiss. It is a reasonable speculation that both men acted out of an inherited sense of Christian duty.
7 Norman Hillmer, "Peacekeeping: Canadian Invention, Canadian Myth," in Sunë Akerman and J.L. Granatstein, eds., *Welfare States in Trouble: Historical Perspectives on Canada and Sweden* (Uppsala, Sweden, 1995), 161.
8 J.W. Pickersgill, *The Road Back* (Toronto, 1986) makes this point forcefully.
9 Lester B. Pearson, *Mike*, Vol. III: *1957–1968* (Toronto, 1975), 128.

LESTER B. PEARSON AND THE MEANING OF POLITICS

1 I am very grateful to Dr. Jennifer Smith (who knows far more about political thought than I), of Dalhousie's Department of Political Science, for her perceptive comments and advice during the drafting of this paper.
2 On John English's account, Pearson actually styled himself as a "British-Canadian Conservative" during his early years as a teacher of British

history at the University of Toronto. See John English, *Shadow of Heaven: The Life of Lester Pearson*, Vol. I: *1897–1948* (Toronto, 1989), 130.

3 The secondary source material on Pearson is voluminous. For present purposes, particular attention has been paid to his own published works, among them *Democracy in World Politics* (Toronto, 1955); *Diplomacy in the Nuclear Age* (Toronto, 1959); *Peace in the Family of Man: The Reith Lectures 1968* (Toronto, 1969); *Words and Occasions* (Toronto, 1970); and the three volumes of *Mike: The Memoirs of the Rt. Hon.Lester B. Pearson* (Toronto, 1972–5). Also pertinent is his "Introduction" to J.W. Pickersgill, *The Liberal Party* (Toronto, 1962). John English's two-volume biography is indispensable. See *Shadow of Heaven*, and *The Worldly Years: The Life of Lester Pearson*, Vol. II: *1949–1972* (Toronto, 1992). Also essential is Geoffrey A.H. Pearson, *Seize the Day: Lester B. Pearson and Crisis Diplomacy* (Ottawa, 1993). Apart from the memoirs of his various colleagues in both the foreign service and public life, there are the more "popular" accounts of journalists and others. See, for example, John Robinson Beal, *The Pearson Phenomenon* (Toronto, 1964); Peter C. Newman, *The Distemper of Our Times: Canadian Politics in Transition, 1963–1968* (Toronto, 1968); Patrick Nicholson, *Vision and Indecision: Diefenbaker and Pearson* (Toronto, 1968); Peter Stursberg, *Lester Pearson and the Dream of Unity* (Toronto, 1978) and *Lester Pearson and the American Dilemma* (Toronto, 1980); and Bruce Thordarson, *Lester Pearson: Diplomat and Politician* (Toronto, 1974). Almost every account of the conduct of Canada's foreign affairs in the postwar period makes mention, of course, of Pearson and his work.

4 At the University of Toronto in the middle 1920s, Pearson taught British history, British constitutional history, and international relations (a "special subject" course in which he focussed on competing interpretations of the causes of the First World War). See English, *Shadow of Heaven*, 124.

5 Pluralist political thought is usually associated with liberalism in the American, rather than the British, tradition, and Americans tend to regard it as their own creation. They trace it back to James Madison in *The Federalist* (No. 10), but there have been recurrent elaborations by American political scientists in the 20th century. Among the most notable examples: Arthur F. Bentley, *The Process of Government* (Chicago, 1908); David B. Truman, *The Governmental Process: Political Interests and Public Opinion* (New York, 1951); and Robert A. Dahl, *A Preface to Democratic Theory* (Chicago, 1956). An account of the intellectual history of the rise of pluralism as a theory and as an ideology can be found in Theodore J. Lowi, *The End of Liberalism* (New York, 1979), ch. 3. See also Robert A. Dahl and Charles E. Lindblom, *Politics, Economics and Welfare* (New York, 1953). A University of Toronto political scientist contributed to the *genre* a year before transplanting himself to Columbia University in New York. Pearson would

have known him. See R.M. MacIver, *The Modern State* (London, 1926). Harold Laski struggled with the pluralist view in his *A Grammar of Politics* (London, 1925), and numerous subsequent editions. In the more recent political science literature in Canada, the approach has been evident primarily, but not solely, in studies of interest groups. See, for example, A.P. Pross, *Group Politics and Public Policy*, 2nd ed. (Toronto, 1992) and Hugh Thorburn, *Interest Groups in the Canadian Federal System* (Toronto, 1985). A rather different model, focussing on elites, is offered by Robert Presthus in his *Elite Accommodation in Canadian Politics* (Toronto, 1973).

6   Pearson, *Words and Occasions*, 89.

7   Ibid., 90.

8   Ibid.

9   Ibid., 92.

10 Ibid., 89–90. See also his introduction to Pickersgill, *The Liberal Party*, ix–x.

11 Pearson, *Words and Occasions*, 91.

12 Ibid.

13 Pearson, *Democracy in World Politics*, 48. He goes on here to extend the argument to the international environment: "The same principle should apply in the relations between nations who are working together for common and good purposes."

14 Some of these themes are discussed in the context of a comparison with the American experience in one of Pearson's early addresses on "Canada and the United States." See *Words and Occasions*, 29–31. His conception of Canadian nationalism as something that had to be founded on "the recognition of differences" and a pride in diversity was very evident in the only historical article that he wrote while on the faculty of the University of Toronto. See English, *Shadow of Heaven*, 136.

15 Some would say it made even *moderately* nationalist projects hard to sell – as Walter Gordon and eventually the Trudeau government found out. Of the aircraft they attempted to fly, many failed to get off the ground. Most of the others soon crashed.

16 Ulric Barthe, ed., *Laurier on the Platform 1871–1890* (Quebec, 1890), 72.

17 Anyone with doubts should examine the concluding paragraph of Pearson's April 1934 address to a church group in Ottawa. See *Words and Occasions*, 14–15.

18 See his January 1942 lecture on "The Road to War," ibid., especially 40 ff.

19 In liberal thought, of course, the two are inextricably linked together.

20 I have already commented on the Madisonian tradition in American political thought. But Pearson had come to his somewhat similar position by a very different route.

21 Geoffrey Pearson's *Seize the Day* provides a rich store of demonstrations upon which to draw. His work follows a case-study pattern similar to the one contained in Robert W. Reford's *Canada and Three Crises* (Toronto,

1968), although Reford associates the behaviour with Canadian dispositions more generally, rather than with Pearson specifically.

22 Peter Gellman, "Lester B. Pearson, Collective Security, and the World Order Tradition of Canadian Foreign Policy," *International Journal* 44 (Winter 1988-9): 68-101.

23 See English, *Shadow of Heaven*, 125-6.

24 Pearson's analysis of the Abyssinian crisis is discussed at length in Gellman, "Collective Security." For English's treatment, see *Shadow of Heaven*, 177-84. For the full tale of the Canadian response, see James Eayrs, *In Defence of Canada: Appeasement and Rearmament* (Toronto, 1965), 3-33; C.P. Stacey, *Canada and the Age of Conflict: A History of Canadian External Policies*, Vol. II: *1921-1948: The Mackenzie King Era* (Toronto, 1981), 179-90; and Richard Veatch, *Canada and the League of Nations* (Toronto, 1975), 143-69.

25 For Pearson, the sovereignty principle was a kind of blight upon the international body politic. But he knew it would not go away. See his January 1948 address on "Some Principles of Canadian Foreign Policy," in *Words and Occasions*, especially 67-8.

26 English, *Shadow of Heaven*, 287.

27 Ibid., 289. The Australians were more feisty.

28 Pearson, *Words and Occasions*, 62-7.

29 Pearson's involvement in the construction of the Food and Agriculture Organization (FAO) and United Nations Relief and Rehabilitation Administration (UNRRA) are discussed in *Mike*, I, 248-58. See also John W. Holmes, *The Shaping of Peace: Canada and the Search for World Order*, Vol. I: *1943-1957* (Toronto, 1979), 50-2, and 79 ff.

30 Pearson, *Words and Occasions*, 67-9.

31 The "operational code" concept began with Nathan Leites, who was a student of the politics of the USSR. See his *Operational Code of the Politburo* (New York, 1951). Other analysts subsequently experimented with it in relation to other targets. For examples, see Ole Holsti, "The 'Operational Code' Approach to the Study of Political Leaders: John Foster Dulles' Philosophical and Instrumental Beliefs," *Canadian Journal of Political Science* 3 (March 1970), and David S. McLellan, "The 'Operational Code' Approach to the Study of Political Leaders: Dean Acheson's Philosophical and Instrumental Beliefs," *Canadian Journal of Political Science* 4 (March 1971).

32 Pearson, *Mike*, II, 34.

33 Pearson, *Democracy in World Politics*, 56-7.

34 Ibid., 58-9.

35 Pearson, *Mike*, II, 103.

36 Ibid., 117.

37 Ibid., 218.

38 Ibid., 182–3.
39 The best treatment of this episode to date is John English's "Speaking Out
   on Vietnam, 1965," in Don Munton and John Kirton, eds., *Canadian Foreign Policy: Selected Cases* (Scarborough, 1992), 135–51.
40 Pearson, *Words and Occasions*, 69.
41 Pearson, *Mike*, III, 149.
42 Ibid., 149–50.
43 See English, *Worldly Years*, 271–8. See also Denis Smith, *Gentle Patriot: A
   Political Biography of Walter Gordon* (Edmonton, 1973).
44 Pearson, *Mike*, III, 236.
45 Ibid., 237.
46 Ibid., 237–8.
47 Interestingly, he later concluded that the one mistake his government had
   made in drawing up the commission's terms of reference was in its failure
   to give sufficient recognition to "the problems of multi-culturalism." See
   Pearson, *Mike*, III, 240–1. The difficulty of striking the right balance is with
   us still.
48 Even here, however, there was evidence of considerable flexibility at the
   practical level. See The Honourable Paul Martin, Secretary of State for External Affairs, *Federalism and International Relations* (Ottawa, 1968).

PEARSON AND DIEFENBAKER

1 John English, *Shadow of Heaven: The Life of Lester Pearson*, Vol. I: *1897–1948*
   (Toronto, 1989), 44–7; Denis Smith, *Rogue Tory: The Life and Legend of John
   G. Diefenbaker* (Toronto, 1995), 22ff. At the Pearson Centennial Conference
   in Ottawa, 22–23 April 1997, journalist and former Co-operative Commonwealth Federation/New Democratic Party MP Douglas Fisher noted
   that Pearson was close to MPs who had served in the Great War; he specu-
   lated that this was because Pearson had some guilt that his war had been
   relatively easy.
2 National Archives of Canada (NA), Historical Personnel Records, RG 32
   C2, vol. 536, W.P.M. Kennedy to secretary, Civil Service Commission, 18
   May 1928. George Smith, chair of history at the University of Toronto,
   more sensibly added that Hume Wrong was Pearson's superior as "an of-
   fice-man and administrator." Ibid., Smith to Secretary, 19 May 1928. For
   his part, Pearson told the Civil Service medical examiner that he drank a
   bottle of beer a week and that his maximum use of spirits in the last year
   had been four ounces. In one day. Ibid., Medical Examiner's Report, 25
   September 1928.
3 Thad McIlroy, ed., *Personal Letters of a Public Man: The Family Letters of John
   G. Diefenbaker* (Toronto, 1985), 25–6.
4 NA, L.B. Pearson Papers, vol. 48, Pearson to W.D. Mathews, 29 June 1944.

5 J.L. Granatstein, *A Man of Influence: Norman A. Robertson and Canadian Statecraft, 1929–1968* (Ottawa, 1981), 104–7.
6 NA, C.D. Howe Papers, vol. 4, file S4–12, L.B. Pearson, "A Review of Measures to Promote Canadian Exports ... ," 19 April 1950.
7 Smith, *Rogue Tory,* 207.
8 Thomas Barman, *Diplomatic Correspondent* (New York, 1969), 252–3. Barman, a British journalist, saw Pearson in Parliament in the spring of 1959 where he "made a deplorable impression on me. It was impossible to resist the conclusion that Pearson the international statesman was altogether out of his depth in the Canadian domestic field. It made me squirm to see how easily he was disarmed by that political mountebank, Diefenbaker."
9 A.D.P. Heeney, *The Things That Are Caesar's: The Memoirs of a Canadian Public Servant* (Toronto, 1972), 98.
10 Ibid., 351–2; Ellen Fairclough, *Saturday's Child: Memoirs of Canada's First Female Cabinet Minister* (Toronto, 1995), 126; Fairclough interview, 3 November 1968.
11 Granatstein, *A Man of Influence,* 373; Mrs. N.A. Robertson interview, 23 October 1978.
12 *Globe and Mail,* 29 April 1966. John English, *The Worldly Years: The Life of Lester Pearson,* Vol. II: *1949–1972* (Toronto, 1992), 355, notes that Pearson "inexcusably" raised the contents of the RCMP file on Munsinger with Diefenbaker "in a fashion that was threatening."
13 NA, Pearson Papers, N4, vol. 35, file 100.2, Munsinger, Diary, 10 December 1964; ibid., Memorandum, "The Munsinger Case," 4 May 1966; Smith, *Rogue Tory,* 522. Smith has the date of this meeting as 11 December.
14 Paul Hellyer interview, 29 March 1983. Pearson would take a decision in Cabinet, Hellyer said, but Walter Gordon would see him afterwards and the decision would change.
15 George Pearkes, Diefenbaker's first defence minister, recalled that "Dief would much rather talk than listen; and when you went in to see him you would start to explain things and then he'd start telling you ..." University of Victoria Archives, George Pearkes Papers, vol. 7, Pearkes interview transcript, 12 July 1967.
16 Canadian Institute of International Affairs, John W. Holmes Papers, file c/IV/3, Holmes to T.W.L. MacDermot, 7 July 1965.
17 Norman Hillmer and J.L. Granatstein, "Historians Rank the Best and Worst Canadian Prime Ministers," *Maclean's,* 21 April 1997, 34–9.

THE UNLIKELY GLADIATORS

1 The material in this paper is based on personal observations of the Diefenbaker/Pearson era. Remembered details were checked with newspaper

and magazine articles published at the time, with voluminous papers in my possession, and with several academic studies of the period. The most helpful of these were Denis Smith's *Rogue Tory: The Life and Legend of John G. Diefenbaker* (Toronto, 1995) and John English's *Shadow Of Heaven: The Life of Lester Pearson*, Vol. I: *1897–1948* (Toronto, 1989) and *The Worldly Years: The Life of Lester Pearson*, Vol. II: *1949–1972* (Toronto, 1992).

2 John Guare, *Six Degrees of Separation* (New York, 1992).

3 See the author's articles: "How Much Longer Must We Put Up With The Hypocrisy Of Our Divorce Laws?" *Chatelaine*, April 1961, 35, 140–5; "The Dismal Failure Of Our Welfare System," *Chatelaine*, November 1961, 34, 56–60; "Canada's Eskimos – A People Trapped Between Two Worlds," *Chatelaine*, November 1960, 34–7, 94–100; "How The Class System Works In Canada," *Maclean's*, 17 November 1962, 18, 68–73; "The Canadian Americans," *Maclean's*, 27 July 1963, 9–13, 38–40; "Olive Diefenbaker at Home," *Chatelaine*, June 1961, 32–5, 85–9; "Mrs. Lester Pearson's New Life in the Limelight," *Maclean's*, 7 March 1964, 26–8, 30–3.

4 Author's conversation with Marta Wasserman in Ottawa, circa April 1964.

5 Hon. Louis Robichaud, in a television conversation with Charlotte Gobeil, part of her CTV series, "*Political Memoirs*," re-broadcast on CKCO, Kitchener, 20 July 1997.

LESTER B. PEARSON AND THE CONUNDRUM
OF NATIONAL UNITY, 1963–1968

1 Peter H. Russell, *Constitutional Odyssey: Can Canadians Become a Sovereign People?* 2nd ed. (Toronto, 1993).

2 Michael Bliss, *Right Honourable Men: The Descent of Canadian Politics from Macdonald to Mulroney* (Toronto, 1994); J.L. Granatstein, *Canada's War: The Politics of the Mackenzie King Government, 1939–1945* (Toronto, 1975).

3 Kenneth McRoberts, *Misconceiving Canada: The Struggle for National Unity* (Toronto, 1997), 31–54.

4 Guy Laforêt, *Trudeau et la fin d'un rêve canadien* (Sillery, Qué., 1992), 101–2, 114–6.

5 Stéphane Dion, "Explaining Quebec Nationalism," in R. Kent Weaver, ed., *The Collapse of Canada?* (Washington, D.C., 1992).

6 Philip Resnick, *Toward a Canada-Quebec Union* (Montreal and Kingston, 1991).

7 John English, *The Worldly Years: The Life of Lester Pearson*, Vol. II: *1949–1972* (Toronto, 1992), 299.

8 Ibid., 302.

9 John Ross Hurley, *Amending Canada's Constitution: History, Processes, Problems and Prospects* (Ottawa, 1996), 32–5 and Appendix 3, 185–8, for the formula.

10 Gérard Boismenu, "La pensée constitutionnelle de Jean Lesage," in Robert Comeau, dir., *Jean Lesage et l'éveil d'une nation* (Montreal, 1989), 91–100.
11 English, *Worldly Years*, 298.
12 Jacques-Yvan Morin, "Jean Lesage et le repatriement de la constitution," in Comeau, *Jean Lesage*, 116–36.
13 Tom Kent, *A Public Purpose: An Experience of Liberal Opposition and Canadian Government* (Kingston and Montreal, 1988), 266–72, 296–7.
14 Ibid., 276–81.
15 Mitchell Sharp, *Which Reminds Me ...: A Memoir* (Toronto, 1994), 135–42. The quotation is from 139.
16 Kent, *A Public Purpose*, 255–9.
17 Ibid., 259–66.
18 Ibid., 281–2. The plan would reach maturity in ten years (as Ottawa wanted), would entail higher contributions with a basic deduction and higher payouts as in the Quebec proposal, and be adjusted to cost-of-living changes of up to two percent a year. Quebec agreed to the constitutional amendment required to include survivor and disability pensions.
19 English, *Worldly Years*, 296.
20 Ibid., 342.
21 Ibid., 314–27.
22 Ibid., 328.
23 Ibid., 343.

LESTER B. PEARSON AND CANADIAN UNITY

1 This article is a translation by Christine O'Nions of a paper written originally in French.
2 House of Commons, *Debates*, 14 April 1964, 2145.
3 Ibid., 17 December 1962, 2723.
4 Ibid., 2725.
5 Order in Council, 17 July 1963, creating the Royal Commission on Bilingualism and Biculturalism.
6 House of Commons, *Debates*, 20 February 1964, 64.
7 Ibid., 14 April 1964, 2144.
8 Ibid.
9 Ibid., 20 January 1966, 70.
10 Ibid., 6 April 1965, 44.
11 Ibid., 14 April 1964, 2144.

PRESCIENCE, PRUDENCE AND PROCRASTINATION

1 National Archives of Canada (NA), Brooke Claxton Papers, MG 32 B5, vol. 83, file Political Comments, Gordon to Clarion, "Draft Memorandum

for Discussion," 4 December 1957. This paper is based on research conducted for the author's book, *Planners and Politicians: Liberal Politics and
Social Policy, 1957–1968* (Montreal and Kingston, 1997).

2 David MacDonald, "Who Will Lead the Liberals into the Campaigning to
Come?" *The Globe Magazine*, 4 January 1958.

3 See Reginald Whitaker, *The Government Party: Organizing and Financing the
Liberal Party of Canada, 1930–1958* (Toronto, 1977). Whitaker characterized
this form of relatively decentralized goverment, in which individual Cabinet ministers are allowed enormous latitude in interpreting both national
policies along regional lines and the regional sentiment for central party
consumption, as "ministerialism."

4 NA, Claxton Papers, vol. 83, file Political Comments, "The Political Situation," August 1957.

5 NA, National Liberal Federation Papers, MG 28 IV 3, vol. 876, file J.J. Connolly, Dunning to Connolly, 13 November 1957.

6 NA, Claxton Papers, vol. 83, file Political Comments, Gordon to Claxton,
"Draft Memorandum for Discussion," 4 December 1957.

7 Tom Kent, "Liberalism and Canada's Future," *The Canadian Liberal* 9, no. 4
(1957).

8 NA, National Liberal Federation Papers, vol. 875, file Duncan MacTavish,
pt. 3, 4th National Liberal Convention, L.B. Pearson acceptance speech, 16
January 1958.

9 NA, C.D. Howe Papers, MG 27 III B20, vol. 109, file Politics – General,
pt. 8, Howe to Walter Harris, 5 May 1958 [misdated 5 April 1958].

10 Ibid., vol. 107, file Political – General, Howe to James Gardiner, 24 May
1958.

11 Ibid., Gardiner to Howe, 11 December 1958.

12 NA, L.B. Pearson Papers, MG 26 N2, vol. 108, file Study Conference on National Problems, pt. 3, J.R. Stirrett to Pearson, 2 October 1959.

13 NA, Peter Stursburg Papers, MG 31 D78, vol. 37, file Sharp, 26–7–76, Stursburg interview with Mitchell Sharp, 26 July 1976.

14 NA, CCF-NDP [Co-operative Commonwealth Confederation-New Democratic Party] Papers, MG 28 IV 1, vol. 494, file Liberal Party, T.W. Kent, "Towards a Philosophy of Social Security," July 1960.

15 NA, Pearson Papers, vol. 108, file Study Conference on National Problems,
pt. 4, "Study Conference on National Problems," minutes, 8 September
1960.

16 Paul Martin, *A Very Public Life*, Vol. II: *So Many Worlds* (Toronto, 1985),
344.

17 J.W. Pickersgill in Peter Stursberg, ed., *Lester Pearson and the Dream of
Unity* (Toronto, 1978), 64; Martin, *A Very Public Life*, II, 344.

18 NA, National Liberal Federation Papers, vol. 886, file Rally – announcement, Pearson statement (draft), 15 June 1960.

19 "Report on Kingston," *The Canadian Liberal* 9, no. 5 (1960).
20 Denis Smith, *Gentle Patriot: A Political Biography of Walter Gordon* (Edmonton, 1973), 70; Montreal *Star*, 20 October 1960.
21 Queen's University Archives (QUA), Tom Kent Papers, vol. 1, file Correspondence, September-December 1960, Gordon to Kent, 4 October 1960.
22 NA, Pearson Papers, vol. 22, file 313.30, Kent to Pearson, 16 November 1960.
23 QUA, Kent Papers, vol. 1, file Correspondence, January-April 1961, "The Health Plan of the Liberal Party," as approved 10 January 1961.
24 Tom Kent, *A Public Purpose: An Experience of Liberal Opposition and Canadian Government* (Montreal and Kingston, 1988), 92.
25 NA, Lionel Chevrier Papers, MG 32 B16, vol. 8, file 16, "Campaign Strategy," February 1962.
26 NA, National Liberal Federation Papers, vol. 685, file Weekly Reports, 1962, Weekly report from Keith Davey, 30 August 1962.
27 NA, Privy Council Office Papers, Cabinet minutes, 9 May 1963, 7–8.
28 QUA, Kent Papers, vol. 3, file Correspondence, October 1963, Johnson to Kent, 6 October 1963.
29 Ibid., vol. 7, file Federal-Provincial Conference on Pensions, 12–25 November 1963, Kent to Pearson, 25 November 1963.
30 Ibid., vol. 3, file Correspondence, April 1964, Kent, "Pension Discussion with Quebec, 11 April 1964."
31 Private Collection, Walter Gordon Papers, Pearson to caucus, 27 January 1965.
32 NA, Walter Gordon Papers, MG 32 B44, vol. 16, file 11, Gordon to Pearson, 28 January 1965.
33 Ibid., Gordon to Pearson, 31 March 1965.
34 Kent, *A Public Purpose*, 366.
35 NA, Department of Finance Papers, RG 19, vol. 4854, file 5508–02, pt. l, A.W. Johnson to R.B. Bryce, 16 July 1965.
36 Interview, A.W. Johnson, 21 November 1991; Bryce was also cautious in regard to the coordination of the categorical programs in the Canada Assistance Plan. See Rodney S. Haddow, *Poverty Reform in Canada, 1958–1978: State and Class Influences on Policy Making* (Montreal and Kingston, 1993), 50–60.
37 Interview, A.W. Johnson, 23 August 1991.
38 NA, Department of National Health and Welfare Papers, RG 29, Acc. 85–86/343, vol. 59, file 3401–2–2/65–1, Federal-Provincial Conference, "Opening Statement by the Prime Minister of Canada," 19 July 1965.
39 NA, Department of Finance Papers, Acc. 87–88/011, vol. 27, file 5935–08–1, pt. 1, Johnson to Bryce, 3 August 1966.
40 NA, Privy Council Office Papers, Cabinet minutes, 18 January 1968.
41 Ibid., 1 February 1968.

42 Among those voting to defeat the proposed delay of Medicare were MacEachen, Marchand, Gordon and Benson. Private Collection, Gordon Papers, Walter Gordon, "Re the Book – Sharp's Troubles," 8 March 1968.

"IT WAS WALTER'S VIEW"

1 Remark at L.B. Pearson Centennial Symposium, Ottawa, 22–23 April 1997.
2 Statistics Canada, *Canada's International Investment Position: Historical Statistics, 1926 to 1992* (Ottawa, 1993), 226–7, 232.
3 National Archives of Canada (NA), Peter Stursberg Papers, MG 31 D78, vol. 36, Stursberg interview with Geoffrey Pearson, 30 May 1978.
4 Bruce Hutchison, *The Far Side of the Street* (Toronto, 1976), 251.
5 Library of Parliament, Peter Stursberg interview with James Coutts, 22 April 1977.
6 NA, Lester B. Pearson Papers, MG 26 N5, vol. 46, file 113–118, transcript no. 114, Chris Young interview with Pearson, 11 June 1970.
7 NA, Walter L. Gordon Papers, MG 32 B44, vol. 16, file 11, memorandum, 5 December 1965.
8 Pearson Papers, vol. 46, file 113–118, transcript no. 115, Chris Young interview with Pearson, 11 June 1970; ibid., vol. 46, file 136–141, transcript no. 138, Bernard Ostry interview with Pearson, 21 October 1970.
9 Royal Commission on Canada's Economic Prospects, *Preliminary Report* (Ottawa, 1956), 90–3. See also Royal Commission on Canada's Economic Prospects, *Final Report* (Ottawa, 1957), 393–7.
10 Gordon Papers, vol. 37, file 2, "Our Changing Economy," speech to the Ontario Federation of Labour, 13 February 1960. See also Walter Gordon, "Some Facts We Must Face for the Long Term Progress of Canada … ," *Financial Post*, 27 February 1960, 9.
11 Gordon Papers, vol. 37, file 2, "The Challenge of Change," speech to the Canadian Manufacturers' Association, 6 June 1960.
12 Walter Gordon, *A Political Memoir* (Toronto, 1977), 85.
13 Ibid., 81.
14 John English, *The Worldly Years*, Vol. II: *The Life of Lester Pearson, 1949–1972* (Toronto, 1992), 389.
15 Interviews with E.J. Benson and Jane Glassco; Library of Parliament, Peter Stursberg interview with Tom Kent, 30 March 1977; Tom Earl interview with Mitchell Sharp, 19 January 1984; Mitchell Sharp, *Which Reminds Me … A Memoir* (Toronto, 1994), 89.
16 Library of Parliament, "Study Conference on National Problems," [transcripts of the sessions].
17 For Barkway's paper, see Gordon Papers, vol. 14, file 3, Michael Barkway, "How Independent Can We Be?" presentation to the Study Conference on National Problems, Kingston, 6–10 September 1960.

18 Ibid., Walter Gordon, "How Independent Can We Be?" presentation to the Study Conference on National Problems.

19 Pearson Papers, N2, vol. 108, file Study Conference, pt. 3, "Study Conference on National Problems" [summary of the discussions]; Gordon Papers, vol. 14, file 3, Harry G. Johnson, "External Economic Relations," speech to the Study Conference on National Problems; Library of Parliament, "Study Conference on National Problems."

20 "Not Liberal," *Winnipeg Free Press*, 20 October 1960. See also Harold Greer, "The Conference at Kingston Leaves Mr. Pearson as Darling Only of the Eggheads," *Globe and Mail*, 14 September 1960.

21 NA, J.W. Pickersgill Papers, MG32 B34, vol. 104, National Liberal Rally, "Policy Statements," 17 January 1961.

22 Gordon, *Political Memoir*, 97.

23 Walter L. Gordon, *Troubled Canada: The Need for New Domestic Policies* (Toronto, 1961), 88–9, 94, 130.

24 Pearson Papers, N6, vol. 38, memorandum to members of the Liberal caucus, 15 October 1962.

25 Stursberg Papers, vol. 33, Stursberg interview with Tom Kent, 30 March 1977; interviews with Mitchell Sharp and J.W. Pickersgill.

26 Interview with Allan J. MacEachen.

27 Gordon Papers, vol. 16, file 11, Gordon memorandum, 5 December 1965.

28 Gordon, *Political Memoir*, 139.

29 Stursberg Papers, vol. 33, Stursberg interview with Maurice Lamontagne, 24 August 1976.

30 Gordon Papers, vol. 16, file 11, Gordon memorandum, 5 December 1965.

31 Peter Stursberg, "Ottawa Letter," *Saturday Night*, September 1964, 9.

32 Gordon Papers, vol. 16, file 11, Gordon memorandum, 26 January 1966.

33 "Will the Real Liberal Please Stand Up?" *Globe and Mail*, 30 September 1965, 6.

34 NA, Gordon Blair Papers, MG 32 C11, vol. 23, file economic policy, Mitchell Sharp, "Strengthening Canada's Independence," speech to the Annual Conference of the Association of Canadian Advertisers, Toronto, 4 May 1966.

35 "An Issue Mr. Winters Cannot Dodge," *Toronto Star*, 14 October 1965.

36 NA, Records of the Department of Finance, RG 19, vol. 5170, file 8580–00–1, pt. 1, Robert Winters speech to the 20th International Banking Summer School, Kingston, Ontario, 24 August 1967.

37 NA, Records of the Privy Council Office, RG 2, vol. 2698, file trade & commerce, "Letter from the Honourable Robert Winters to the Chief Executives of Foreign Company Subsidiaries in Canada," 31 March 1966.

38 Pearson Papers, N6, vol. 14, file Liberal party caucus, "Memorandum re Special Caucus Conference," 23–24 September 1967.

39 Gordon Papers, vol. 17, file 13, Judy LaMarsh, speech to the Canadian District West of Civitan International, Niagara Falls, 4 February 1967.

40 "Benson Promises 'Foreign Control,' " *Calgary Herald*, 10 February 1967, 26; "US Money, Progress Stymies Canada's Plans Marchand Says," *Quebec Chronicle-Telegraph*, 16 January 1967, 3.

41 Interview with E.J. Benson.

42 "Once Again, Here's Walter," *Monetary Times*, May 1966, 46.

43 Walter L. Gordon, *A Choice for Canada: Independence or Colonial Status* (Toronto, 1966), 114–5, 117.

44 Jack Cahill, *John Turner: The Long Run* (Toronto, 1984), 111.

45 Blair Papers, vol. 23, file economic policy, Mitchell Sharp, "Strengthening Canada's Independence." Although this speech was given the day before *A Choice for Canada* appeared in the book stores, Sharp must have benefitted from a leaked copy of the book, as his comments were clearly aimed at Gordon.

46 Ibid., Mitchell Sharp, Cutler Lecture, University of Rochester, Rochester, New York, 5 May 1966.

47 Arthur Blakely, "Sharp-Gordon Power Struggle Moves Into the Open," *Montreal Gazette*, 10 May 1966.

48 Gordon Papers, vol. 9, file 12, "The Role of Foreign Capital in Canadian Economic Development," [September 1966].

49 Sharp, *Which Reminds Me*, 145.

50 Anthony Westell, "Liberals Reject Gordon's Nationalism," *Globe and Mail*, 12 October 1966, 4.

51 Pearson Papers, N4, vol. 159, file 391, pt. 3, "Plenary Sessions Decisions," October 1966.

52 Quoted in Peter C. Newman, *The Distemper of Our Times: Canadian Politics in Transition, 1963–1968* (Toronto, 1968), 416.

53 Gordon Papers, vol. 11, file 15, Gordon to L.T. Pennell, 26 October 1966.

54 Ibid., vol. 14, file 6, Gordon to Earl H. Orser, 26 October 1966.

55 "Two Voices ... ," *Calgary Albertan*, 23 January 1967.

56 Bob Cohen, "Winters Reaffirms Foreign Investment Welcome," *Ottawa Citizen*, 25 January 1967.

57 "P.M. Assures Business on Investment Curbs," *Globe and Mail*, 2 February 1967.

58 Records of the Department of Finance, vol. 5170, file 8580–00–1, pt. 1, Robert Winters, speech to the 42nd Canadian Purchasing Conference, Montreal, 10 July 1967. Ibid., Maurice Sauvé speech to the Club St-Laurent Kiwanis de Montreal, Montreal, 1 March 1967. Records of the Privy Council Office, vol. 2699, file Mitchell Sharp, Sharp speech to the Manitoba Division of the Canadian Industrial Management Association, Winnipeg, 21 February 1967.

59 Interview with Mel Watkins.

"A GOOD MAN FOR THE MIDDLE INNINGS"

1 See Patrick H. Brennan, *Reporting the Nation's Business: Press-Government Relations during the Liberal Years, 1935–1957* (Toronto, 1994), ch. 6 and 167–8; Christina McCall-Newman, *Grits: An Intimate Portrait of the Liberal Party* (Toronto, 1982), 30.

2 National Archives of Canada (NA), Lester B. Pearson Papers, MG 26 N1, vol. 6, Hutchison file, Hutchison to Pearson, 21 January 1953.

3 Michael Bliss, *Right Honourable Men: The Descent of Canadian Politics from Macdonald to Mulroney* (Toronto, 1994), 221.

4 McCall-Newman, *Grits*, 33–4.

5 Pearson Papers, N2, vol. 22, R.S. Malone file, Malone to Pearson, 25 July 1961 and enclosed undated Hutchison memo. Also vol. 126, Hudson-Hyndman file, Pearson to Hutchison, 14 September 1960 and vol. 133, V file, Pearson to Vining, 25 May 1960; John English, *The Worldly Years: The Life of Lester Pearson*, Vol. II: *1949–1972* (Toronto, 1992), 215–6; interview with Bruce Hutchison.

6 Pearson Papers, N2, vol. 28, O'Hagan file, O'Hagan to Davey, 5 September 1961; Allan Levine, *Scrum Wars: The Prime Ministers and the Media* (Toronto, 1993), 243–5.

7 Wilfred Kesterton, "Journalism," in John Saywell, ed., *Canadian Annual Review for 1963*, (Toronto, 1964), 407; interviews with Arthur Irwin and Bill Wilson.

8 Kesterton, *Canadian Annual Review for 1963*, 409.

9 Ibid.

10 Peter Newman, *The Distemper of Our Times: Canadian Politics in Transition, 1963–1968* (Toronto, 1968), 14; NA, Escott Reid Papers, vol. 34, Hutchison file, Hutchison to Reid, 22 July 1964; interviews with Graham Fraser, Bruce Hutchison and Arthur Irwin.

11 NA, Richard Bell Papers, vol. 110, Personal-misc. 1964 file, Bell to Macdonnell, 12 May 1964; Kesterton, *Canadian Annual Review for 1963*, 410.

12 On Ferguson's attitude, interview with Carl Goldenberg; on Fraser's, interviews with Escott Reid and Arthur Irwin; and on Hutchison's, interview with Arthur Irwin.

13 Levine, *Scrum Wars*, 246–8; Pearson Papers, N5, vol. 47, CBC interview, n.d.; Bliss, *Right Honourable Men*, 240; Richard Doyle, *Hurly-Burly: A Time at the Globe* (Toronto, 1990), 201.

14 Keith Davey, *The Rainmaker: A Passion for Politics* (Toronto, 1986), 46; interviews with Douglas Fisher and Peter Newman.

15 Paul Rutherford, *When Television Was Young: Prime Time Canada, 1952–1967* (Toronto, 1990), 403; Wilfred Kesterton, "Journalism," in John Saywell, ed., *Canadian Annual Review for 1964* (Toronto, 1965), 480–1.

16 David Taras, *The Newsmakers: The Media's Influence on Canadian Politics* (Scarborough, Ont., 1990), 46–7.

17 Rutherford, *When Television Was Young*, 403; interviews with Roy Faibish and Arthur Irwin.

18 Robert Fulford, *Best Seat in the House: Memoirs of a Lucky Man* (Toronto, 1988), 149–50; interview with Fulford and Levine, 259.

19 Taras, *Newsmakers*, 61; interviews with Charles Lynch and Bill Wilson.

20 Levine, *Scrum Wars*, 259–60.

21 Views of Douglas Fisher in Taras, *Newsmakers*, 133.

22 Kesterton, *Canadian Annual Review for 1963*, 410. As a rookie Co-operative Commonwealth Confederation (CCF) candidate in 1957, Fisher had defeated C.D. Howe. He now wrote columns for the politically conservative Toronto *Telegram*.

23 English, *Worldly Years*, 286; Peter Newman, *Home Country: People, Places and Power Politics* (Toronto, 1973), 17; Pearson Papers, N4, vol. 109, Dornan to Pearson, 25 November 1966; Levine, *Scrum Wars*, 256–7.

24 *Globe and Mail*, 18 February 1965.

25 "Backstage at Ottawa," *Maclean's*, 21 March 1964; Kesterton, *Canadian Annual Review for 1964*, 436–7.

26 Ibid., 437–8.

27 Davey, *Rainmaker*, 57.

28 Newman, *Distemper*, 49–50.

29 Levine, *Scrum Wars*, 238–9; Lester B. Pearson, *Mike: The Memoirs of the Rt. Hon. Lester B. Pearson*, Vol. III: *1957–1968* (Toronto, 1975), 163–4.

30 Ibid., 205; interviews with Charles Drury and Paul Martin.

31 Newman, *Distemper*, xii.

32 Tom Kent, *A Public Purpose* (Toronto, 1988), 214 and 251–2; Judy LaMarsh, *Memoirs of a Bird in a Gilded Cage* (Toronto, 1969), 5; interviews with Charles Drury and Paul Martin.

33 McCall-Newman, *Grits*, 37–8 and 44–5; Kent, *Public Purpose*, 334; interviews with Davie Fulton, Alvin Hamilton and Mitchell Sharp.

34 Newman, *Distemper*, 316 and 336; Levine, *Scrum Wars*, 262.

35 Richard Gwyn, *The Shape of Scandal: A Study of a Government Crisis* (Toronto, 1965), 244; McCall-Newman, *Grits*, 44–5.

36 Ibid., 48; Levine, *Scrum Wars*, 262–3.

37 Wilfred Kesterton, "Mass Media," in John Saywell, ed., *Canadian Annual Review for 1965* (Toronto, 1966), 480–1.

38 CBC TV Program Recordings [AVCA], *The Sixties*, 15 November 1965 [01V1CV 8201 036–1], post-election commentary by Blair Fraser, Ron Collister (Toronto *Telegram*) and Charles Lynch (Southams).

39 *Toronto Star*, 13 October 1966.

40 Interviews with Douglas Fisher and Bruce Hutchison.

41 Newman, *Distemper*, 353; Bliss, *Right Honourable Men*, 228–9; McCall-Newman, *Grits*, 47.

42 Bliss, *Right Honourable Men*, 228; English, *Worldly Years*, 313.

43 *Toronto Star*, 30 May 1966; Rutherford, *When Television Was Young*, 403 and 409–14; interviews with Roy Faibish and Patrick Watson.

44 Fulford, *Best Seat*, 171.

45 Pearson Papers, N4, vol. 228, LaPierre to Pearson, 19 February 1965 and Pearson to LaPierre, 9 March 1965.

46 CBC TV Archives [Toronto], *This Hour Has Seven Days*, 20 March 1966 [11803]. This episode included a Watson interview with a very depressed Fraser. Ibid., 13 March 1966 [11802], another panel discussion with Fraser, Charles Lynch and Douglas Fisher.

47 Newman, *Distemper*, xiii; interviews with Bruce Hutchison, Charles Lynch and Bill Wilson.

48 Wilfred Kesterton, "Mass Media," in John Saywell, ed., *Canadian Annual Review for 1968* (Toronto, 1969), 433.

49 Christina Newman, "This Month: National Affairs," *Saturday Night*, September 1968.

50 Davey, *Rainmaker*, 32.

51 Newman, *Distemper*, 37 and 71–4.

52 Ibid., 9 and 42.

53 Bliss, *Right Honourable Men*, 243.

MINDING THE MINISTER

1 John F. Hilliker and Donald Barry, *Canada's Department of External Affairs*, Vol. II: *Coming of Age, 1946–68* (Montreal and Kingston, 1995), 250–6.

2 Pearson's efforts to encourage Canadian policy-makers to re-think their approach to NATO is explored in my piece, "Domesticating NATO: Canada and the North Atlantic Alliance, 1963–68," *International Journal* 52 (Summer 1997): 445–63.

3 Department of Foreign Affairs and International Trade (DFAIT), Department of External Affairs (DEA) file 20–22–Viets–2–1, "Minutes of Rusk-USSEA Meeting, 30 April 1964."See also Telegram from the Department of State to the Embassy in Vietnam, 1 May 1964, *Foreign Relations of the United States, 1964–68*, Vol. I: *Vietnam 1964 (FRUS)*, (Washington, D.C., 1992), 281–2.

4 "Memorandum for the Record of a Conversation Between President Johnson and Prime Minister Pearson, Hilton Hotel, New York, May 28, 1964, 6: 15–6: 45 p.m.," *FRUS*, 395.

5 Ibid. In his memorandum of the conversation, Sullivan thought that Martin's nervousness about the domestic consequences of escalation was worth drawing to the attention of Ambassador Lodge. See *FRUS*, 395, n. 5.

6 DFAIT, Historical Section Records, Tom Delworth, "A Study of Canadian Policy with Respect to the Vietnam Problem, 1962–1966."

7 George C. Herring, *America's Longest War: The United States and Vietnam, 1950–1975* (New York, 1986) 118–9.

8 L.B. Pearson, *Mike: The Memoirs of the Right Honourable Lester B. Pearson,* Vol. III: *1957–1968* (Toronto, 1975), 137–8.

9 DFAIT, DEA file 20–22–Viets–2, Washington to Ottawa, Tel No 2821, 5 August 1964.

10 Ibid., Ottawa to Saigon, Tel No Y-682, 28 September 1964.

11 National Archives of Canada (NA), L.B. Pearson Papers, MG 26 N3, vol. 281, file 845/IV666 Crisis 1964, H.O. Moran, Memorandum for the Minister, 21 September 1963. As a member of the Colombo Plan for Southeast Asian economic development, South Vietnam received $700,000 worth of assistance in the 1963–64 fiscal year. It would increase to $1.2 million in 1964–65.

12 John English, *The Worldly Years: The Life of Lester B. Pearson,* Vol. II: *1949–1972* (Toronto, 1992), 360.

13 Pearson, *Mike,* III, 126–7.

14 Patricia Smart, ed., *The Diary of André Laurendeau* (Toronto, 1991), 127.

15 L.B. Pearson, "Address to the Canadian Club of Ottawa." 10 February 1965, *Statements and Speeches* 65/6. American observers missed this slight shift in Canadian policy and reported that Pearson, who "displayed a full understanding of the U.S. position and the western stake in the Vietnam situation," had "[c]ome down strongly in support of U.S. objectives in Vietnam." See United States National Archives (USNA), RG 59, box 1989, file POL 15–1 CAN, American Embassy Ottawa to State Department, Airgram A-616, 15 February 1965.

16 DFAIT, DEA file 20–Viets–1–4, New York to Ottawa, Tel No 349, 8 March 1965.

17 DFAIT, DEA file 20–22–Viets–2, Moscow to Ottawa, Tel No 324, 24 March 1965; Moscow to Ottawa, Tel No 334, 26 March 1965; Warsaw to Ottawa, Tel No 162, 23 March 1965.

18 English, *Worldly Years,* 367.

19 Escott Reid, *Radical Mandarin: The Memoirs of Escott Reid* (Toronto, 1989), 372.

20 NA, DEA file 20–Canada–9–Pearson, Paul Martin, "Memorandum for the Prime Minister," 29 March 1965.

21 Cited in DFAIT, Historical Section Records, Donald Barry, "Canada's Department of External Affairs," draft chapter 10.

22 Pearson, *Mike,* III, 138.

23 J.L. Granatstein and Norman Hillmer, *For Better or For Worse: Canada and the United States to the 1990s* (Toronto, 1991), 231.

24 Charles Ritchie, *Storm Signals: More Undiplomatic Diaries, 1962–1971* (Toronto, 1983), 79–80. American anger was compounded when they

compared the circumstances surrounding Pearson's speech with those surrounding a speech that George Ball, the under-secretary of state, was invited to give in Toronto in March. After consulting Canadian officials, Ball accepted Ottawa's advice and declined to make the speech lest it embarrass the government. See Lyndon Baines Johnson Library, Austin, Texas, Johnson Papers, National Security Files, Country File Canada, vol. 3, box 166, State Department to Ottawa, Tel No 1074, 6 April 1965 and Ottawa to State Department, Tel No 1258.

25 Ibid., State Department to Ottawa, Tel No 1074, 6 April 1965.

26 Pearson, *Mike,* III, 156–7.

27 DFAIT, DEA file 20–22–Viets–2–1, Marcel Cadieux, Memorandum for the Minister, 6 August 1965.

28 Interview with Basil Robinson, 7 June 1994.

29 George C. Herring, *The Secret Diplomacy of the Vietnam War: The Negotiating Volumes of the Pentagon Papers* (Austin,Texas, 1983), 173.

30 Interview with Alexis Johnson, 8 June 1992.

31 Confidential interview.

32 Interview with Basil Robinson, 7 June 1994.

33 Herring, *The Secret Diplomacy of the Vietnam War,* 171.

34 Ibid, 176.

35 DFAIT, DEA file 20–22–Viets–2–1–1, Saigon to Ottawa, Tel No 184, 11 April 1966. For Ronning's account of the discussions in Hanoi see Chester Ronning, *A Memoir of China in Revolution: From the Boxer Rebellion to the People's Republic* (New York, 1974), 255–69.

36 DFAIT, DEA file 20–22–Viets–2–1–1, Saigon to Ottawa, Tel No 184, 11 April 1966.

37 Cited in Herring, *The Secret Diplomacy of the Vietnam War,* 123.

38 DFAIT, DEA file 20–22–Viets–2–1–1, Washington to Ottawa, Tel No 838, 21 March 1966.

39 Herring, *The Secret Diplomacy of the Vietnam War,* 179.

40 DFAIT, DEA file 20–22–Viets–2–1–1, Ottawa to Washington, Tel No Y-288, 22 April 1966. The American record is reproduced in Herring, *The Secret Diplomacy of the Vietnam War,* 187. Martin also raised the matter of a second Ronning mission with Averell Harriman on 20 April 1966. See USNA, RG 59, box 1984, file POL 15–1 CAN, Harriman, Memorandum of Conversation, 20 April 1966.

41 DFAIT, DEA file 20–22–Viets–2–1–1, Ottawa to Saigon, Tel No Y-349, 14 May 1966 and Saigon to Ottawa, Tel No 409, 21 May 1966.

42 Herring, *The Secret Diplomacy of the Vietnam War,* 193.

43 Ibid. See also DFAIT, DEA file 20–22–Viets–2–1–1, K. Goldschlag to Charles Ritchie, 24 May 1966.

44 Ibid., Ottawa to Brussels (for secretary of state for external affairs (SSEA)), Tel No Y-114, 4 June 1966.

45 Ibid., "Cannatodel" to Ottawa, Tel No 400, 5 June 1966.

46 Ibid., Saigon to Cannatodel (via Ottawa), Tel No 450, 6 June 1966.

47 Ibid., Ottawa to Cannatodel (for SSEA), Tel No M99, 6 June 1966.

48 Herring, *The Secret History of the Vietnam War*, 192.

49 DFAIT, DEA file 20–22–Viets–2–1–1, Washington to Ottawa, Tel No 1725, 10 June 1966.

50 Ibid., Ottawa to Saigon, Tel No Y-438, 16 June 1966.

51 Johnson Library, National Security Files, Memoranda to the President, vol. 5, box 8, file 5/27/66 – 6/10/66, Rostow to the President, 8 June 1966.

52 Herring, *The Secret Diplomacy of the Vietnam War*, 197.

53 USNA, RG 59, box 1984, POL 15–1 CAN, William Bundy, "Memorandum for the Record," 22 June 1965. See also United States Freedom of Information (FOI) Request No. 9202977, P.H. Kreisberg, Memorandum of Conversation: Visit of Ambassador Ronning to Hanoi, 21 June 1966.

54 DFAIT, DEA file 20–22–Viets–2–1–1, A.E. Ritchie, "Note for Mr. Collins," 28 June 1968.

55 Ibid., Ottawa to Washington, Tel No 4476, 30 June 1966.

56 English, *Worldly Years*, 357. See also NA, Walter Gordon Papers, MG 32 B44, vol. 16, Gordon, Memorandum: Lunch with LBP, 30 March 1966.

57 English, *Worldly Years*, 347.

58 Paul Hellyer, *Damn the Torpedoes: My Fight to Unify Canada's Armed Forces* (Toronto, 1990), 209.

59 FOI Request No. 9202977, American Embassy Ottawa to the Department of State, 6 January 1966, Airgram A-38.

60 Johnson Library, White House Confidential Files, CO 45, Canada, box 19, Robert E. Kantor, "Memorandum For the President," 17 June 1966.

61 FOI Request No. 9202977, Benjamin H. Read, Memorandum to Ambassador J. Leddy.

62 Johnson Library, Rostow Papers, vol 2, box 7, Dean Rusk, "Memorandum for the President," 7 May 1966. See also, for Butterworth's views, FOI Request No. 9202977, American Embassy Ottawa to Secretary of State, Tel No 1455, 27 April 1966.

63 USNA, RG 59, box 1984, file POL 15–1 CAN, Robert McClintock to George Ball, 12 May 1966.

64 DFAIT, DEA file 20–1–2–USA,"Summary of Prime Minister's Meeting with President Johnson, August 21, for Consulates in the United States," 30 August 1966.

65 Johnson Library, Johnson Papers, National Security Council Files, R. Smith, Memorandum of Conversation: Communist China and Admission to UN, 21 August 1966.

66 DFAIT, DEA file 20–1–2–USA, H.B. Robinson, "Memorandum for File," 24 August 1966.

67 DFAIT, DEA file 20–China–14, P. Martin, Memorandum for the Prime Minister, 28 June 1966.

68 Ibid., Mary Macdonald to J.E. Hadwen, 11 July 1966 (emphasis in the original) and Marcel Cadieux, Memorandum for the Minister, 22 July 1966.

69 Ibid., H.B. Robinson, Memorandum for File, 22 September 1966.

70 Ibid., [P.A. McDougall], Chinese Representation: Notes on Three Possible Courses of Action, 21 October 1966.

71 FOI Request No. 9202977, Dean Rusk, Memorandum for the President, 5 November 1966.

72 NA, Pearson Papers, N4, vol. 7, file 821/C359.1.Conf., Dean Rusk to L.B. Pearson, 9 November 1966.

73 DFAIT, DEA file 20–China–14, H.B. Robinson, Memorandum for the Prime Minister, 11 November 1966.

74 Ibid., H.B. Robinson, Memorandum for the Minister, 17 November 1966.

75 NA, Papers of the Privy Council, Cabinet Conclusions, 18 November 1966.

76 DFAIT, DEA file 20–China–14, H.B. Robinson, Memorandum for UN Division, 21 November 1966.

77 Norman St. Amour, "Sino-Canadian Relations, 1963–1968: The American Factor," in Paul M. Evans and Michael B. Frolic, eds., *Reluctant Adversaries: Canada and the People's Republic of China, 1949–1970* (Toronto, 1991), 120.

78 FOI Request No 9202977, Department of State to American Embassy Taipei, Tel No 91450 and W.J. Stoessel Jr., Memorandum of Conversation: Secretary's Conversation with Canadian Foreign Minister Martin: Chirep, 25 November 1966. During this conversation, Rusk showed some signs of irritation about the lack of consultation about the evolution of Canadian policy.

79 DFAIT, DEA file 20–China–14, J.G. Hadwen, Memorandum to Far Eastern Division, 30 November 1966.

PEARSONIANISM

1 Peter C. Newman, *The Distemper of Our Times: Canadian Politics in Transition, 1963–1968* (Toronto, 1968), 205.

2 John English, *The Worldly Years: The Life of Lester Pearson*, Vol. II: *1949–1972* (Toronto, 1992), 385.

CONTINUITY

1 Norman Hillmer and J.L. Granatstein, "Historians Rank the Best and Worst Canadian Prime Ministers," *Maclean's*, 21 April 1997, 34–9.

2 A 65-year-old anglophone night watchman, Wilfred O'Neill, was killed by a FLQ bomb blast in Montreal, 12 days after Mr. Pearson's election as prime minister on 8 April 1963.

3 G. Bruce Doern and Richard W. Phidd, *Canadian Public Policy: Ideas, Structure, Process* (Toronto, 1983), 196–8.
4 "Striking a Balance Working Group Synthesis Report," in Health Canada, National Forum on Health, *Canada Health Action: Building on the Legacy; Synthesis Reports and Issues Papers – Final Report*, Vol. II (Ottawa, 1997), 16.
5 Northrop Frye, "Conclusion," in C. Klinck *et al.*, eds., *The Literary History of Canada* (Toronto, 1965), 848.

REFORMISM

1 See my "Debating the Public Good: Afterthoughts," in Tom Kent, ed., *In Pursuit of the Public Good: Essays in Honour of Allan J. MacEachen* (Montreal and Kingston, 1997); "How a Democracy Can Best Invest in its People," *Inroads, A Journal of Opinion* 6 (May 1997); "How to Strengthen the Welfare State," in R.B. Blake, P.E. Bryden, and J.F. Strain, eds., *The Welfare State in Canada* (Concord, Ont., 1997). For a longer perspective, see Tom Kent, *Getting Ready for 1999: Ideas for Canada's Politics and Government* (Montreal, 1989).

UNITY

1 Lester B. Pearson, *Mike: The Memoirs of the Rt. Hon. Lester B. Pearson*, Vol. III: *1957–1968* (Toronto, 1975), 236.
2 Ibid.

Acknowledgments

This book has been made possible through the financial assistance of The CRB Foundation-Heritage Project, the C.D. Howe Foundation, and the Pearson Trust, as well as the Bank of Montreal, Bill and Cathy Graham, NOVA Corporation, Petro-Canada and Rogers Communications. The Rt. Hon. Jean Chrétien graciously agreed to write the preface. The idea for a critical re-examination of the Pearsonian role and legacy as prime minister came from his valued assistant, Mary Macdonald, and Maurice Foster, who succeeded Pearson as member of Parliament for Algoma East. Geoffrey Pearson was tolerant as I tinkered with his father's reputation, and I owe other and considerable debts to Ron Hallmann, Senator Dan Hays, Anne Hillmer, Michael Hillmer, Annette Kennedy, Pierrette Landry, Hector Mackenzie, Noni Maté, Gordon Shields and Boris Stipernitz. Brenda Donaldson and Roger Sarty skilfully prepared the manuscript for publication, while Philip Cercone, Joan McGilvray and the staff at McGill-Queen's University Press saw it through to its finished state with cheerful professionalism. Stephen Azzi created the index.

I dedicate the book to my sister-in-law, Elizabeth Trowell, a magnificent researcher and gifted writer who was a senior policy analyst with the Department of Transport at the time of her tragic death on 11 January 1998.

N.H.
Ottawa, Ontario

Contributors

STEPHEN AZZI is executive assistant to a Canadian member of Parliament and teaches history at Carleton University.

THE HON. MONIQUE BÉGIN is professor emeritus of health sciences at the University of Ottawa. She was the first Quebec woman elected to the House of Commons, serving as minister of national health and welfare, 1977–79 and 1980–84.

MICHAEL D. BEHIELS is professor of history, University of Ottawa.

ROBERT BOTHWELL is professor of history and director of the international relations program at the University of Toronto.

PATRICK H. BRENNAN is associate professor of history at the University of Calgary.

P.E. BRYDEN is assistant professor of history at Mount Allison University.

ROSS CAMPBELL is senior partner, Intercon Consultants Ltd. He was a leading member of the Canadian foreign service while L.B. Pearson was prime minister.

THE RT. HON. JEAN CHRÉTIEN became prime minister of Canada in 1993. He was first elected to the House of Commons in 1963, and was parliamentary secretary to L.B. Pearson, 1965–66.

ANDREW COHEN is a foreign correspondent for the *Globe and Mail*, and is based in Washington, D.C.

GREG DONAGHY is a historian at the Department of Foreign Affairs and International Trade and editor, *Documents on Canadian External Relations*.

J.L. GRANATSTEIN is director and chief executive officer of the Canadian War Museum, and Rowell-Jackman fellow at the Canadian Institute of International Affairs.

NORMAN HILLMER is professor of history at Carleton University and co-editor of *International Journal*.

A.W. JOHNSON is special advisor, South Africa/Canada Program on Governance. He was assistant deputy minister of finance, 1964–68.

TOM KENT is visitor, School of Policy Studies, Queen's University. He was the Pearson government's chief policy strategist, 1963–66, and deputy minister of manpower and immigration, 1966–68.

CHRISTINA MCCALL is a Toronto writer and editor, and a winner of the Governor General's Literary Award for Non-Fiction.

H. BLAIR NEATBY is professor of history *emeritus* at Carleton University.

GORDON ROBERTSON was clerk of the Canadian Privy Council and secretary to the Cabinet, 1963–75.

CLAUDE RYAN was editor-publisher of *Le Devoir*, 1964–78, and then active in Quebec politics, notably as leader of the Liberal party, 1978–82, and a government minister, 1985–94.

DENIS STAIRS is McCulloch professor of political science at Dalhousie University.

Index